Praise for *Leadership: Tl*

"Lee Thayer has followed his own leadership convictions and insights in writing a book that is itself the art of leadership. It is refreshing, authentic, and has a penetrating integrity. Don't take it lightly."

– Max De Pree,
Chairman Emeritus, Herman Miller, Inc.,
Author of *Leadership is an Art*

"It's a great book (or 'guidebook,' as the author calls it), reflecting years of hard-won experience doing what he reports on here. And he's done his homework, as well. It's an original, very creative. If you can't learn how by applying the leadership lessons here, you probably can't learn how. It's superb!"

– James O'Toole
Author of *Leading Change*

"When we first met Lee Thayer, our company was growing slowly at about 10% per year. Within a couple of years of following his ideas, our growth rate was 100% per year. Our customers became raving fans. We were receiving prestigious awards. Most importantly, our employees were more productive, full of life, and dedicated than they ever were before ... Some of his concepts were initially hard to grasp. But I came to see that he was right ... The concepts presented in this book (which we didn't have the advantage of – we only had the author!) work. Once you begin the journey to high performance, nothing else will suffice."

– John T. McBeth,
President & CEO,
Next Century Corporation

LEADERSHIP
Thinking, Being, Doing

New and Revised Edition

Lee Thayer

WME BOOKS

a division of
Windsor Media Enterprises, LLC
Rochester, New York
USA

Leadership: Thinking, Being, Doing
New and Revised Edition
Copyright © 2007 by Lee Thayer
All rights reserved. Printed in USA.

ISBN-10: 1-934229-01-6
ISBN-13: 978-1-934229-01-9

Editor: Yvonne DiVita
Cover Design: Karin Marlett Choi
Page Layout/Design: Tom Collins

Published by:
WME Books
Windsor Media Enterprises, LLC
Rochester, New York
USA

Available online at: www.WMEBooks.com, as well as other booksellers
and distributors worldwide.

Special Sales:

This and other WME Books titles are available at special discounts for bulk purchases, for use in sales promotions, or as premiums. Special editions, including personalized covers, excerpts of existing books, and corporate imprints, can be created in large quantities for special needs or projects.

For more information, please contact:

Special Book Orders
Windsor Media Enterprises, LLC
282 Ballad Avenue
Rochester, NY 14626

1-877-947-BOOK (2665)

info@wmebooks.com

For K.T., for every reason.

*As long as people exist, some will
always strive for the best.
And some will attain it.*

– Historian Barbara Tuchman

Preface to the Revised Edition

No book is ever "finished." Most could be improved upon indefinitely.

The first edition of *Leadership: Thinking, Being, Doing* was probably somewhere around its 4th or 5th iteration. I was always thinking of better ways of doing it. And, since I am a rabid learner, it always seemed to me that the particular version of the manuscript I was working on was already superseded by what I had learned last week. In this sense, books are like still pictures. They reveal what your thinking was back then.

This case is different. The book is out there. It has had many readers, and lots of fans. They have told me, directly or indirectly, that it is not an easy book to read. The main reason of course is that it requires readers to read and to think in ways that they had forgotten – or never learned in the first place. There's not much I can do about that one. People who are not superior readers and thinkers are not likely to become leaders anyway.

But the feedback illuminated some occasionally inadequate handling of key concepts, a few ambiguities, and some just plain counter-intuitive concepts. About these, something can be done.

So the book editor and I went through the book, from the first sentence to the last, and changed whatever needed changing to make the book and its sometimes contrarian concepts easier to comprehend. And to make it more obvious how they might be implemented. What's "new and revised" is that the whole book has been re-edited, and rewritten if called for, based on reader feedback – *and* on the insights an author gains by distancing himself from the book for a period of time.

Perhaps the most obvious or notable improvements are that I have added at the end of each chapter a short list of "Points to Ponder." Not actually a summary of the chapter, but provocations for thinking about some of the main ideas in the chapter. Also added: an index, making it easier to find what you are looking for in the book when you want to revisit certain topics that you want to think more about.

My intention was not to make the book larger, but simply better. The basic concepts remain the same. In some cases better explained, but still the concepts that have been field-tested successfully many times. The improvements include, for example, better explanations of the way change evolves out of how compellingly the leader tells his or her story of the future; more on dumb vs. smart systems; why most of the "dragons" that impede our journey are internal; that the only way to really understand high-performance organizations is to make one; how the victim mentality seeps into organizations from the pop culture, and how that creates a kind of "corporate welfare"; more definitive explanations of why pre-packaged "recipes" don't work; and many more.

Some parts have been kept intact. Readers have dog-eared the page at the end of Chapter 1, "How to Have a Mediocre Organization." It's as if they've been there, done that. Once they "get it," readers have the feeling of being confronted by the blindingly obvious, even though they may at first have disagreed. Such revelations ensure their retention.

As it says here and there in this admittedly very unconventional book about making high-performance organizations (and what leadership has to do with that complex undertaking), what I know comes primarily from what I have learned doing it. There are the "trenches" in which I continue to work alongside my clients to make it happen. And then there are the "trenches" involved in trying to learn how to describe it.

Neither will ever be perfectly done. Neither can be reduced to a recipe. But what I can guarantee you is this: that if you will work as hard at getting your head around this alien paradigm as I have in learning about it and trying to share that learning with you, you will be equipped to make a great organization. And to lead it in the extraordinary ways required.

I would like to make it easy. But it's not. It is not easy to think about it rightly. And it is certainly not easy to do it. But every great journey has a base from which to go forth prepared. It is my intention that this revised edition of the book will provide just that for you.

Lee Thayer
Flat Rock, NC
January, 2007

Executive Orientation

Leadership: Thinking, Being, Doing ... you may be thinking a little explanation is in order.

Here it is: You can't learn to be a "leader." History decides that. All you can do is be prepared if you are "called" to provide leadership.

Leadership is a specific role in a specific ongoing story. The leader's role is to change the course of that story. Since you can't learn to be a leader as such, how do you change the course of the story? You can learn how to *perform* leadership, to *prepare* to fulfill that role, if it happens that you are called to fulfill a specific leadership role.

So, about the title: If you intend to equip yourself to provide leadership – when, where, and how it's needed – this is your comprehensive guidebook. How successful you can be depends upon how you think, because that determines who you are. And who you are determines how you will do what you do. Thus the title: *Leadership: Thinking, Being, Doing*. If those three don't hang together rightly within you, your leadership won't amount to much.

There is no point in learning about leadership unless you have a *cause* that demands extraordinary performance. All the words about leadership ever written are worthless unless a great and worthy cause is at stake. This book is about high performance and the kind of leadership required to pursue a great and worthy cause.

You have been referred to this book, or drawn to it because there is nothing else that can provide you with all of the thinking, being, and doing tools you will need. You need to know not only what the territory looks like when you are traversing it, but the whys and the wherefores. The ideas and navigational tools provided here were forged in the trenches, working directly with the executives who were, and are, actively working to make it happen. Those tools come as well from many years of seeking out the best that has ever been said or written about the subject of leadership.

The only people who really understand what it takes are the people who have done it. These are the people who can effectively equip others to do it. I'm here before you after more than four decades in the trenches being directly involved in making it happen, with some successes and some failures, which will always be the case. What you need are the hows and the whys – what works and what doesn't. That's what you have here.

Is the journey difficult? More difficult than you can imagine.

Is there a simple formula? Only the ones provided by the business press, which simply don't work – for most people, most of the time.

In this book, we won't shrink from the difficulties of what's required, no matter how counter-intuitive they may seem to be, or how difficult to implement. You will meet up with the most tough-minded, realistic perspectives on leadership ever brought to life by those who had what it takes to reflect honestly on their successes and their failures. It is not the ideas that make it happen. It is the person who deploys them in her thinking and being, and thus in her doing.

You can't be who they were. But you can learn how to develop your own capacity for thinking, being, and doing when trying to forge *your* way.

Finally, is this a "how-to" book? Yes, in a way. But it is not a book about how others did it. It is a book about how it can be done ... by you.

Leadership is an art. It requires you to have a compelling cause. That's your part of it. For real success, you need to be informed by someone who has been there, done that. That's what I am providing here.

A guidebook for learning how to do it ... by doing it.

Who Should Read This Book?

Anyone who is seriously interested in optimizing his or her leadership capabilities.

It is for practicing CEOs and high-level executives. It is for anyone who presides over any type of organization or institution – commercial, government, voluntary. It is for anyone who intends to be the "best" in his or her roles in life, from managers and coaches to athletes and musicians to lovers and parents. It is for anyone who intends to perform optimally in any role. While the specific circumstances may vary, the kind of thinking required to make it happen is universal.

It is for anyone who wants to improve his or her ability to lead – herself or others – in any enterprise or venture in life. It is about life. It is about achievement. It is about living with purpose, which is the only reliable source of quality of life and of rewarding engagement with life there is.

One Caveat

You may be inclined initially to disagree with some of the perspectives offered in the pages that follow. That is understandable. Much of what undergirds leadership thinking is *counter-intuitive*. It simply runs contrary to much "common" knowledge. If you want something other than conventional results, then you have to learn to think in certain unconventional ways.

You can't be successful in a leadership role if you think like everyone else does. You have to see the world as leaders see the world. If you take this book to heart, and if you practice, you can prepare yourself for a leadership role.

How to Use
This Book

A couple of suggestions about how you might maximize your take from what's available here:

The first is that you want to be able to dip into this guidebook at any place it may seem personally advantageous or necessary to do so. But to be able to determine this most effectively, I would suggest that you first carefully read *Openers* and *Part I: How To Think About What Needs Thinking About*. This will give you a perspective on the rest of the book and provide a basis for where you might dip into it for your personal advantage from there on.

The second is that you can use the *Annotated Chapter List* as your guide. There may be enough description there to take you where you need to go at any time, given your personal needs and interests.

Since this is a guidebook, you will want to have it around, easily accessible, to refer to certain key sections to help you think about and implement the ideas that most appeal to you in your situation. You won't always get what you need with one reading, particularly a once-over-lightly. What's here is here to be studied and internalized, not merely "read" – to make it bear fruit for you, in the form of your improved performance as a leader.

It's impossible to write a book that is personally for the one individual who is reading this now. In your use of this book, it is necessary for you to seek out and incorporate what you need.

It's here. You just have to find it and put it into practice. Your real learning lies not in what is here, but in how you apply what is here.

If your learning journey is not fun and exciting, it will not bear fruit.

Some chapters, and some parts of those chapters, will appeal to you more than others. That's as it should be. Let your appetite, your needs, and your present circumstances be your guide. Explore. Be pulled by your own needs.

However: It is very important that you invest in the early chapters (about how to think about what you need to think about). They inform everything else in this book. If you don't get the thinking part down, you may not gain the perspectives that will make all the rest of it work for you. It's not for the casual reader. It's for those who seriously want to equip themselves to fulfill a leadership role. It's a matter of gaining as much as you can of what you need – of all of this distilled experience and knowledge about how it's actually done – to prepare you for your own journey to real achievement.

Reading this book is not a measure of much. But using it to achieve great and worthy goals ... that will be the measure of what you did with what's here.

ANNOTATED CHAPTER LIST

Openers: Some Preliminary Stretching Exercises   1

Offers an issue-by-issue overview of the unconventional paradigm one has to be familiar with in order to pursue extraordinary achievement – in any human endeavor, individual or collective. Sets forth how this book aims to lay out that paradigm and its implications, for any person who is serious about learning what has to be understood in order to achieve high performance.

PART I: HOW TO THINK ABOUT WHAT NEEDS THINKING ABOUT   19

Takes the reader on an expedition that explores, in the most fundamental way, *how* to think about what needs thinking about. What is it the leader of any endeavor to excel needs to be able to think about, and how?

Chapter 1: Gearing Up: Some Preliminaries That Need Your Attention   21

Offers a very comfortable introduction to some of the main terms and concepts that structure the mind-set required.

undertake leading a change in that direction, as Machiavelli warned back in the 16th century. And yet a few are successful in changing "the order of things." How do they get past those obstacles and barriers?

Chapter 5: Dragons   113

From the earliest recorded history, adventurers and heroes have always encountered *dragons* on their quests. However, it was understood then (less well today) that those "dragons" were mainly internal. What people imagine is going to happen to them on the path to any goal or destiny bears more upon whether or not they set out, and how easily they are discouraged, than do any actual obstacles they might encounter. How do leaders deal with their dragons?

Chapter 6: The Way You Think About Things   123

Nothing is more important than the way a person conceives of him or herself relative to his or her goal or cause. That's because this is what determines how that person will perceive their path given the obstacles encountered, and also determines how others will perceive that person. There are pratfalls in the way leaders think, such as the fact that much of what comes with being the *boss* is addictive. If those addictions cannot be overcome, the prognosis for success as a leader is very low. This is but one of several such obstacles dealt with in this chapter.

Chapter 7: The Drivers, Right Or Wrong   135

This chapter examines in detail what actually drives human behavior (not the conventional ideas about this subject). If you're thinking about this rightly, you will be successful. If you're stuck in the wrong ideas about them, you won't. If you have misconceptions about the "drivers," yours or others', those misconceptions will function as a barrier to your becoming the person who leads the way to high performance.

Chapter 8: Under-Empowerment   **147**

People are under-empowered if they are not fully competent to do what they do, or want to do. People are *empowered* by their own competence at what they do. This is not something you can confer on yourself or on others. It has to be earned through effort, discipline, and diligence. This is one of the keys to achieving extraordinary performance. This chapter sets forth the obstacles that "under-empowerment" presents, and what has to be done about it.

Chapter 9: Dumb Systems   **159**

Another barrier to the pursuit of high performance or of excelling is that of trying to support the endeavor with systems that work against the cause they are supposed to be aiding. These are "dumb" systems. Success depends upon learning how to identify dumb systems and to replace them with smart systems. This chapter explains what systems are, and how to distinguish the "dumb" ones from the "smart" ones.

Chapter 10: "Pop" Culture   **169**

One of the most potent obstacles to great achievement is *popular culture* – the "formulas" for living that people consume when they attend to popular music, popular television or radio, popular magazines and newspapers, and the popular folklore that emerges in all of the talk that gets generated by the universal consumption of this fare. This chapter focuses on the false ideas that people pick up there and bring to their lives or their workplace, and how those need to be displaced by unconventional ideas – the ones required for any elevated level of achievement and performance. Pop culture will take you in some direction other than the direction you need to be going to achieve extraordinary results.

Chapter 11: Perversity   185

The world we live in is almost infinitely more *perverse* than people believe. It is a person's own perversity that keeps him or her from carrying out even the most mundane of their dreams or goals in life. Assuming one can overcome his own perversity, it is still the case that the world does not aid people in their endeavors, but usually throws more perversity in their way. For leaders, this is a paradox: they must overcome their own perversities in order to see clearly the perversities they will encounter daily in pursuit of their cause. And leaders have to have the "weapons" to slay or defend against those perverse dragons that will otherwise defeat them.

PART III: HOW IT'S DONE   201

So, we've come to what some readers would consider the good parts – the how-to-do-it parts. For some, what follows might be the main target. But this book does not pander to what readers think they want. You get plenty of that in the sop being spoon-fed to you in the hundreds of *how-to* and *recipe* books being hyped week after week. This book is intended to provide readers with what they *need:* as much real-world from-the-trenches reality about this whole process as they can stand. There is an even more compelling reason for why this part of it comes now. Most attempts fail. They fail in large part because those who tried to apply the recipes did not fully understand what was required on their part to make those ingredients (tools) work. The better you understand the tools and what can be done with them, the more effective you will be. Using a tool not fully understood, to accomplish something not fully understood, is the formula for failure. There's a good reason why first things are first in this book. Leaders steep themselves in what they need to know first. This makes them who they *are.* Then they act. Your performance will be no better than your preparation, which is why all of those preceding chapters came first.

Chapter 12: What It Takes   203

This chapter is about what it takes to perform superbly: preparation, luck, being *had* by one's cause or mission (as contrasted to "having" one), inexhaustible enthusiasm for that cause and, for leaders of enterprises – surrounding oneself with the people who are going to make it happen by casting the right people in the right roles. Then, the four covenants between the leaders and those people who are going to make it happen. This requires engaging people *directly* and *necessarily* in what has to happen. Sounds easy? It's not. Most people give up and start looking for an easier way almost immediately. They remain on the lookout for "fairy dust" or some other panacea. There are none. What's required to make it happen is what has always been required, as this chapter makes clear.

Chapter 13: More Of *What It Takes*   215

What else does it take? Dealt with in this chapter: a robust plan, telling the story of how we get from here to there compellingly, and the role each person plays in that story. Keeping up the impetus and sustaining the change. The *power* required to make it happen. Some right-headedness about communication and why communication can't do what you'd like it to do. And why leadership and communication are so intricately interrelated.

Part IV: Some Tools For Making It Happen   229

The preceding chapters described what it takes for the leader to *think about* how to put together the people, the organization, and the systems to make it happen. The next three chapters describe some of the manifest and tacit tools leaders use to align others with their mission. It is the competency of the user that makes any great tool effective. These tools will not work for those who have not equipped themselves (along the lines of the preceding chapters) to be extremely competent in wielding the tools that will "make it happen."

Chapter 14: The Basic Tools   233

The basic tools are those that contribute to making elevated performance *possible*, and those that contribute to making the required level of performance *necessary*. Making higher levels of performance possible requires (a) developing the competencies of people in their roles, (b) making the systems in which those people are embedded smart enough to both encourage and accommodate higher levels of performance, and (c) having a critical mass of leaders who exemplify the kind of culture that makes higher levels of performance simply the order of the day – day after day. The most basic tool is that of "Role Descriptions." This chapter describes in detail how this extraordinary tool is conceived, and how to use it.

Chapter 15: More Tools   251

The next most basic tools for raising performance are "Performance Goals" and "Learning Plans." Role Descriptions provide an idealized description of what a virtuoso in that role would accomplish over the long term. Performance Goals describe mutually-agreed-upon accomplishments, objectively measurable, on a time-line. These are integrated with the goals of the organization, top to bottom and side to side. Learning Plans address the competency shortfalls exhibited by any role-holder. Again – the measure of achievement is *demonstrated accomplishments*, on a time-line. Other tools dealt with in this chapter include measurement, how problems can be used for development of people and of systems, how organizations can be composed as a tool, and a thorough exploration of smart systems, which could be considered as "meta-tools."

Chapter 18: Values & Beliefs: The Tacit Mediators 303

People do not maneuver *by* their values and beliefs. They are the pawns *of* their values and beliefs. A person's values and beliefs, imported largely form the cultures and sub-cultures to which that person belongs, are the tacit mediators of the world the person "sees" and understands. All of a person's thinking, doing, and saying are mediated by those cultural values and beliefs. They determine not only a person's performance. They also determine over time that person's destiny. It is the collective and common values and beliefs of the people who comprise an organization that determine the organization's performance and *its* destiny. If you can't get them right and internalized, you can't arrive at your chosen destiny. This is where the transformation has to come from.

Chapter 19: The Core Stratagems 315

The *core stratagems*, which also operate implicitly – or tacitly – distill most of the key issues from throughout the book into a handful of very broad strategically-oriented concepts. Get these right and you get most of the rest of it right. They are not a summary of all the other ideas in the book. They are more like key foundation stones, which enhance the fit and function of all that precedes this chapter.

Part VI: Envoi 331

One meaning of envoi: A message to send you on your way. That's what this chapter is for.

Not exactly a summary of all that has come before.
More like a capstone. This is short. The more it reminds
you of what was here to be learned, the more useful it will
be to you.

Openers:
Some Preliminary
Stretching Exercises

Although it is also about *real achievement* in any form, this guidebook is mainly about making high-performance organizations, and the kind of leadership required to do so.

The kind of achievement we're talking about is a little bit like winning at Wimbledon or the Masters. If you haven't done so, it may be because you don't know how. If you do know how but haven't actually done it, it amounts to the same thing.

There's so much to think about, much to learn. A mental "stretching exercise" occurs when you encounter something you haven't encountered before. There's much in this guidebook that you haven't encountered before. The other kind of stretching exercise occurs when you have to accommodate a way of understanding something that runs contrary to the way you've always understood it.

You will find that much of this book is devoted to challenging you to understand something you already understand – but to do so in a different way. Most people avoid both kinds of stretching exercises as ingeniously as they can.

The sheer fact that you have come this far – the sheer fact that you are even skeptically open to being stretched into the mental shape you need to be in to accomplish what you want to accomplish – is evidence that you are an unusual person.

Most people take for granted they *could* do "it" (especially this "it") if they "wanted" to badly enough. They would be wrong.

Most people's minds are already made up about what can and can't be done. Their position is: "Don't confuse me with the facts." But it is precisely the *facts* that call for the rethinking that has to be done. Here's an example of a stretching exercise to get started on:

- People can't figure out what they need to know. People can figure out only what they are personally capable of figuring out. So they seek advice. And here a paradox rears its ugly face: *If you know the difference between good advice and bad advice, you don't need advice.*

In other words, the most useful advice is the kind that helps you to develop your capacity for distinguishing good advice from bad advice. Therefore a lot of the advice you are likely to be exposed to is *bad* advice because it doesn't raise your own abilities for discerning the good from the bad.

The more you think about this, the more effective your mental muscles will be. In what follows in this guidebook, you will encounter, page after page, the kinds of challenges to your thinking, based on the *facts,* to put you in the mental shape you need to be in to accomplish what you want to accomplish.

Just for fun, here is another stretching exercise that can produce great benefits to your thinking (what you believe), your being (who you are), and your doing

- *Conventional wisdoms always and inevitably produce conventional results.* This means that if you perceive some problem or some opportunity in a conventional way (just because that's the way your mind works), you will come up with a conventional solution. But high performance, real achievement, is far from being the norm, far from being conventional. So the implication is that if you want to achieve extraordinary results, results that are not more or less average, you have to produce those results out of some fairly unconventional wisdoms. This guidebook is full of the kind of unconventional wisdom you need to achieve high performance. You have to stretch your mind to accommodate some of the counter-intuitive thinking that will challenge you in the pages ahead. You have to be open to the kind of stretching required to get into the mental shape necessary to make it happen. And to practice, practice, practice. The more different a different way of thinking seems to you, the more you have to consciously practice it.

Some Immediate Challenges

Here are some immediate challenges. Exercising your thinking on these will help you to get in good mental shape, ready to take full advantage of all that follows in the rest of this guidebook.

- One is that *many try, few succeed.* How ought you to understand this? Why are there so few successes when there are so many who long for real achievement, at work or at home? You're going against the odds. Two-thirds to three-fourths of business organizations in the U.S. have tried some formula for becoming excellent. The "key," the blurbs blare, is TQM, or reengineering or "transcompetition" or "open book management," or simply "teaching the elephant to dance." There have been as many proprietary schemes for easy success sold as there have been people who thought they could make money off of them – off of you. But of all who have tried, in less than 10% of those attempts was there any noticeable improvement. In the case of "reengineering," there were many organizations that ended up worse off.

There is clearly a hunger for getting better, or of transforming into excellence. Those who buy the panaceas of the month gobble up a lot of empty calories.

There's no trick to beating the odds, here or at the game table. You just have to know what the odds are. And you need to be able to see through to the reason why they are what they are. You can change *your* odds by avoiding the reasons others have failed.

The main reason is probably this: those consumers of the panacea of the month are led to believe that the logic required to become high performance is the same logic that is required to become average or mediocre. It is not.

3

Another basic reason for these failures is that those who undertook some scheme for producing real achievement didn't understand that being great at something requires that you be *different*. Most of the people you know would like to be superior, but only if they can be like everybody else. In other words, trying to be different by being the same just doesn't work, no matter what the recipe says.

Another reason: Wimpy or inconsistent commitment. People get all fired up, and then lose their enthusiasm. Something to think about here: Enthusiasm without relentless commitment and devastating competence never produces much of anything worthwhile.

Still another reason: It's nice to think that if you really want to achieve high performance, to make an organization that is hands-down the best, you'll get a lot of support from other people and from the rest of the world. You would be wrong. You will encounter daunting obstacles and barriers at every step of the way. And you can't look to the world to make it easier for you just because you've undertaken to try. As Yoda says in *The Empire Strikes Back*,

"There is no try. There is only do or do not."

Some Additional Stretching Exercises

Well, that's but one stretching exercise, and some examples for thinking how to go about it. Here are some additional stretching exercises. The better you can think through them and get yourself in the mental shape required, the better your odds.

• In spite of how seductive the "13 Secrets" or the "49 Steps" or the "8 Habits" may be, there are no easy answers. Any real achievement requires great effort, sacrifice, pain, and utter, utter determination. If you can't or won't pay the price, you will fail.

  • The difficulty of making a high-performance organization, of fulfilling any great and worthy cause, has never been *over*-estimated. It is mediocrity that is easy, not excellence.

- The media will lead you into confusing what's merely in fashion with what actually works. There have never been any fashions in what it actually takes to excel.

- The *answer* to something is never the same thing as accomplishment. There are words, and there are real accomplishments. Dilettantes and pundits deal in words. Those who are actually doing it are too busy to talk about it.

- If you think you can buy a process or a technique that is going to do it for you, you would be as wrong as you can get. The best tool works only if wielded by the best wielder.

- The number of recipes increases as the overall competencies of cooks decrease. The less able people are to do something, the more the predators will feed them about how to do it.

- If you don't know what real achievement *is*, if you don't know what it looks like and what it feels like, and how radically different it is from luck, or talent, or magic, you are not ready to launch *any* effort.

- It doesn't really make any difference whether or not you can talk a good story. The only thing that makes a difference is what you accomplished with your understanding.

- What you think this book is about is not what you think it is about. It is about what it *is* about. To learn, sometimes you have to un-learn.

- There are many things we do in life that we can learn to do only by doing them. Walking would be an example. Making a high-performance organization, and developing the kind of leadership required to do so, would be another.

- The "how-to" industry (books, magazines, seminars, talk shows) are not there to solve your problems. They exist to solve *their* problems. Which includes taking your money

for ideas or theories that don't work because they need
your money again next month.

- Real achievement is not an idea. It is an accomplishment.
They are measured very differently.

- The more people there are who believe in the latest panacea,
the less likely it is that you can make it work for you.

- In the past twenty years, there have been more than
10,000 books published on how to manage and how
to lead. Why does the failure rate remain more or
less constant?

- How is it possible that a recipe for how to be "the best"
can be a best seller? Is it even possible that the question of
how to be "the best" could have 10,000 answers?

- How is it possible that your organization could be unique
if you think like everyone else does?

And so on. You get the point. But unless you think through and
then think through these issues again and again, you won't have
done the mental exercises that you need to do to get in the mental
shape you need to be in to go on. *Have* you?

Revisiting the Lobby

Entering this (or any) book is a little like entering a building.
You arrive first in the lobby. There you have your first glimpse
of what the building is like. And your question is always, How
am I supposed to navigate this book (building)? What are my
impressions thus far? How can I develop a mental model of this
place so I can use it to my advantage? How do I assess what kind
of advantage is here for me?

Fair enough. Let's leave the exercises for a bit and go back to
the lobby. You'll encounter some of these mental exercises again
later on.

This book is all about what you need to know – and do – in
order to be successful at making a high-performance organization.
Such real achievement is something most heads-of-organizations

who have tried have failed at. So what is it you need to know, standing right here in the lobby, that will tell you whether or not this is for you?

After four-plus decades of being intimately engaged in this effort, with scores of those who run our organizations of every size and type, here and abroad, I'm convinced (in spite of how more or less adequate many are) that most American organizations are plagued by many of the same problems. Some of those perennial problems are at least implied in the stretching exercises you have just considered. But to cut to the chase, there are at least three basic impediments. If you cannot honestly see yourself overcoming these, this book can't be of much help to you. Here they are:

1. People who sign up to make this happen fizzle or fail because they did not have or could not muster the level of commitment required. It turned out they didn't have the overriding passion for it, or the level of perseverance required.

2. Those who didn't make it either (a) didn't have what it takes to make it happen, or (b) didn't have what it takes to develop in themselves those extraordinary ways of thinking, being, and doing that are simply necessary.

3. They never had a deep appreciation of what was required to make it happen.

The first of these impediments is totally your problem. You can't get the gumption required from reading a book about it – not even this book. You can't get the needed passion, zeal, or stick-to-itiveness from reading a book – no, not even this book. You either have those or you have what it takes to perform them whether you actually have them or not. Real achievement cuts you no slack on these. If you don't have what it takes to see it through, then you may be better off not commencing the journey.

By this time, you've already figured out that the second of these impediments also belongs to you – with some collaboration here. If you don't right now have what it takes to develop those extraordinary ways of thinking, being, and doing, you've come

7

to the right place. With an experienced guide (distilled in this guidebook), you *can* develop in yourself what needs to be developed to make it happen.

The most valuable thing I can provide you with is how to really understand what is required to make it happen. That level of understanding is indispensable. If you don't really understand how to do something, it's unlikely you'll be able to do it. So if you do your part, you can depend upon this guidebook to help you with all the rest of it.

It *can* be done. Not by belief. Not by faith. Not by desire or ambition or effort alone. It requires understanding. Real understanding. And that requires a significant level of collaboration between you and me, represented here by the tough and challenging perspectives and facts presented in this guidebook. If you can do your part of it, then you're in the right place.

Why Would An Otherwise Sane Person Take This Path In Life?

If you persist, you will find yourself wondering, when the going gets tough, Why am I doing this? It's the right question.

There are three basic reasons why a few people in history have committed themselves to real achievement:

One is fairly recent, but it's for money or notoriety. A large proportion of those who fail come from this category. That's because you can't buy anything that is really worthwhile. You can't "buy" real achievement. And fame is fickle. Those who head up businesses are often like shooting stars. The belief is that if you pay them enough money, they can make real achievement happen. But for the person on whom so much depends, if the primary focus is on money, then it won't be on achievement. The media, more full of myth than substance, identify their celebrities of the month. Then they move on. Sustained achievement isn't newsworthy.

Two, some people are just naturally perverse enough to pursue greatness for their own reasons. They are internally driven to compete and to outperform their peers. These "Lone Ranger" types also disproportionately contribute to the ranks of the failures. That's because they often can't get along with other people – the very people they would need to make a high-performance organization, or to sustain it.

Three, there are those who see it as a *moral obligation* – if for any reason they end up in charge of an organization, to make of that organization all that could possibly be made of it. To make it great. These are the same people who deeply believe that they have a moral obligation to make of themselves all that could be made of that unique raw material they happen to have. It seems clear that most of the real successes come from this category. That may be in part as follows: Anyone who seems to be seriously engaged in the pursuit of outstanding performance these days (either individually or organizationally) is looked upon by other people as marginally insane. So you are always going to get the question, "Why in the world are you doing this?" Presumably it is unthinkable that a person would choose that difficult, less materially-rewarding path rather than the easy path of self-indulgence, greed, or of "balance." To be able to answer, "Because I have to," may limit the conversation so each can get back to the different paths they have chosen.

Other replies that reveal possible success:
• "Because, for me, it's the only right thing to do."
• "Because I wouldn't be able to live with myself if I didn't strive mightily to be the best."
• "Because there's a high road and a low road, and I personally have to take the high road."
• "Because I can't take my toys with me but I can leave behind a legacy that will affect other people for years to come."

These are some of the kinds of answers you might get from a person who is rightly cast and fully dedicated to his or her role in making it happen. For most other people, it is usually a matter of doing much the same thing, over and over again, while hoping for a different outcome. You may recognize that as an old Chinese description of insanity. So there may be a real question about which one is insane – the person who does what is necessary in order to achieve what is possible; or the person who does the same thing over and over again, but merely "hopes" for a better result.

The Immediate and Inevitable Challenge

If this is the path you choose – of doing whatever is necessary to achieve some great and worthy purpose – you will be quickly challenged by other people who might have to be involved. Those other people are going to ask you: "Why should **I** be doing this? Why should **I** buy in? What's in it for **me**?"

If you don't have a convincing answer, if they can't read you as *being* the answer, your attempt to achieve a high-performance organization will essentially be dead in the water. You have to understand right from launch that a high-performance organization, while it can be measured in many other ways, is fundamentally an organization that is *good* for people. Most people work in organizations that are unhealthy, and for bosses who are not good for them. Most people go to work in the morning and come out at the end of the day no better off as human beings than they were at the beginning of the day. Many are worse. If the people who work at your place are not measurably better human beings at the end of the day, or when they get their 10-year pin, then you do not have a high-performance organization.

It is not just money, although they will have more of that. It is not just the fact that they will have far more control over the conditions of their lives at work, although they will have much more of that. It is something very counter-intuitive in the American culture. It is that the one condition that predicts to happiness and to relevance in life – to the very meaningfulness of life – is *competence*. The more competent people are in their roles in life, the more stimulated and satisfied they will be in their lives. And a high-performance organization is based in the competence of the people in every role in the organization. To have a competent organization, you have to have competent people in every role.

Seeking happiness directly, as we all know now, is the surest possible way of not getting it. That's why the more you try to provide for people's happiness or satisfaction at work, the less likely it is to happen. It doesn't come from what people are given. It comes from how competent people are to live their lives at work (the bulk of the day). So what is needed for an organization to be extraordinarily competent at what it does is the competence of every person in that organization. Thus it is win-win.

Here are some stretches:

- Most people don't know what you have just read. It is part of the power of every compelling leader who has ever lived.
- The less competent people are at work, the more they lose interest in their work and in everything around them. No wonder the day seems so long to less-than-fully competent people!
- Competence is the only thing people have that is portable. They certainly cannot take their "politicking" gains with them to some other organization, which many failed CEOs have learned to their dismay.
- "Work" is not a way for a person to sell her time or soul for a paycheck. It is an integral part of one's life. The better a person is at it, the better a person's life will be for it.
- As someone's boss, if you are not good for yourself in this sense, you won't be good for other people – the kiss of death for any would-be leader. If you can't effectively and advantageously lead yourself, then there's little hope that you can lead others.

Will those people be clamoring for you to make it necessary for them to be more competent at what they do? Not bloody likely. They will resist you every step of the way. After all, you resisted *you* in much the same way. If you didn't win with you, you aren't going to be good for them.

The more broadly and deeply you can understand how to answer their questions and their objections, the more likely you are to succeed in your venture. This guidebook can supply you with the way of thinking you will need to be able to do this. You just have to make it a part of who you *are*.

"Wanting" Vs. Doing

In the top executive seminars I conduct around the world and where I sometimes talk about such things, I'm frequently asked, "How many top executives can actually do this, based on your experience?"

My answer? "All of them *could*. Are you asking how many will actually carry it off?"

"Yeah," they say. "That. And, what's the difference? What do you mean, all of them *could*?"

"By 'all of them could,' I'm acknowledging the fact that whether they can or not depends ultimately on whether they did or not. And we've all been surprised from time to time by our judgments of people and what they actually do. In all cases, it's possible. It might take one person a few years and considerable effort. It might take someone else a lifetime and incredible effort. But perseverance counts for more than potential. So how many will actually produce great outcomes? Out of every ten or so who really, really *want* to be responsible for great achievements, maybe three or four will actually make some progress. But it's likely that no more than one out of ten will see it through."

"So it's not potential? It's not motivation?"

I have to answer as follows, "It's not potential. More potential goes to waste than anything else. But, by itself, what we're calling potential won't do it.

"Motivation? I don't even know what that means. It's a weasel word. People use it to excuse themselves and put others' achievements into the hands of psychological fate. It's nonsense. A person either accomplished what she set out to accomplish or didn't. Nothing is added by saying, 'She was motivated to do so.' The key point to focus on here (a stretching exercise for readers) is

12

that *wanting* to do something and *doing* it aren't even in the same universe. People who aren't going to do it will waste everyone's time by talking about how much they *want* to do it. They are delaying, in the hope that someone or something will do it for them. The person who is going to do it just does it. Nothing is added by saying, 'I want to do this or that.' It's more like a way of bonding with other people who would rather talk about what they *want* than to make the effort needed to bring it about."

There is nothing easy about being the best at something. And there is nothing easy about *learning* how to be the best at something. "Wanting" is the easy way out. "Doing" is what it's all about.

Then comes another often-asked question, "So how do you decide who you're going to work with? If you're picking one out of ten, how do you do that?"

"I don't always do a good job of picking the winner. By the time an executive has made it to the top, he or she is really good at deceiving other people. So I've been had – mainly by enthusiasm, as we all are. It is very intuitive, like Michael Jordan's decision to shoot this one or that one is ultimately intuitive. Based on experience. Asking a lot of questions. But it probably comes down to how much experience the candidate has had at strategizing and putting whatever effort is required into accomplishing the impossible. It may not seem so at the outset, but it won't be long before a task will appear that seems to be impossible. That's what will separate those who do from those who don't."

The key, certainly, is preparedness. If you read carefully and apply the distilled lessons available in this handbook, you can be optimally prepared. Beyond that, there are factors over which no one has any control.

Competence And Control

People often talk about competence or "talent" as if it would permit you to control things over which you do not and cannot have control. Competence alone will not ensure your success.

Competence optimizes only your preparedness. The real world will go on functioning as it does, immune to your will. The real world is oblivious to your wants and needs, even to your competencies. Real achievement has to be pursued in that world, not the world of fairy-tale success stories. The real world favors those who are best prepared, because they are prepared for both good "luck" and bad "luck."

It is frequently the case that people try to control what they cannot control. And fail to control what they can control. What they can control are their own capabilities and competencies. To be fully competent does not give you any more control over the uncontrollable than others. What it does provide is being prepared for whatever happens. And competent people have contingency plans.

There is no way of creating superhuman people or organizations that can bend the world to their will. Increasing one's competence every day in every way is the only reliable means there is of coping effectively with a world that operates by its own logic – not yours.

You will never be omniscient or invulnerable. The best you can do is never ceasing to develop your competencies, and/or those of your organization. No book can provide you with immortality or certain success. But, if thoughtfully internalized and practiced, it can help you immensely to equip yourself to be prepared. If you bring unremitting passion to bear, the mental tools and provisions offered here will provide you with what you need to make the journey.

Thinking Tools

*As you think, so will you **be**.*
*And as you are, so will you **do**.*

I've met many top executives who simply did not have the mental horsepower to avoid getting into a problem in the first place.

Or the exceptional mental wherewithal to extract themselves from it once they had gotten themselves into it.

In that sense, most of the problems such leaders face are self-inflicted. If they had the thinking tools needed, they could have avoided, or at least anticipated, most of the problems that predict to their future. If they had the kinds of thinking tools they needed, they might have been able to avoid or to get around the problems they face, and move on.

This is a book of *thinking tools*. You need to think in a certain way to provide the kind of leadership required for the pursuit of real achievement. If you intend to be the primary cause of making a high-performance organization, you have to think in a high-performance way. The logic that enables the achievement of high-performance is not the logic that leads to being "good enough."

Reading an advertisement about a new tool does not thereby equip you to use it effectively. You have to learn, thoroughly, what the tool does and how. And you have to learn what you and the tool can do collaboratively.

Many of the thinking tools you will encounter in this handbook may be expressed as axioms. Like the one above. The most generally-applicable axiom I know of, and the one which best explains what most needs explaining for leadership, is this:

> *Most people prefer a problem they can't solve*
> *to a solution they don't like.*

To put this in the immediate context, what this means is that most people will go on being pretty much like they are. If their problem was how to create a great organization, or even a reliably effective one, they will be likely to have that same problem next week and even ten years from now. The reason: The effort required to eliminate that problem and to get involved in real achievement just looks like more effort than they feel like putting out. It just looks more difficult than they want to deal with. So they deal with the problems of mediocrity – and all of the insoluble problems that go with the nurturing of, or tolerance for, mediocrity.

This is a difficult book because the process is a difficult one. You could buy a book that promises success in a couple of minutes or by simply owning the panacea.

Well, there are none that will work for you regardless of how you think and who you *are*. And I would be insulting your intelligence and further tarnishing your credulousness by making it look easy. It never was. It is not now. It never will be. Can you buy an answer that does not, ultimately, depend on *you*? You can, but it won't work.

So Who Is This Book *For?*

Good question. It may be for you if you've got what it takes.

Or, if they've got what it takes, it may also be an invaluable handbook for anyone put in charge of any kind of human endeavor; for anyone who has to achieve something great through themselves or other people. Thus, by definition, it is for parents, for coaches, for military leaders, for private sector leaders, indeed for the would-be leaders of any human endeavor that has some great and worthy aim, or purpose, or mission. It is for teachers, for mentors, and for any kind of role model.

It is for anyone who has to carry out real achievement, whether by choice or by happenstance. There are, after all, no *leaders*, at least not until historians dub them thus. There is only "leadership." That's what's required when one can take on that role for purposes of changing history.

That could be you. That's because it could be any one of us. But only if we are competent and prepared to fill that role. You could be. You could make this a better world – for yourself, but as well as for all the rest of us.

Leadership: Thinking, Being, Doing is your guidebook for how to do that. Bring your passion, your zeal, your determination. The pursuit of real achievement is the pursuit of real life.

16

So let's get on with what will work. If you can incorporate the thinking tools you need, then you will be the person you need to be. Only then can you do what needs doing.

N.B. You will meet up with some of those tools more than once in the pages that follow. This is not careless repetition. It just means that internalizing a tool and how to use it usually requires more than one encounter. But, then, most people prefer a problem they can't solve ...

PART I

How To Think About
What Needs Thinking About

This first part takes you on a trip. A mental expedition to explore, in the most fundamental way, how to think about what needs thinking about – and why. It will turn out to be indispensable.

You will like it if you have a keen interest in great performance. Or in leading your organization on the long and difficult journey to great achievement.

And then only if you have what it takes to undertake such a rigorous and challenging journey. Only if you have what it takes to learn what needs learning, and to persevere.

Chapter 1 offers you some essential provocations to help you get into the needed frame of mind for what's to come.

Chapter 2 provides a series of "think pieces" – brief engagements with what needs thinking about – and how.

Chapters 3 and 4 put before you a few key terms and how you may have to understand them if you are to provide the leadership required. Real achievement requires understanding basic terms, but sometimes in an uncommon way. How you define things (your lexicon) will determine who you are, and how you do what you do.

Chapter 1

Gearing Up:
Some Preliminaries That
Deserve Your Attention

If you were to read every book ever written about real achievement, about organizational excellence, and about the leadership required even to undertake such audacious causes – even if you were to memorize them all – that still would not enable you to do what has to be done. You have to learn how *by doing it*. Even then, it would still depend upon who you *are*. And then, upon how doggedly determined you are to fulfill your mission in life. And even then, upon how well you can surround yourself with the people who are going to make it happen. And having a strategy for getting there. And, always, upon a certain amount of the right kind of "luck."

No scheme for making you "successful" – even your own – comes with an iron-clad guarantee. The reason is simple. The only person who can make you successful in a venture such as becoming extraordinary is you. Your personal mental and emotional resources may be superior, or not. Your timing may be fortuitous, or not. Your people may be better equipped, or not. If your business or personal strategies are wrong – forget it. If you do not pursue your mission in life ruthlessly enough you will simply get whatever is dealt to you, good or bad. About "luck," that's easy. Good fortune favors the best prepared. That's accomplishable for those who are incorrigibly determined – and willing to pay the price.

A large part of that price is how you think about the things that make a difference. That's what this book is for. To help you think about what needs thinking about.

This *book* will not transform you into a high-performance person or your organization into a high-performance organization. Nor will this *book* make you into the leader you would need to be. No book, no seminar, no "program" can do that.

But, if you internalize the way of thinking this book offers, and if you implement these ideas by putting them into daily practice until they are habits, then you will have the necessary wherewithal for undertaking the journey of becoming "the best" – a leader of a truly high-performance organization, or a world-class achiever.

Once again, this *book* won't do it. But if you take what is offered here to heart and mind, *you c*an become the leader you need to be. These ideas are like the launching pad and the vehicle. *You* have to be the one to power the ideas. *You* have to make it happen. *You* have to be the engine. That "launching pad" cannot be made of words. It has to be dug down to bedrock – to belief, to habit, to a commitment from which you cannot escape or abandon, to a way of thinking and doing that comes from who you *are*.

It's not these words – these or any others. It's the passion and the competence behind the words. It's not the understanding – yours or anyone else's. It's the passion and the competence that focuses the understanding, like an overwhelmingly powerful magnet that is unfailingly energized by how you think about the things that makes a difference. It's about what you do with that thinking – how you put it into everyday practice.

If you're ready, willing, and able, let's collaborate in the building of this "launching pad."

1. Create the habits that make the difference.

Behind, under, and before every perception, every feeling, every decision and every action, there are habits. Habits of mind, habits of perception, habits of feeling, habits of action and reaction.

"The world" about which we speak so loosely does not "inform" us. We are "informed" by our own thinking and feelings about what that world is like and what is going on in it.

In short, the first and last leadership lesson is this:

We are led by our *habits* – of feeling, of thinking, of perceiving, and of understanding.

Get those right, and everything beyond becomes possible. Get those wrong, and the outcomes will always be something you didn't choose.

A leader's perceptions, thinking, and feelings about the world inside or outside are informed by that leader's cause in life. Most people believe that the world around them is a given, that when they look at it they are seeing what's there. That what people say about it constitutes reality. The true leader knows that a perception or an interpretation of something is never more than just that. Reality is not obligated by what we say or fail to say about it.

The leader also knows that people do not choose their trajectories through life. How we live and maneuver through life is not something we can have simply by choosing it. It is our habits that drive the way we think, and feel, and have, and do, and see, and say. We cannot choose our ways of being and doing. But what we *can* choose, within our capabilities for doing so, are the habits that inform our perceptions, our thinking, and our feelings. What makes the leader different is that he or she depends upon the habits *chosen* and developed to drive the direction and the outcomes of life. Not upon "hope." Or "intention." Or "desire." We necessarily go in the direction our habits take us. You can't get what you "want." You can only get what your habits can deliver.

What characterizes the leader is his or her mental models, the heuristics used to assess the world and the strategies for undertaking his or her cause in that world. It is the unique, unconventional habits of thought, feeling, and action that underwrite the leader's success in his or her endeavor.

- You do not acquire those habits of thinking merely by reading about them. Like all habits, they have to be developed.
- Nor do you acquire them by reading what celebrities tell us was *their* recipe for success.
- You get those by working backward from your cause and laboriously building into your thinking and feeling and doing those habits that are going to propel you in the direction of your cause. It is *your* cause that prescribes the habits you need.

Thinking. First things first. It is how you think that determines what you do. Habits of thinking produce habits of seeing and doing.

2. You have to be dissatisfied.

You have to be sufficiently dissatisfied with yourself and your performance in your roles in life to do something about it. We will talk more about "roles" later on.

To be satisfied with the habits that will determine your life is to endorse them and to acquiesce to wherever they take you. Most people seem to prefer whining about their lives, or their work, or their friends, or the world, than doing something about the only thing they have the prerogative to do something about – themselves. Leaders understand that they cannot get to a place they have chosen to get to by being victimized ... by *themselves*, which opens the door to being victimized by all the rest of the world.

- The leader changes the world by who he or she *is*. That *might* occur as the result of some one-in-a-billion genetic or historical accident.
- The only leadership worth pursuing is not achieved by accident. It's achieved by the habits of thought, feeling, and by the action required by the circumstances.

24

3. Understand your interdependencies.

The leader understands that pursuing any significant cause in the "real" world requires doing so in a complex web of interdependencies. The stand-alone hero who single-handedly achieves what appears to be impossible goals exists only in myth, in the movies, in the imaginations of lazy journalists, or in our dreams.

We all need someone who will make us do what we ought to do. If you have a powerful conscience, that will function as the "other." Or, if you have the kinds of habits that make it necessary for you to do what you *ought* to do (your "duty"), those will also function to make it necessary. For the rest of us, what's required is surrounding ourselves with the kind of people who will not let us default ourselves, who will make it necessary for us to do what we have to do in order to pursue our cause in life. Without an inner or outer context that absolutely makes it necessary, we will, more likely than not, fail by defaulting.

The leader is **first** of all interdependent with the historical moment. If the timing is right, he or she may become "the leader." If the timing is not right, if there is not a compelling need sensed by potential constituents for that person's leadership, that person will be unknown to history.

Second, "the leader" (of course we're talking about the would-be leader) is totally interdependent with those people on whom the success or failure of his or her cause depends. You've all heard the sing-song-y thing about "For want of a nail, the shoe was lost/For want of a shoe the horse was lost …" and so on, until it is revealed that the battle was lost. That's the kind of interdependence we're talking about here. Patton understood that his success as a field general depended upon the competencies of the lowliest recruits. That's why he paid so much diligent attention to the development of the competencies they would need under adversity.

Third, "the leader" and the success of his or her cause will always be interdependent – inseparable – from the strategies and tactics put in play to make it happen. If they're "right" for the historical moment, there will be success. But it will never be known whether or not those strategies were the "right" ones until the results are in. No guarantees. Just intricate and inescapable interdependences.

Fourth, any leader will remain over the course of the endeavor interdependent with whatever happens along the way. These may be happenstances. These may be a competitor's counter-moves or strategies. These may result from the fact an alarm clock didn't go off. Stuff happens. And the test of the leader is how nimble he or she is with respect to improvising and moving on, whether it is only oneself involved, or thousands of other people.

The fancy term for all this is *systems*.

- What this concept enables us to understand is that everything that happens – certainly everything that happens in the human world – has to happen in the context of other things that are constantly happening.

- Linear thinking won't work for leadership. What's required is thinking "systemically" – that is, understanding that everything is related to everything else. In *some* way.

- The leader understands that everything is what it is because everything else in the system is what *it* is.

- That may sound like gobbledygook to you. If you can't make it fundamental to your way of thinking, you'll never have the leader's edge.

- Not cause-and-effect. But interdependence, interrelatedness. You will never be more than those on whom you depend will enable you to be. And you will never accomplish more than the circumstances with which you are interdependent make possible.

You can't change that. But you can equip yourself to pursue your cause in *that* world – for the leader, the "real" world.

4. Figure out how to have more LIFE.

Leaders seem to have more LIFE brimming behind their eyes and ears, within them and around them, in the evidences of their "spirit," than the rest of us have.

That's a major part of what makes successful leaders so seductive.

They have so much LIFE in them that they can give it away. They seem to infuse those around them with more of this ... LIFE. What is it? Exuberance? Zeal? Passion? Clarity of purpose? Single-mindedness? Openness? Whatever it is, it seems to be infectious. We see it in their eyes. In their movements. In the way they listen and ask questions. In the way they speak and engage others. In the way *they* grab hold of LIFE and won't let it go.

- Does LIFE grab them more? Or do they grab more LIFE?
- Or, given that they are a part of a system that has everything in it that is there for the rest of us, maybe it has something to do with how they *think about things*, or with their habits.
- They inhabit the same *world* we do. So it must have something to do with *them*.
- Maybe the difference is that they had no interest in the difference.
- Maybe the difference emerged from their total immersion in the pursuit of their cause?

5. Interact with change.

There is the perennial issue of *change*. It has become so popular it functions like a "mantra" – people frequently mouth or pen the term but it has ceased to mean much more than suggesting that the speaker or writer is "with it."

Leaders know:

- Things are changing all the time.

- Most of the changes that swirl around us are not within our control.
- Who people *are* – because that is a function of a whole bundle of habits exercised every moment of every day – is a primary source of resistance to change. We will most likely be tomorrow what we were today. For that to happen, the world tomorrow has to be reasonably like it was today.
- That to attempt to change the world, which would require people to change, is (as Machiavelli wrote) the most dangerous and uncertain undertaking there is.
- That it is the appeal of the alternative leaders describe that makes any significant change *possible*.
- But that it won't occur unless it is *necessary*.
- That change cannot be generated or sustained by rational means.
- That systems in which people are embedded are fiercely resistant to change because they are tacit, accessible only by habits of belief.

Leaders understand that they are wholly interdependent with the forces that resist change, **and** with the forces that enable change.

All this because leaders don't *make* change. They midwife it.

6. Measure what counts.

Leaders don't just measure. They measure what counts.

7. Ask what needs knowing.

About *anything* they imagine might bear upon the journey undertaken to fulfill their mission or cause in life, leaders have a minimal threshold. Being intensely curious about anything that might bear, one way or another, on the path they are on, leaders are in the business of asking questions. Asking questions of themselves, of others, of all of the world's wisdoms and its histories and current complexities. Leaders aim not to "know" everything, but only to gather the intelligence they need, from any source that bears upon their cause – beginning with themselves, that can be used to accomplish what needs to be accomplished.

- There is no leadership "trivia."
- Leaders either know what they need to know in order to carry out their mission, or they fail.
- Their communication is that critical.

8. Hold people accountable for ...

What matters? Holding people accountable for the results? Or holding people accountable for how well prepared they are, at all times, for pursuing those results?

Managers seem to prefer the former, leaders the latter.

Something to think about.

9. Become ruthless about ...

Leaders often seem to be ruthless. On themselves? About what? Was there ever a leader who wasn't ruthless – about what might contribute significantly to the success or the failure of their endeavor?

How often have leaders failed by being reasonable? How often have they succeeded by being unreasonable (again, about what really matters)?

Given that most people have no particular aims in life, beyond having a comfortable "job," a comfortable spouse/lover/family, a comfortable house in a comfortable neighborhood with comfortable friends, a surfeit of comfortable leisure, and a comfortable retirement, can you achieve your aims in life by soliciting and indulging those people? Especially if one of them is *you*?

10. Think about your *role* as a leader.

It does hinge profoundly on how the would-be leader *thinks about things,* doesn't it? The leader understands this: *As we think, so we will* **be.**

The leader knows that leadership is not a characteristic of a person. It is a *role* that needs playing in a *story* that needs writing. If it isn't the *leader's* story that gets written, the leader knows that it will be someone else's story, and that he or she will be no more than a bit player in those other stories.

It is only when this kind of outcome is intolerable that the irresistible desire to lead gets born. The leader knows that leadership, being a role that needs to be played, is, metaphorically, a performing art. How the would-be leader plays that role will determine whether or not there are followers, and thus whether that leader's aims make a difference ... or not.

It may be that "All the world's a stage," but the only one that matters is the one on which you appear. And upon how well prepared you are for that role.

- Prepared with a way of thinking that makes a difference in *your* performance.
- Unconventional.
- A way of thinking that powers your performance.

The leader understands people better than most. The leader understands, for example, that if you want to know how a person *really* wants to live, you look at the way that person lives. If you want to know what people mean by what they say, observe what they *do.*

Much more ahead on this.

11. Understand mediocrity.

How to have a ***mediocre*** organization (for some variations on this, see my book, *How Executives Fail: 25 Surefire Recipes for Sabotaging Your Career):*

- Be a conventionally-minded manager or executive. Think like your peers do. Put your own immediate interests and feelings first.
- Make sure you have a conventionally-designed organization, with conventional systems, processes, and procedures that take precedence over performance.
- Hire only mediocre people, especially those who put their own immediate concerns and interests first. They will be more comfortable to have around if they have no particular aims in life.
- Navigate solely by the "bottom line." The shorter the time frame, the better.
- Don't expose yourself to excellence, except to critique it.
- Do what you can to force your customers, suppliers, and other stakeholders to "understand" *you*.
- Make sure all of the people and other sources whose opinion you value are no better than you are.
- Get excited only about what has *happened* to you in the past.
- Defer learning to your leisure time.
- Appear always to know everything.
- Use your thought-ways until they become comfortable "ruts."
- Depend on habits that you didn't choose.

That's all worth thinking about. How? Shall we move on?

POINTS TO PONDER

+ Habits take you where they are headed, not where you "want to" go.

+ Habits of thinking determine habits of seeing and doing. And of feeling.

+ If you can't tell your story compellingly, you don't have one.

+ Knowing-about is not the same as knowing-how.

+ Leaders don't depend on what is known. They depend on what can be done with what is known.

+ Reading success stories won't make you successful.

+ It is solely your cause that determines the habits you need.

+ Outcomes are never linear.

+ Be the source of change, or the victim of it.

+ Change has to be made possible, and then necessary.

+ Where their cause is at stake, leaders have to be capable of being ruthless.

+ We all need someone to make us do what we ought to do. Who?

2 Getting Underway ... Think On These Things

This chapter offers you an opportunity to exercise even more of your thinking muscles. What follows is a (minimal) set of "think pieces" to use as examples for how you might think through short quotations or epigrams that (for any reason) intrigue you. They are not intended as recipes for how to think. They *are* intended as exercises for how to think about what needs thinking about.

Let's start here...

1. If you want to know what kind of organization you deserve, look at the one you've got.

Maybe you've never heard chief executives whine about the performance of their organizations – or the people in them. I have. Many times. They seem to be suggesting that they somehow "deserve" better. A little bit like parents trying to get others to agree that they did "the best they could" raising their children, so why those children didn't turn out wonderfully is certainly no fault of theirs.

Here's an example:

I arrive at the office of a client. This client – we'll call him Frank – is livid, enraged. I wait. You should never ask why a person is angry; it encourages them. After a while he says, "I'm absolutely beside myself. Why so-and-so would do such-and-such is beyond me. And, this isn't the first time it's happened. What makes him so stupid?"

My reply (not kind): "Do you mean what makes him so stupid or what makes you so stupid for choosing him and casting him in that role?"

"What do you mean?" Frank turns to squint at me, some of his anger now targeted at me. "He's supposed to know better than that."

"How?" I ask. "By behaving like you do? If everyone behaved as they are supposed to behave, from whose point of view would that be, yours or theirs?"

"Mine," Frank admits, sheepishly pointing the finger back at himself. "But, it just seems like I deserve better." Then, unable to muster the same level of anger at himself, he adds, "You know, smarter performance."

"You probably do," I replied. "Doesn't that begin with you?"

You get the point. Them who can, do. Them who can't, whine about the reality they have surrounded themselves with, using words like "should" and "ought."

If something they consider "smart" happens, they are quick to take credit for it. If, however, something wrong or "stupid" happens, they start pointing fingers at anyone or anything other than themselves.

So, what do people like you and me "deserve"? Better than we are? Better than we have? Contemplate this:

• The people in your organization are there because you directly selected them. Or, because you selected the people who selected them. How people perform throughout the organization is your mandate – directly or indirectly. If you can't get that part of it right, you're going to have trouble getting any of the rest of it right.

- The person who performs in a way that pushes your frustration or anger button is likely not as fully competent to perform his or her role as may be necessary. Who is ultimately responsible for *that*?
- The attitudes and the performance of every person in your organization is directly or indirectly (through *your* choice of *their* boss) influenced by who you *are*, because who you *are* determines how you do what you do.
- If you overlook performance shortfalls or the failure to grow in your role until you finally "blow up," that makes those shortfalls and failures as much your fault as the other person's fault. From day one, *if there are no consequences forthcoming for sub-par performance, then you are responsible for your own frustrations or anger.*
- Are your expectations clear and mutually understood? As Sun Tzu said, if people do not perform as expected because the expectations were not clear (to them), then the fault lies with the boss – with the leader – with you.

With rare exceptions, the organization you deserve is the one you have.

Think about it.

Shall we press on?

Over time, the organization isn't going to be much better – or perhaps much worse – than its leader. If you want an organization, or an athletic or musical performance, that ranks you among the "best," you have to be the kind of leader who *deserves* that outcome. And what needs to be changed at the outset is not the organization. It is the leader.

If you can't become the kind of person with all of the capabilities required to lead a great or high-performance organization, then you will not have a high-performance organization.

If you can't put your organization on – and keep it on – the path to becoming "the best," then you are not – **yet** – the kind of leader who deserves such an organization.

Fix that first. The rest will follow.

This brings us full circle: If you want to know what kind of organization, or performance, you "deserve," look at what you've got. If you're not sure what you "deserve," ask your followers. They will know what you "deserve."

2. Like it or not, believe it or not – it will all depend first and last on who *you are* and thus on your leadership.

It will depend on how you think about what needs thinking about, which is the *source* of your leadership.

Let's revisit this one:

>*Conventional thinking always and inevitably leads to conventional ways of doing things.*
>
>*And conventional ways of doing things always produce conventional results.*

Short version: Conventional thinking always leads to conventional results. It's always easier to think like everyone else thinks. That way you never have to justify your ways of thinking or of doing. And you'll end up in the middle of the pack, like most everyone else. How to have the most ordinary life? Think like everyone else does.

Second stanza: It's always easier to think like you have always thought. Thoughts – ways of thinking – are like the paths sheep make on the hillsides, as they follow in one another's footsteps. Your thoughts follow each other like those sheep, in paths well-worn with many previous footsteps. The more you think today the same way you thought yesterday, the more ingrained your thoughts become and the harder they are to change. We get deeply into our mental grooves and resist any happening or any person who challenges them. We twist present reality so that it fits past "experience." We'll think like we've always thought.

One of my clients was a very smart fellow, a good engineer, a person who wanted to be an adequate – or better – CEO. I arrived in the middle of an almost plant-wide involvement in figuring out why a certain machine wouldn't "register" – it just wouldn't perform the sophisticated operation it was "supposed" to perform. The CEO, his staff, and several other "experts" were engaged in trying to figure out why the machine wasn't doing what it was "supposed" to do. They had even called in the machine manufacturer's people, and a consultant or two.

I asked, "Why are you doing this?" In fact, I asked two or three times, looking right at him.

Finally, he said, "Okay, you keep asking me that question. I'm trying to fix a problem. So, what the hell do you mean, 'Why am I doing this?'"

At least I had his attention. "You're a good engineer," I said. "If you figure out why the machine isn't 'registering,' will that tell you how to make it do so?"

"Well ... no," he said, thoughtfully.

"Let me ask another question, then. If you wanted to make this product, could you set up a plant across the street and just do it?"

"Yes, I reckon we could."

"In that case," I said, "why don't you do it that way? Why don't you take a blank sheet of paper and figure out what has to be done to fabricate that product? Why are you wasting your time looking for a cause of something that went wrong when knowing the answer won't in itself tell you how to do it right?"

I waited. He was deep in thought. Then he took a blank sheet of paper, called a couple of his key people in, and they "solved" the problem. Not by going head-on at it, but by going around it.

Sometimes people just do the same thing over and over again, but "hope" for a better outcome. As retired Army General Gordon Sullivan and many before him have observed, "Hope is not a method." Thinking and doing in the same ways over and over again, while trying harder and hoping even more for a better outcome is, as ancient wisdom has it, a form of insanity. But you have observed this kind of insanity many times, maybe even being involved in it.

There are two traps here: One is that conventional ways of thinking are simply easier. They are likely to go unchallenged by others who think the same way. Or by others who have come to expect us to think or act in those familiar ways.

The other is that a way of thinking that may have resulted in some modest success is likely to take root and defend itself against any alternative. We come up with a success paradigm and then use it to fit all circumstances until we fail by applying it where it does not fit.

Here's the corollary: If you want something other than conventional results, you have to start with something other than conventional wisdom, like, "Experience is the best teacher." Your interpretation of some past success is a very unreliable prescription for future success.

Conventional thinking is a byproduct or a symptom of the inability to think afresh about a common problem. Thinking afresh requires:

- Being totally accomplishment minded, not being shackled by routines.
- Having great mental resources honed on great thinkers, and
- Having the sort of disciplined mind that enables you to be creative, to *invent* or improvise ideas and stratagems that enable you to leapfrog current thought and beliefs.

The more commonplace the "stuff" you feed your mind, the more commonplace will be your thinking, and thus the results of your thinking. If you want uncommon wisdom, you have to go after it ruthlessly. And you may have to invent or improvise a way of accomplishing what needs accomplishing.

Leader's lessons …

- An accomplishment is always in the future. Exactly what is it? And what is the most expedient path from here to there? Leaders often have to **create** the outcomes they seek. If those could be had from experience, or by prescription, we'd all have been successful long ago.

- Leaders have to calculate what needs to be done in always-unique and ever-changing circumstances, *given their own aims*. If you're looking at circumstances *in terms of* your own aims, it will quickly become obvious that prepackaged ways of thinking won't work.
- Leaders are the makers of the world and its consequences for their purposes. They are not the victims of it. Change the world? Change your thinking.

Here's another corollary: There is no competitive advantage in doing *anything* conventionally. That simply places the outcome directly in the clutches of chance or "luck." When everyone thinks like everyone else, the winner is determined by the roll of the dice. Maybe what drives leadership is a loathing for living that way. The success of your vision could hardly be at the end of the widest and most-worn path. What's been done has been **Think about it.** done. The future you need to create hasn't occurred yet. What's the "recipe" for creating something that hasn't existed before?

3. Here's an easy one: There is no quick fix.

We all know that's true. Yet why do so many executives, so many "wannabe" leaders, continue to lust after the latest and greatest of the "quick fixes" being hyped by the business press – or by one another?

Not only is there no quick fix, there certainly isn't a one-size-fits-all prescription for greatness, for unparalleled success. Why? Because no two leaders are ever that much alike. And the circumstances in which it all has to be worked out are *never* the same. Add the fact that very few leaders have ever been able to replicate their success at another time and in different circumstances. So the imagined prescription which made them successful won't even work for them in changed circumstances. And they are themselves different from who they were previously.

There are no shortcuts. There is no fairy dust. There are no "secrets" to be revealed if you just buy this or that magazine or book or seminar. Your fantasies do not in themselves transform you into a James Bond (or even a Warren Buffett). Every day you are offered all kinds of "magic wands" to wave over your organization to make it wonderful. As someone once said, "Hope springs eternal." We seem to be seduced by every panacea that gets hawked by the panacea-hawkers. Why?

There is only one way to achieve something intended that is really worthwhile. And that is the hard way. To achieve great things, you have to pay the price. That's just the way it is. The "price" is not in fairy dust, or agreements. The price is in the long-term investment. That requires great effort and dedication. Extraordinary achievements require discipline, smarts, diligence, and an unwavering passion to achieve.

Here's the reality. Becoming "great" is not a goal to be reached. It is a way of life, gained and maintained by superlative discipline of mind, body, and spirit. It is character. It is pursuing a purpose or a cause even when it requires more than your own lifetime.

It might take a hundred years. So what? There is no better way to live than by what is required to be solidly on the path of becoming – forever *becoming* – the best at some truly human, and humanizing, endeavor. This way of life makes "getting there" a non-issue. At the end of the day, whether or not you are securely and irreversibly on the path is the only thing that matters.

I hear someone mumbling something about quarterly financial statements. A quarterly financial statement is certainly important. It has frequently been observed that you can't have a future unless you are healthy in the present. But making any short-term measure the only one that counts will guarantee that you are not on the path of becoming anything other than short-term. You will be pushed here and there like a reed in the economic winds. You will always be a victim.

A short fable:

> There was this CEO who said that things were not going well because "the economy is weak." There was this same CEO who, when "the economy" was robust,

said, "Look at what **I** did!" Which "theory" are you going to believe? Taking credit for good results, but placing blame for poor results, is a prescription for failed leadership.

Consider these:
- You have to be up to something great in order to have any possibility of making progress in that direction.
- If you are not interpreting the world in terms of your own designs on it, then it will interpret you in its terms.
- If you don't know (or care) where you are going, you're likely to end up someplace else – but with tons of advice about how to get there.
- To compete on any criterion other than becoming "the best" leaves you vulnerable to even the poorest competitors.

There is no "quick fix." Sure, you *can* buy a quick fix today, and then another one tomorrow, and another one the day after. You can be known as the person who pursues "the flavor of the month." Or ... you can get on the path of real achievement, which means practicing today in order to perform "perfectly" tomorrow. And then tomorrow you practice again. So you are forever practicing in order to do *everything* better. That's the path to ... real achievement and leadership.

If most of your focus is on the short-term, in pursuit of quick-fixes or just ways of accommodating the posture of firefighting, then thinking about what truly needs thinking about – to get where you have chosen to be – will never become a priority.

You will put it off until your own aims and intentions have atrophied.

It helps to remember that a "quick fix" is the one you need before you need the next one.

Think about it.

4. Getting from here to there requires getting into a different "paradigm."

The "here" refers to the present you. And to the present circumstances of your organization. The "there" refers to the point at which you are irrevocably on the path of determined achievement. A "paradigm" refers to your standard way of looking at and thinking about yourself and your organization – and the world in which both function.

Why a different "paradigm"? Well, if you use the same "paradigm" every time, you will be doing the same thing over and over again. Or, at best, you will be on the path of the ordinary, of carrying out whatever is inevitable in your present paradigm. Your destiny is either given or chosen. To choose requires moving into a way of thinking and doing that is different from the one that presently holds you hostage.

This means that there has to be a "leap of faith" for the first person to transition from the "here" lily pad to the "there" lily pad, from the one way of thinking to the other way of thinking. This would be the leader. Once there – thinking and doing – in this different paradigm, he or she can reach out a helping hand – provide a bridge – from the one to the other. It is only the leader who must believe in his or her vision of that future way of life. It helps if the others – particularly your other leaders – also believe. But, *ultimately, they have no choice.* They can choose *not* to make the journey. What they cannot do is choose to make the journey, yet fail to make the leader successful in the expedition. No one can be along for the ride.

Some key points to consider:

- Leaders are roused to commitment and action through *dissatisfaction.*
- Dissatisfaction with the status quo, with being merely adequate, with being victimized by whatever happens, with the deadly suffocation of mediocrity, with the mundane same-old, same-old, has to be the leader's driver.

- Leaders *lust* to live in the rarefied atmosphere of being exceptional.
- The faith required, the effort required, the perseverance required – all fade to irrelevance in the face of the raging dissatisfaction of being no more than a pawn in the clutches of yesterday, forever recycled.
- To attempt to write your own story, you have to be powerfully dissatisfied with the one you're in.
- That's part of what it takes to lead the struggle from "here" to "there."

A reminder: You can't live in the conventional world, wallowing in a conventional lifestyle, with its conventional orientations and attitudes, and still expect to be a real achiever. A would-be leader who does not have the courage to follow that proverbial "path less taken" will not make much of a difference in his or her own life, or the lives of others.

In spite of a persistent myth to the contrary, history is not made by the masses of people who do not have to think because their thinking is done for them. It is the leader who derails inevitability by refusing to let the past determine the future.

You need followers. Radical followers – people who will make your vision into reality in spite of your own shortcomings and weaknesses and regressions. Without leadership, they have no aim, no direction, nothing toward which to channel their energies and their pursuit of something greater than their present lives. Without those radical and unreasonable followers, the leader's cause will be stillborn.

The journey from "here" to "there" is a matter of *realizing* – of making the mere vision into an absolute reality. How incorrigibly committed the leader is will determine the life – or the death – of a cause, a vision, a dream. **If** it is life or death for the leader, that leader will attract the followers needed to turn the vision into reality.

We humans have to understand the world by looking at the past. But we have to live it going forward. The future is not subject to past analyses. It gets created by what people say and do every day. We can neither predict nor control that. But we can align people to a cause. It will never be perfect. But it's all we have. The leader makes allegiance to the present "paradigm" difficult or even *impossible*. And, the leader makes saying and doing consistent with the alternative "paradigm" *necessary*.

You can't align people by exhortation. You have to make the thinking and doing that will get you from "here" to "there" **necessary**. For people to go their own way cannot be an option. If it is, the leader's vision is doomed.

What's required of our thinking and doing is not more of the same. It is not a comfortable extension of present thinking and doing. What's required is a profound shift in orientation and attitude to what's going on, made necessary by where we're going – from "here" to "there." This is, at the outset, what the leader makes necessary – the kind of thinking that gets people out of the old paradigm and into the new.

For example, here are some faulty assumptions:

- Working "harder" at being a manager will turn you into a leader. Hasn't happened yet.
- Whatever makes us adequate could make us "the best" if we just worked harder at it. Won't happen.
- Knowing-*about* is almost the same as knowing-*how*. Never.
- An adequate organization could evolve into a great organization. No. That won't happen.
- The future we desire will be produced by our desire. Does anyone *really* believe that?
- Most people are willing to leave their comfort zones of their own volition. Does it work that way for anyone you know?
- The future is determined by the past. One of the historians' fallacies.

You have to be overwhelmed, totally seduced by your zeal to get from "here" to "there." Those who cling to their present paradigms like shipwreck victims to anything that floats are not neutral. They will thwart you if they can. Ever try to save a drowning person? They will welcome you with open arms only to take you down with them.

You have to think and do in a way that will make your cause come to fruition, whether they welcome you or not. Great achievements are always *in spite of*, never "because of." Change is brought about by the unreasonable person.

More to ponder:

• It's tough. The road signs are all on the well-traveled road being taken by most others.

• *You* have to make your own road signs. You have to *make* the road, not take one.

5. Most people, and thus most organizations, are *event-driven*. Leaders, and their organizations, are *purpose-driven*.

What this means: In an event-driven organization (or life), the day begins with the first event that occurs, followed by the second, and then by the third, each more or less random event being superceded by the next more or less random event until, at the end of the day, people are exhausted. "Fighting fires" is not very inspiring or energizing work. People finish one day of being event-driven, only to look forward to another day of the same. It is like a squirrel-cage – a squirrel-cage being cranked by a problem that you look like a target for.

One thing leads to another. You sort them out according to which one seems the most threatening, *or* has the least risk, *or* whatever one's random feelings are for dealing with these random events at the moment.

Well ... you've been there, done that. You know how it feels and how it leads to nothing other than more of the same. If you like that, forget the rest of this. If you are really, really dissatisfied, read on.

What's different about being *purpose-driven*? After all, the same events can occur whether you are event-driven or purpose-driven. The primary difference is that you look at those events in terms of their relevance to your purpose, your aim, your cause in life. You interpret events in terms of their bearing on outcomes you have chosen, not in terms of those events themselves. A "fact" is a fact only because it relates to some purpose or cause. To deal with it as a thing in itself is exhausting because it is meaningless, a mere exercise in getting through the day. For the purpose-driven, one's purpose is the measure of an event, not the other way around.

In a purpose-driven organization, the agenda precedes events. Events get put into a more meaningful context – in terms of their relevance, not to people, but to the larger purpose – the reasons for the organization's existence and its destiny. Leaders help us to put the horse before the cart, the context before the event.

As follows:
- To be event-driven is to measure things by *their* demands.
- To be purpose-driven is to measure life through *accomplishments* that move you toward your purpose.
- Preparing yourself, and then others, to get on the path of real achievement is being purpose-driven. Mere *activities* diminish everyone to a life of being event-driven.
- If it gets on your agenda without your permission, or is not a means to **your** ends, it is because you prefer being event-driven.
- A person who is event-driven will never become a leader.

6. The pursuit of a cause is not a goal. It is, however, the best way of life.

The pursuit of a great and worthy purpose in life is an endless *journey*. The world will not stop just because you got a little better. There are those who are struggling to overtake you, always. You will not be exempt just because you tried.

Real achievement is not a place. It's an attitude, a set of habits, a way of life.

Think on these things:
- Those who seriously pursue a purpose in life cannot afford to tarry at any level of "success."
- Getting better, making progress, is about preparing today for tomorrow's trials.
- If this striving ends before you do, you have failed.
- It is the striving that enhances our lives, not the arriving.
- The question, "Are we there yet?" is the kiss of death for your mission in life.

The quality of the life you have while pursuing your goals is more important than achieving them. You can be successful by accident, by sheer "luck." And you can fail through no direct fault of your own. But you cannot pursue a purpose in life except by choosing to do so. It is the character that comes as a byproduct of being committed to your own purposes in life that measures the quality of one's life – or an organization's life.

Here's the critical difference: the pursuit of a great and worthy purpose in life requires you to develop and maintain an increasing capacity for learning. Learning produces growth. And life is always enhanced to its current limits by growth, which in turn increases its limits. By putting people on this path, the leader incites and inspires their lives. Having something larger than themselves to live for generates and raises the sheer quality of life. The leader is a life-maker, first his own and then the lives of followers.

Arriving is a form of death. It is the end of something. *Striving* requires forever *beginning*. There is more life in beginnings than in endings. There is more life in striving to achieve something great than in being forever buffeted by "events."

A client once said to me, "We're not getting there."

There's only one answer to that: "You're not getting there *today*? What are you doing *today* about that?"

Or, let's put it as follows:
- To live in the thrall of the habits required to pursue a great and worthy purpose in life generates endless adventure.

- Achieving one's goals too soon or too easily is the end of the adventure that life could be.
- To compete with the best in order to surpass the best puts you in the "best," the most exciting, company.
- The schoolyard game "King of the Hill" teaches us that being the one on top is temporary, at best. It was those who were trying to knock you off your perch who were having the most fun.
- But, the critics say, suppose we "fail." Fail? At what? At having richer and more rewarding experiences of life?
- Where's the downside? If you don't do it, how much life will go un-had, unrealized?

7. You like "practical"? Here's an extremely practical one: *Take your eye off the bottom line.*

That must look like some whack-o advice. It's ancient advice. It is advice not much heeded in our world. We're "bottom line" people. But you'd be surprised by how valuable this simple bit of advice can be.

Some managers believe that the numbers tell them what they need to know. How wrong they could be! The conventional bottom-line numbers may tell you a little bit about the current and most recent financial history of the company. They may tell you where you are relative to where your forecasts were.

But those numbers won't tell you where you *ought* to be. They won't tell you what's wrong. They won't tell you what to do about what's wrong. They won't tell you what the situation might be if you had prepared differently. They won't tell you, won't even give you a clue, about what your purpose in life ought to be. They won't tell you how to get from "here" to "there," or even where "there" is.

Those numbers will tell you something about your current state of purely financial health (and you have to read that into them). But managers who don't have a fairly accurate intuitive grasp of that without the numbers are not going to learn much by any literal interpretation of the numbers. Those numbers won't tell you whether or not you got to the present situation out of incompetence, stupidity, or (good or bad) luck. They won't tell you how good your competitors are, or where the next real threat is coming from. They won't tell you if you have the right business strategy. They won't tell you whether or not you have the right people in the right roles (including the CEO), or the right organizational design for what you want to accomplish.

The "numbers" are a conventional talisman produced by a conventional accounting practice. Here's something accountants won't tell you about "the numbers": that they do not, can not, partial out the contribution of the environment from the contribution of the organization to "profit." Thus some organizations do all the right things, but fail. Other organizations do all the wrong things, but succeed.

The numbers may tell you *something*. But they won't tell you what you did right, or wrong. They won't tell you what you need to do next, beyond doing whatever it takes to make the numbers measure up to some preconceived pattern.

Enough? The point is that taking your eye off the bottom line (except as you might use a thermometer) sets you free to put your eye on what *drives* the bottom line. Things like towering competence. Like intensity and zeal. Like preparedness for whatever happens (or doesn't). Like reserve energy and acumen. Like the kind of intelligence that matters. Like being committed to a level of performance that forever pulls the bottom line along in its irresistible wake. Like focus, or the right strategy, or the right organizational design. Like "smart" systems that underwrite exceptional performance. Like practice. To reframe:

- Bottom lines do not improve by analysis or interpretation.
- They are produced. What produces them is measurable.
- Put your eye on what *drives* the bottom line, develop those capabilities, and the numbers will always meet or exceed your expectations.
- What's most easily counted is rarely what counts most.

The financials are the result of many forces – some of which are controllable, some of which are not.

Leader's lessons:

- Those who pursue real achievement will focus on what *is* controllable, what *is* developable.
- Leaders focus on being the *best prepared* players in the game.
- Better than this, you cannot do.

8. Don't let what you can't do define what you can do.

People who have abandoned themselves to mediocrity or merely being average do this all the time. What most people get good at is explaining why something can't be done. They use their arguments about why they think something can't be done to define what they think can be done. Unacceptable. (You've probably never been in a meeting where this has been the M.O. – right?)

Leaders think about this as follows:

- There are *always* ways of figuring out what has to be done if the obvious tactic doesn't work.
- You just have to be determined and smart enough to figure out what that alternative tactic is. As we old engineers used to say, "There's more than one way to skin the cat."
- If ingenuity or determination are lacking, then you are doomed to succeed – or fail, in no more than an ordinary way – that is, merely by chance.
- You have to measure *capabilities* by figuring out how to do something that others have considered "impossible."
- Give us the difficult. What's easy brings no honor, no joy, no glory.
- Never confuse an activity with an accomplishment.
- Never let what someone assumes we can't do define our future.

9. What drives extraordinary performance is necessity.

NOT threats. A boss's threats are a symptom of a bankrupt manager.

NOT blackmail. Not "rewards" or "punishments."

NOT exhortation. None of these engenders any real *necessity*. These are games that require no more than the complicity of the other players. They are testimony to a bankrupt imagination.

What, then?

The kinds of necessity that make a difference in thought, feeling, or behavior take many forms and have several sources. Here are some of them:

- The most pervasive and powerful of all the forms of necessity is **habit**. It is our habits that behave us. We are merely the visible evidence of their pushes and pulls. Our habits function as the necessity that produces what we do (or don't do), what we think, what we feel, and what we say. There is rarely any possibility of compromise. We dance to the music of our habits, not our hopes.

- A person's **competencies** are also a source of considerable necessity for that person – for you, for others. The more competent people are to do something, the more likely they are to do it. Conversely, a person who is not competent to do something is not likely to do it.

  Incompetencies work like this: The more *incompetent* a person is to do something, the more necessary it is *not* to do it. What a person is capable of doing, that person will do. What a person is not capable of doing, that person will not only *not* do, but will avoid. Our incompetencies provide one kind of necessity. You will never observe people doing what they cannot do, or thinking in a way they cannot think, or feeling in a way they cannot feel, or seeing in a way they cannot see. It is *necessary* for them *not* to do so. Looking at the positive side of it we see that it is simply *necessary* for people to do what they are competent to do, and in the way they are competent to do it.

Practical implication: If you are not (or any other person is not) performing at the required level, it's most likely that you or they are simply not competent enough to do so. Fix that first. For the most part, you can only fix performance by first fixing that person's competence to perform at that level. Don't rail at reality. Do something about it. If that doesn't fix the performance problem, replace the person.

You can't know for sure if there is another explanation – laziness, for example – until you fix this competence shortfall. In other words, fix first what's fixable. Some people are more conscientious than others, and about different things. Some people would never cheat a friend, but might be stealing time from you.

• A person's **conscience** is a formidable source of necessity for that person. The more conscientious a person is, the more necessary is his or her way of doing things.

Conscientiousness requires self-control. People who have developed significant levels of self-control live by a greater sense of personal necessity than do those who feel far less responsible for themselves.

• There is a **destiny** in every way of thinking. There is a destiny in every person's history and present circumstances. There is a destiny in every organization's history and structure and mode of operation. Everyone belongs to a culture and to one or more subcultures. These are evolving in some direction. The people who "belong" to them will be greatly influenced in their future destinies by virtue of their membership in them. Who you hang out with, who you talk to, what you read, will affect your destiny. Your mind works the way it does because it is interdependent with the other minds it associates with. The way a person's mind works is a form of necessity.

If you seek a certain destiny, you have to have aligned the conditions that will produce that destiny. Necessity is in the way circumstances work themselves out. You have to put in place *all of the factors* that will produce a *necessary outcome*. Necessity is far more powerful than theories, or mere desire or effort.

• **Consequences**. Of all of the sources of necessity, none is more potent than the imagined or foretold consequences. We like to think that children become more like little angels when they are told at Christmastime that good behavior gets the goods, and bad behavior takes stuff off their list. We like to think that the sticks and carrots we use makes people perform better in the long term. Wrong. In the short-term, maybe. But when the sticks and carrots are the end-game, people will play to those and not to something beyond them.

If there are no long-term consequences for that person's life, if people don't imagine consequences that are worse than what needs be done to avoid them, then there is no real necessity. My own father bought basketball shoes for me (6th grade, proper shoes required) with the proviso that I would be first-team. Guess what? (Yes, he would have taken the shoes back if I had failed to keep up my end of the deal. My basketball *career* would have ended there.)

When there are no consequences for poor performance, there is little that a CEO can say about consequences that will carry any necessity. You see the point. It is that the level of performance a person regularly demonstrates will reflect the level of necessity operating for that person, internal and external combined.

For these and like reasons, the leader knows –

• That the best path for gaining predictable and enhanced performance forever is to surround oneself with people for whom that level of performance is simply *necessary*.

- Or to inculcate that level of internal necessity, which requires more leadership capabilities than most people can muster.
- Or to be the kind of seductive leader who so enchants followers that they *assume* the necessity for always pleasing that leader with their performance, and never displeasing that leader.
- The leader knows … that it must be one of these ways. And that extraordinary performance will always be a function of *necessity*.

10. It isn't the recipe. It's the cook.

Like necessity, this is an underlying theme throughout this guidebook, so we don't need to spend much time on it here. So let's just recap at this point:

You'll recall this basic caveat:

Many have tried. Few have succeeded.

There are three reasons. The **first** is that the person who undertook to make it happen was not the leader he or she needed to be. It may have been a shortfall of passion, of dedication, of necessity, of competence. Whatever it was, something was missing in the person who had the role of leading the charge.

The **second** reason for the fact that most attempts fail is that the leader did not persevere. Thinking of real achievement as a destination rather than a way of life may have contributed.

Third, that person didn't have what it takes to implement the process – to "make it happen," which is about 95% of the process. What has to be done to make it happen has to be done by the leader(s) in place, in the context of the condition of the organization and the circumstances of the real world at that moment in time.

You can't put that in a bottle, a can, or a nutshell. It cannot be reduced to a recipe. One size does not fit all.

We suffer especially in our civilization from the delusion that knowing *how* to do something – like having a recipe or a set of "secrets" revealed by a celebrity – is all that's required. Wrong. It takes much more than following a recipe. Ask any chef. Or champion golfer. Or great lover.

People are not interchangeable with respect to a set of instructions. We want to "buy" something (like a pill or a technique) that will compensate for our personal inadequacies. That might work with unimportant things. But the greater the aim, the greater the personal capabilities required.

There is no all-purpose technique that can overcome individual ignorance or incompetence. You may even have tried it yourself.

Let's cut through this. The best recipe in the world in the hands of an incompetent person will produce a poor product or service. Are we to believe, after 30 years or so, that computers have made us all a lot smarter? Or our organizations significantly more capable? Isn't the failure rate of businesses about the same as it always was? If our productivity has actually *decreased* during the hi-tech era, why do we cling to the myth?

Do we get better "customer service" (that's the claim) because our calls are handled electronically? Why are we *less* literate than the pioneers? Do we really make better marriages, better families, because we watch Dr. Phil? Have these new recipes that we are bombarded with every day, by the business press, enabled us to make *better* – more competitive, more resilient, more prepared, more secure – business organizations in this "global" economy? Have all of our problems gone away yet?

The ancient wisdom is simple enough:

"Talk does not cook rice."

Here is how leaders understand this:

• There is no recipe that is better than the cook.
• Great cooks, like great leaders, are well beyond recipes. Recipes are for amateurs.
• There is no recipe that will turn out the same regardless of the cook. Poor cooks can ruin the best recipes; great cooks can make great food out of the most mediocre of recipes.

- No recipe or scheme or theory the leader can buy will be any better, in its implementation, than is the leader.
- Great leadership cannot be taught. *But it can be learned.*
- The key variable will not be a recipe. It will be *you.*
- In the hands of a great leader, *any* recipe will work. And has.

Think about it. These are but examples of how to use "think pieces" to your advantage. They can come from anywhere. Whenever you come across a quotation or an epigram or even an offhand comment that runs contrary to what you believe, do what we've just done here. Think through what you could advantageously make it mean to you on your journey on-behalf-of your cause in life.

Here are a few more to whet your appetite:

- Exceptional performance is not "because of" but "in spite of." Turning the lights on does not make people smarter. Put your money on the person who is going to accomplish what needs to be accomplished … regardless. The *bricoleur.*
- People don't learn from "experience." They learn from their *interpretations* of their experiences. What they learn will be no better than their interpretations.
- Most people prefer a problem they can't solve to a solution they don't like. Observe carefully a person who does not make his or her problems go away and you'll see why this is so.
- Good enough is the *enemy* of better performance. It is not a step in that direction.
- The most important things have to be learned by doing them. That's the great chasm between "knowing-that" and "knowing-how."
- People love doing what they do in direct proportion to how good they are at it. Pop psychology will have you

exactly backwards on this, suggesting that if people can find something they "like" to do, they will therefore be good at it. No one who ever got to be really good at something believes this. So why does the myth persist?

• Security "kills."

Or, as Thoreau said:

> *"What can the person who is*
> *dissatisfied with himself not do?"*

POINTS TO PONDER

+ "Hope" is the method of choice for the marginally competent.

+ Recollections of past success are just as fanciful as are dreams of future success.

+ You don't become a leader by becoming a better manager.

+ The future is determined more by imagination than by history.

+ Railing at reality propels you out of it, backwards.

+ When "sticks and carrots" are the modus operandi, *they* become the end-game.

+ Off-the-shelf panaceas, no matter how popular, can never compensate for incompetence.

+ There is no quick fix for defects in thinking or performance.

+ There is no recipe for creating something that has not existed before.

Chapter 3

The Leader's Lexicon: I

Be patient. We're all eager to get to the good parts – like the how-to-do-it stuff. That includes me.

But we need to put depth of understanding first. Think about it this way: Many more people fail than succeed. And the main reason for this … is that …

> *a technique that is not supported by a superior understanding of why things work the way they do is a technique that will likely fail.*

We're all eager to do things. Are we all not urged to read the instruction book first? But most don't. Most people launch into things with the shallowest understanding. They consult the instruction book only when all else fails.

Where people and the dynamics of doing life and business are concerned, no technique can be any better than the depth of understanding of the person who exercises that technique. No matter how prestigious the source. Imagining that a great idea offered by a guru will solve all your problems is a (widespread) delusion. People imagine that, because they read somebody's words, they now know all they need to know to do it. But no mere reading of John Wooden's thoughts on coaching will make a better basketball coach of anyone. He was the one who gained the potent understanding. It is *his understanding of the game* that you need, not his words. It is *this* understanding of the game you need, not just the words. Reading the book merely provides you with insights about what you need to do next. Most people need some coaching – a guide, a mentor.

If doing is not profoundly supported by understanding, it will, in any critical test, fail. That's why we have to dig down into the *understanding* part of it.

We cannot dismiss the importance of this guidepost. The more difficult and challenging the journey, the more critical are the preparations and the provisioning. All great achievements require intense preparation and provisioning.

Most of those preparations and provisioning have to do with *your* thinking, *your* attitudes, and *your* overall readiness for the journey. That's what all this upfront stuff is for. The more thoroughly you understand and internalize these provisions for your thinking, the better able you will be to *implement* your leadership aims. "Measure twice, cut once," is the carpenter's wisdom. This means that the most important part of your journey is *your* preparation for it. That's what all of this up-front preparation is for – it is for equipping yourself for your journey.

So, it is not simply a matter of being patient. It is a matter of being thoroughly equipped – mentally and emotionally – before you are put to the test.

What we want to delve into and understand here are some critical terms for your thinking. We think with the terms we have available to think with. If we get them right, we get our thinking right. Most of them are common enough terms. But, as you will recall from the last chapter, conventional thinking always leads to conventional results. You want *unconventional* results. So you have to start with more powerful ways of understanding certain terms that you will use every day.

An example would be "thinking" itself. Most people think they can think. But most people can't. They've lost that ability – through misuse, or disuse, or by being "dumbed-down" by the millions of words, ads, images, and other information they are exposed to every day. Many people believe that being able to tell others what they heard on the news, or from other people, constitutes "thinking." Not even close.

When someone begins a sentence directed your way with, "I think ... this or that," you can be fairly certain that what they are saying is something like "The way my head works, I couldn't help coming up with what I am about to say to you." In other words, don't be led to believe that there is any significant thinking behind the use that other people make of the phrase, "I think ..."

As Henry Ford put it:

"Thinking is the hardest work there is,
which is probably why so few engage in it."

Thinking requires great depth and breadth – of real intelligence, and the tools for combining and recombining pertinent facts creatively. Thinking is perhaps a little like improvising in music. All of the fundamentals have to be at your command without thinking about them. Years of practice may enable you to "think out of the box" – to use your unique tools with your unique stockpile of knowledge and your unique capacity for putting your imagination to work on a difficult or "impossible" outcome. Are you asking what imagination has to do with it? Einstein, a great thinker himself, reminded us that,

"Imagination is more important than knowledge."

And knowledge is far more important than facts.

Here's another angle: Picasso insisted that computers are not good for anything. All they can give you, he said, is the answers. What's wanted in "thinking" isn't coming up with the answers but with the questions – the kinds of questions that lead you to insights, ideas, and solution paths that would otherwise not be available to you. The important thing, as Einstein also suggested, is never to stop questioning. That's what thinking is for: to take you where you have never gone before. "Thinking" is not opinion. It is not someone's interpretation of something. It is not bringing to bear what one already knows on a situation never before encountered. It is the capacity to take you mentally to a more advantageous point of view, a more powerful perspective on things.

So it is dangerous to imagine that others are offering you their "thinking." In all likelihood, they are offering you something they just happen to know, hoping that will do. They haven't learned how to think. As Ford said, it's hard work. As for your own thinking – don't give credit where it is not due. If you pay careful attention to this and the following pages, you'll be thinking better than you ever have in your life. It'll be a start for the great journey of learning how to think – your prerequisite for the journey to any great achievement – including compelling leadership.

Let's start with the obvious. **We are led by words**.

A better way of putting this, perhaps, is, *You* are led by how you understand the words that are used – whether your words or others' words. Words are merely tags by which you invoke your concept of things.

What this means is that the way you understand things determines what you are going to do about them. Your understanding goes far toward determining how things are going to turn out for you. Given the range of possible outcomes, there are better ways and worse ways of understanding the terms by which you describe present and future circumstances.

Let's look at some of these (common) terms, and consider some better ways of understanding how they reveal the world to us. Before we do, are you wondering whether or not people can change or improve their thinking abilities? If so, that's a good question. The answer is … yes. But how much people can change, how good they can really get at this business of thinking, depends upon how determined and how ruthlessly they are committed to some future great achievement – as in this case, becoming a compelling leader. Lukewarm desires and intentions will produce little, if anything. Many people want certain outcomes. They would probably even like to be able to think. But getting there requires hard work, *change*, passionate dedication to the outcome, and discipline.

What's provided here are ways of disciplining your mind. Learn to *lead yourself* with these ways of understanding. If you don't have these characteristics in sufficient measure, you have two choices. Develop them. You can use what follows to do that.

Or forget it.

Communication and Reality

You can't talk about the one – sensibly – without talking about the other one. But here, just for ease of thinking hard and usefully about them, we look at each and then put them back together where they belong.

Reality. We often talk as if we are dealing with reality. But this never happens. We are stuck dealing with what we *say about* reality, with what we think about reality. What's in our heads is not reality. It has already been transformed into what things *mean* to us – given our own mental models. The world we see is a virtual reality. It is reality as we interpret it.

This is not a philosophical issue. There is nothing even academic about it. It's as practical as we can get. The concept may be hard to get but if you don't come to grips with this one, you will be forever disadvantaged in your pursuit of becoming an effective leader.

The world is, in and of itself, no matter the object or the event, meaningless. It is we, we people, who render it meaningful. We have to. Our minds – the only tools we have ever had for dealing with the world – work only with the meanings of things. Think about anything which is meaningless to you, and you will get the point. I'm betting you can't do it.

So our talk about reality, your grasp *of* reality, is necessarily limited to the way our own minds work. We might both wish it wasn't that way. And maybe we have been able to become comfortable with the fact that reality is what we think it is. There is another "reality" out there, but it exists for us only as we talk about it, only as we conceive of it, only as we interpret it.

Different takes on what people agree is reality may permit us to exercise more – or less – control over some aspects of it. We can nullify the limits of our natural capabilities by inventing airplanes. Or, by contacting each other electronically. But the realities of the world in which we have to perform, with all of its social/economic/technological/political ramifications, are things we can understand only by thinking about them in the way we think about them. And no one of us controls the twists and turns of the economy or of society. Oftentimes, we can barely control ourselves. We certainly cannot control one another.

So what's the point? Here are a number of them, given the way leaders have to understand them:

- All human conflicts can be reduced to the struggle over whose realities will prevail. Who has the power – or the good fortune – to determine whose realities will prevail?
- All misunderstandings come down to the fact that one person's view of reality was not the same as some other person's view of reality.
- More people (and thus organizations) get misled more by their misassumptions about reality than by any other single thing.
- Our take on reality consists of hypotheses, hunches, and assumptions about it. We can never know at the moment whether they are right or wrong. We can only know and assess where they took us.
- "Truth" is always a red herring. Truth is whatever we agree it is. There is no test beyond a test that we might devise, which will be as fallible as we are.
- What's in your head (your way of seeing and thinking about things) isn't reality. It just happens to be the way you think about things. Inescapably, it's just the best any of us can do.
- You either have to trust your view of reality, or someone else's. You are no more infallible than they are.
- How you happen to see things doesn't obligate things to be that way.
- Your sense of certainty that you're right doesn't make you right.
- People try to understand the existing world. Leaders try to make an alternative world. If, as Einstein suggested, *"Imagination is more important than facts,"* we are left with the questions, "Whose imagination?" "Whose facts?" The person who becomes the leader is the answer to those questions.

Any argument over whether something is true or not is, more often than not, a waste of time for leaders. The issue is simply this: Where is this way understanding things, of looking at things, going to get us? For the leader, all of our thinking, all of our talking, all of our claims on reality come down to the consequences for doing so one way rather than another. The question is not, "Which interpretation is the true one?" but "Which interpretation is going to get us where we want to go?"

Whether someone is right or wrong is given in how things turn out. Every other argument is an academic one. No conflict ever determined whose opinion about reality was right. It merely determined whose view was going to prevail.

Practicing this orientation is immensely worthwhile. Try it. You'll have a clear sense of how much more potent it is.

Communication. Let's cast the same lens on communication.

When people think (talk to themselves) or talk to one another, they are always and inevitably talking from their perspectives on reality. People can only tell you what they know. They can't tell you what *is*. What something means is what it means to that person. When people talk a lot with each other, they come to have similar meanings for things. They come to see the world in similar ways. Their realities have the same furniture and similar understandings, assumptions. When people want to collaborate for some mutual purpose – becoming lovers or partners, for example – they try to make sure they are on the same page. They want their views of reality to coincide. So they talk to determine how compatible their views of reality are.

We acquire from other people and other sources the intelligence we imagine we need to pursue our interests. We have maps and signs and reports to tell us where we are. We read books, and ask others, to figure out who we ought to be, and how we ought to go about it. We tell other people what we think might bring us closer together or otherwise enable us to manipulate them in some way to our advantage. That's what advertisers do. That's what buyers and sellers do. That's what politicians do. That's what artists do. That's what writers and television producers do. That's what we people do.

The real world is the one people construct when they talk to themselves or to one another. It carries no warranty with respect to our lives. But that's as good as it gets. It's the world that exists in our minds. It's the one we work from when we observe, or assess, or debate. We are stuck with the way our minds work – which is the product of communication.

The point: People may presume to refer to some reality when they talk with you. But if they can think about it or talk about it, it has already been appropriated to their way of thinking or of talking. When they talk, they are not referring to some reality that is independent of them. They can only describe the way they understand it, the way they see it. They can't tell you what's in the world. They can only relate what's on *their* minds.

So we're back again to the all-important criterion. What something means ultimately lies in the **consequences** for having or applying that meaning. What you infer from your perception of the world, or of what others say to you, ultimately lies in the consequences of those interpretations. Here are some practical applications:

- When you observe something first hand, it is your interpretation that you come away with. When you listen to others, it will be your interpretation of their interpretations. (I know that is awkward. But how otherwise to put it?)

- Your ability to provide yourself with the interpretations you need to get where you are going – whether these interpretations are yours or others' – will determine whether or not you can get there.

- Yes, indeed. You have to know what the present circumstances are, as best you and/or others can assess them. But those will still be no more than interpretations.

It's just that some are better (or more relevant for your purposes) than others. But not even a perfect assessment of present circumstances will be of any help if you don't know where you are going. The value of any communication lies in its **consequences**. For you. For your cause.

- Some people believe that communication is a way of solving problems. They forget: that's how we got into the problem in the first place.
- The more flaws there are in your perception/interpretation of yourself, the more flaws there will be in your interpretations of others – and of the world of which you are both a function.

So you can see how the concepts of reality and communication can fruitfully be seen as two aspects of the same thing.

Knowing and Believing

Another bugbear. A "bugbear" is a problem that won't go away because we're not seeing it the way we need to, by not knowing how or not wanting to go to the source. Consider this: You say something to someone. That person nods in agreement, adding, "I know." Dilemma: Just because two or more people agree doesn't mean that you can't be wrong, or that all of you can't be wrong. Agreement validates what you know. But it doesn't guarantee that what you know is what you need to know.

In a leadership coaching session where we were talking about this, a favorite client said, "Okay. What's your point?" Not a very satisfactory one, I'm afraid. It is this: that there is no necessary correlation between what you know and what the actual situation may be. The correlation lies in the fact that others agree with you. This guarantees nothing. Entire civilizations have disappeared from history, agreeing with one another to the end that what they knew was what they needed to know.

You can't "fix" this dilemma. It's just part of being human. People in power always imagine that their view is the right one. In many instances, their organizations have failed. Whole nations have been created, and failed, because they continued to the bitter end contending that they were "right." There is no happy ending here. The best you can do is to be aware of the following:

- You know what you know basically because people told you so, directly or indirectly. You may have improvised on what you started with. But you had to improvise from what you already knew. So what you had as a source is crucial. As one writer put it, "It makes a lot of difference who you choose as parents." Or teachers. Or friends. Or "experts." Or conversational partners.

- We can live with that. We do so every day. Pretending, probably, that what we know is what we need to know. But that's even more irresolvable. The point is that you don't know whether what you know is what you need to know. Because that evidence is not available until after the fact. Did what you knew get you where you wanted to go? Were you able to achieve your goals? Did what you knew keep you from trouble and harm? The answers to all of these are revealed solely in the **consequences**. Figure out the consequences that matter to you. Then figure out what you would have to know to achieve those consequences. Part of that is knowing what to do and what not to do. No one has ever been able to do better than that.

Not much in the way of consolation, for sure. But it's far better to start with the interpretations needed for effective leadership, no matter how difficult or counter-intuitive they seem to be.

"Knowing" is a sucker's game. How do we get suckered into it?

- By believing you know something you don't know. It's old wisdom, but still not very common: the first step is *being clear about what you do not know.*

- By believing that what you just happen to know is an accurate picture of some reality independent of what you happen to think about it.

- By failing to understand that what you now know is far more determined by what you already knew than by any reality external to you.

- By assuming that what you don't happen to know is probably irrelevant. By ignoring the fact that other people's observations are only their interpretations.
- By not realizing that any argument about who is right and who is wrong may change the future. But it doesn't change present reality one whit.
- By pretending that other people, events, and things in the world are somehow obligated to be as you "know" them.

What you know is what you made of the past in your thinking about it. What you *need to know* is what to make of the present and of how that bears on the future you aim to create.

An aside:
Are you *thinking* about this stuff?

- By concluding that others are "right" to the extent they are certain and outspoken about their opinions, and that you might therefore be "wrong."
- By making the opposite mistake. Just because you believe you know better doesn't mean that you don't. Is there any tougher issue in leadership than when to take others' advice and when to take your own?

Here are the constraints or limits on your "knowing." It pays to know what they are. We are revisiting them here because it is crucial that you understand them implicitly.

The **first** of these is that you can know only what you are capable of knowing. The less capable you are, the more likely you are to be drawing on faulty assumptions. "Knowledge" is a hoodwink. You can know only what you are capable of knowing.

Second, what you know is limited by the words and ideas you regularly consume. You know the saying, "We are what we eat." It applies here.

Third, you can't know everything. You will never know more than a tiny fraction of what might be knowable. What you don't know in this world of ours will always outpace what you do know.

Fourth, what you know becomes a part of who you *are*. And who you are is immensely resistant to change. Habits will trump the facts every time. Add to that: what you know at any point in time precludes what you could know. Especially if knowing something different would call into question what you already know.

Fascinating, these perspectives. Most people avoid ever confronting them in any serious way. The leaders who have made a difference don't have bigger brains or even better luck than you do. But they have confronted these facts about their own knowing – and others' knowing – in a deliberate way. If your aim is to raise your own performance, or the performance of your organization, you will be advantaged by the kind of thinking that accommodates these little rules of thumb about "knowing."

Lessons? Well, you've heard the expression, "Know thyself." And you've heard it said that the leader must first demonstrate self-leadership. That's what those expressions mean. That, where "knowing" is critical, it's far better to ask a provocative question than to offer any statement that represents what you know.

Now … what does **belief** have to do with all this? This one's easy. What you know is already a belief. Otherwise, you would have long ago traded it in on something better.

One last suggestion from all of the leaders who have preceded you. They knew, as you must carefully consider, that people who don't know *how* they know – or *why* – are dangerous people. To themselves, and to you, if they play follow the leader with you. This is the source of "the blind leading the blind" proverb. It's risky to fail to make that central to one's thinking.

Some thought-prodders to have some fun with:

- What you know, or what you believe, is indifferent to whether it is good for you, or bad for you.
- You cannot *know* what the present would be like if past events had been different than they were. Trajectories into the future are created out of what we presume to know (or believe) at the present moment.
- Similarly, you cannot *know* what the future will be if you do "X." You can only speculate.

• What you don't know could be to your advantage. Choose carefully what you do not want to know. Entrepreneurs refuse to believe the prognosis of their enterprises offered by friends and lenders.

• When you're talking to someone else, it is their thinking that constitutes their reality. Not yours.

• What leaders do is create a reality out of their vision of it.

If you need a reminder – the only measure of the value of what you know (or what you believe) is given in what you accomplish with it.

Explaining Things

Of all the creatures on earth, we humans can be best characterized as the species that has an inexhaustible need to *explain* things. This has gotten us to places where we wanted to go. The moon, maybe. A drug for everything, maybe. But it has also gotten us to places where we perhaps didn't intend to go. War after war and every other kind of human tragedy, for example. When spouses start explaining *the other person*, they cease to be lovers. We seem to be unable just to live life. We have to "explain" it.

We explain ourselves and then define everything else in the world to fit that. Or, we explain everything in the world and then define ourselves to fit those explanations. It amounts to the same thing. We describe (explain) our organizations and that defines us in them. Or, we explain ourselves and then define our organizations to suit. It's a bit both ways, isn't it?

Not just that we *have to* explain things, but how we do so has consequences, many of them often unintended. But let's get practical here. How you explain performance bears upon the kind of performance you get, whether individual performance or the performance of organizations.

It's easy to get waylaid by popular explanations. For example: It seems that most problems you face will be traceable to some painful discrepancy between what people said was going to happen, and what actually happened. And most people seem to prefer such problems to even the obvious solutions. Dilbert gets a lot of laughs out of the fact that people are quick to take credit for any success that occurs. But when there is a failure, "it's explanation time!" People don't normally get better at performing. They get better at explaining why their shortfalls were never their fault.

If there is to be reliable collaboration that produces the intended outcome (as is always the case for organizations), two conditions have to be met. One is that the people involved have to be supremely competent in their roles. This means avoiding problems, but also having the capacity to improvise through or around them if they can't prevent them. The second condition is that the "ensemble" – the set of people who are supposed to be collaborating – is supremely competent. They are prepared not only to perform, but to do so in any imaginable contingency (and even unexpected ones). This means that they will have to have a communicative and logistics infrastructure that is adequate to the task.

The point here is a key one. It is that the only measure of performance is performance. Either people (including you) did what they said they were going to do. Or they didn't. (Did they lie?) If you accept an explanation in lieu of the promised accomplishment, that's what you will get more of. Treat an excuse as if it were the same thing as the accomplishment, and that's what you will get more of. In our world, excuses are often equated with accomplishment. But an intention is not an accomplishment. Treat it as if it were, and you'll get far more excuses than you will accomplishments. This is especially the case for the leader, himself or herself.

The *only* measure of performance is performance.

Some thought-prodders:

• Performance is either *necessary* or it isn't.
• If outstanding performance is not necessary, it won't happen.
• Achievers blame themselves first. That's fixable.

• Winning at the "excuse" or explanation game makes losers.
• The way you explain things will be your destiny.
• Competence at explaining shortfalls makes those shortfalls inevitable.

Cause vs. Choice

It all depends on which end you look at it from. Things may be seen to be "caused" by certain events that preceded the outcome. OR, events may be made to conspire to produce a desired outcome … by choice. Examples: You want a "zero defects" organization. You choose that. Then you decide what has to happen to get there. You choose the people and the practices out of which that outcome will be produced. All great athletes do it this way. All great actors and musicians and artists and thinkers do it this way. All great leaders have always done it this way.

When you get hung-up about cause-and-effect relationships in your organization, and go on witch-hunts to find *the* cause, you've got people with their heads buried in the past and not directed at the future.

Cause carries with it a sense of being determined by what happened in the past. Things are caused. So you look for "the" cause. You feel compelled to explain why what happened, happened. If you had chosen the outcome, and put in place the conditions necessary to produce that outcome and it didn't happen, you wouldn't be looking for the cause out there somewhere. It would be reflected in your mirror.

The illusion that what happens in the real world is independent of the people in it and how they think about it may make people feel they are being rational and objective. But if you did this, you would be missing the core causes of things. Those would be: Incompetence, inattention, indifference, and the capacity (in your organization?) to get away with an explanation that puts the blame somewhere else.

Here's what you do: If you take the position that whatever happens is by **choice**, you'll get far more knowing-how and far less knowing-that. It's the *how* that gets you where you want to go. Explaining what-caused-what is a huge waste of time in most conventional organizations. The past is not the issue. The issue is how to get from here to there. The *there* has to be chosen first. Then the how is chosen. If the how turns out not to be quite right, you can change it.

If you are a cause-and-effect thinker, you are a person trying to figure out how you got victimized by what happened to you. Before long, you *will* be a victim of whatever happens. It's a way of looking at things. But it's not the way of looking at things that you need.

Key question: Do people learn from their mistakes? Rarely. That's because there are two preconditions.

First, you *might* learn from your *interpretations* of your mistakes, never from the mistakes themselves. This would require you to be able to see what part of the problem you were. Most people don't look at it that way. So they can't learn from their mistakes. Most people don't want to know what part of their problems *they* are.

Second, learning from your mistakes requires that you have a great and worthy cause in life. Or at least that you have a very specific destination in mind. People who live from day-to-day, without a long-range destination to which they feel obligated, don't learn from their mistakes. What's to learn? They get good – really good – at being victims and expecting the boss or someone or something else to make them happy and secure, to fulfill their hopes and dreams. Or at least to solve their problems for them.

Here, for your amusement and edification, are more thought-prodders:
- If you want to be a part of the solution, make certain you are not a part of the problem.
- The first obligation of competency, therefore, is not to be a part of the problem.

- An explanation tells you more about the explainer than it does about the happenings being explained.
- Practice what needs to be accomplished, not how to successfully explain shortfalls.
- The conditions of our organizations, like the conditions of our lives, were *chosen.*
- If you don't choose them, they will choose you.

We could, of course, predict future outcomes. This would be like explaining things forward. And, like all explanations, would be a mix of hope, ignorance, past explanations, and guesswork. As has often been observed, if you want to predict the future, create it.

That's what leaders do. Perfectly? Never. Determinedly? Totally. They know the outcomes are not controllable. But they also know that their preparation for accomplishing what needs to be accomplished is within their control. So they concentrate on that.

As the prize-winning biologist D'Arcy Thompson famously said about the study of cause in biology:

"Things are the way they are because they got to be that way."

Indeed. And things will turn out the way they do because they turned out that way. Yet *you* could intervene. You could redirect. You could set another direction.

Here's a brief version of a typical exchange about an organizational "problem":

CEO: "Why is this happening?"

ME: "Do you mean you didn't choose this to happen? Are you sure you know what your role is here?"

CEO (huffy, of course): "What do you mean by that?"

ME: "I would have thought your job was to *make* happenings, not to be made *by them.* Anyone could do that."

CEO: "Come on. I don't control what happens."

ME: "Agreed. But did you choose the outcomes and then choose how those outcomes were to be achieved?"

A little more discussion and he got the point. And, by the way, his organization is doing far better than it did when everyone assumed they were just victims, when the best they thought they could do was to figure out why things went wrong.

It's also useful to remember that nothing has a single cause. There's always *The Tipping Point* or "The straw that broke the camel's back." It wasn't the one straw that broke the camel's back. It was the accumulation of weight. Same thing in organizations. Things happen because the conditions are ripe for that to happen. People make mistakes because they are incompetent. Because they weren't paying attention. Because they weren't thinking. Because someone else didn't perform. Fix the conditions first. There is always luck. But being fully prepared makes you luckier.

More interim thought-prodders, if needed:

- The smartest leaders partner with serendipity.
- Nothing that involves people has a single cause.
- Things do not turn out as we *want* them to. Things turn out the way they *have to*. Make that work for you. Luck can't. Hope won't.
- A leader is not the sole cause of anything – not even of himself or herself, although they have more choice there than anywhere else.
- Leaders who make a difference are those who have successfully limited the difference randomness makes.
- Surround yourself with people who are not part of the problem. Then they could be a part of the solution.
- Out of what causes does a person emerge as a leader?

Here's a partial list of questions that help to absorb people's spare time at work, along with a potentially useful alternative formulation:

1. Why *were* those customer deliveries late?

   Try: *What would we have to do to ensure that no scheduled delivery is ever late?*

2. Why didn't we know what our competitors were planning to do?

   How about: *What would we have to do, and how, to be competitor-driven?*

3. Why did the stock market (or the "economy") go up or down? What would you do with *any* explanation of that? Try this: *How can we optimize our immunity to things over which we have no control?*

4. What caused this problem we're faced with?

   Why not: *Do what needs doing in order to be faced with the problems you think are going to get you where you want to go?*

5. How did that accident happen?

   Try this: *Who ought to own the problem of not causing an accident, or of not being a victim of one?*

6. How can we explain the slump in sales? Depends on who you ask, doesn't it?

   Maybe a better question is: *How can we prepare for the ups and downs of our revenues?*

7. Why did the people who said they would buy an Edsel not do so? What would you be able to *do* with an explanation of that? There was only one Edsel.

   How about: *What constitutes a **valid** market estimate?*

8. Why is it that what you tell people to do sometimes doesn't get done?

   Well: *What part of that problem are **you**?*

Did we forget something? Maybe it's this: Outstanding performance is not *because of* (because of the resources provided), but *in spite of* (in spite of any and all impediments). If people don't think that way, they won't be that way. If the *leader* does not think that way, no one else will take on that way of thinking.

You have to make the future out of the present, not out of the past. If you can figure out what causes the right outcomes, use those

causes to drive the future, to *cause* your aims. It's not likely that
knowing what caused the wrong outcomes will enable you to do
this, beyond simply avoiding *those* causes. The leader's challenge:
How do you *cause* something that didn't exist in the past, and
doesn't exist in the present?

> *It isn't that impersonal "cause" is not a perfectly
> useful way of explaining things in the nonhuman
> world (although it doesn't always work there).*
>
> *It is that this way of thinking has steadily eclipsed
> the role of human* choice *in life and social life, and
> especially life in organizations.*

The Founding Fathers of the U.S. were not caused. The republic
they envisioned was not caused. It was chosen. We could choose
how we want it, or our organizations, to be. A person *could* choose
not to smoke or not to overeat. Abe Lincoln thought a person *could*
choose not to be illiterate. But times are a-changing in this freedom-
loving, permissive world of ours. We're raising young people to
believe that they have a "right" to do whatever they want to do
whenever they want to do it. And it's somebody else's problem to
take care of any untoward consequences – parents, social agencies,
the society.

You will have more and more of these people in your
organization. Where everything is your fault because people are
innocent victims of what *happens* to them.

Corporate Welfare

There could hardly be a better term for it. As our government
and private and commercial organizations become more like day-
care centers, we will arrive…where? It may even be an okay idea in
the abstract. But there will never be the heart for the pursuit of great
achievements to emerge from that environment – neither individual
nor collective.

Is it a world you would choose?

I heard a college graduate report, via public radio, that the "American Dream" was dead. He concluded this was the case because no one came to him and offered him the kind of job he thought he deserved.

I understood that the American Dream was that everyone had an equal *opportunity* to make something of themselves and of their organizations. What they might *choose* to make of themselves. We train our young people – at home, at school, in health and illness, and in that welfare state we call our colleges and universities – how to expect and even demand whatever they can imagine they deserve. Not what their responsibilities are but what their "rights" are. All because we've elevated cause above choice, rights (as victims of anything and everything) above responsibilities (to self and others). It is now only barely imaginable that a person could *choose* not to smoke or overeat. Or, to choose a future rather than be determined by past or present. Or, to choose not to be incompetent. Or, to choose not to be an eager victim, *before* becoming addicted to that way of life. Welcome to the world – was it not Socrates who said,

> *"Children today are tyrants. They contradict their parents, gobble their food, and tyrannize their teachers."*

So be it, now and ever more so.

You can see how important your understanding of things – your thinking – can be. As you think about things, so you will be. There's the source of real power – the power of *your* choice.

This concept is crucial to leadership thinking. So we will meet up with it again later on.

Moving On

Here are a couple of thoughts to chew on as you move on:
- If you believe in cause as the all-purpose explanation, then the most important thing in the world for you to know is what causes *you*. If you are caused, put in place what will cause you to be who you intend to be, or who you *ought*

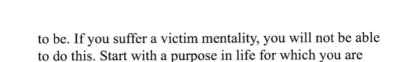

to be. If you suffer a victim mentality, you will not be able to do this. Start with a purpose in life for which you are responsible. Assume there is no one who will excuse you.

- Be had by your own cause. Otherwise, you will be had by others' causes. That is, otherwise you will be a random event. A victim of previous random events. We have become high-maintenance people as a result of our victim mentality.

Passion causes. Does it cause you? Is your passion a cause of others, of a real achievement in the world as given, with the hand you were dealt? Or do you ask the dealer for five other cards?

The leader does not so much seek to know the causes of things as to *be* the cause of something. Is there a "key" here to what needs unlocking?

In this world of ours, you will either make your own path as best you can. Or your path will be made for you by whatever randomly comes your way.

Most people get around this by refusing to choose either way, and thus by pretending to be blameless. Are you prepared to support that habit in yourselves or in others? If so, you need to remind yourself that leadership lies in the opposite direction. Leadership requires competence, responsibility, and performance. The more necessary these can be made to be, the more possible great achievement will be. It's worth thinking about.

POINTS TO PONDER

+ Preparation outperforms passion every time.

+ The only reality we are capable of dealing with is interpreted reality.

+ Where "facts" and interpretations are in question, leaders are the answer.

+ The more you misinterpret yourself, the more you will misinterpret all the rest of your world.

+ Affirming something does not make it so.

+ It is better to be competent than to be "right."

+ You can only know what you are capable of knowing.

+ You cannot learn directly from "experience."

+ Explaining something is not the same as accomplishing something.

+ A victim mentality redefines achievement as luck.

+ If you are not had by your own cause, you will be had by others' causes.

+ Whom you cannot influence will influence you.

4 The Leader's Lexicon: II

We've devoted a good bit of time to examining the idea of cause. For good reason. This is not a philosophical issue. There are two fundamentally *practical* reasons why leaders need to grapple with the idea of cause:

The **first** is that leaders have to know what causes *them*. There is no more direct route to knowing who you are. Leadership is not primarily about what you do. It is primarily about who you **are**, and that is a product of how you think. Where you get the content and the gears matters. Decisively.

The **second** reason is that leaders have to be able to figure out, once they have an accurate perspective on who *they* are, what they can and cannot *cause*. Leaders are caused and leaders can cause things to happen. But only as they are capacitated to do so.

So while it may still try your patience to devote more time to this matter of the leader's lexicon, it's much like practice and preparation for the game: the better you get this stuff, the more effectively you are going to get all the rest of it. To do what leaders do, you have to think like leaders think.

People

Small word, people. For the way you think about it – HUGE consequences. People: the source of all of our problems. And yet, we have no other source for solutions.

So the way you think about people will either preclude or contribute to the problems you face, and will either contribute expediently to the solutions to those problems, or to persistent inabilities to resolve them. In other words, the way you think about "people" will determine what kinds of problems you will have *and* how solvable those problems will be.

Let's start at the beginning. If you don't truly "like" people, it is unlikely you will ever be able to provide leadership, for yourself or for them. If you do not truly **care** about people, it is unlikely you will ever have followers. And it is unlikely that you would ever be able to lead them to extraordinary levels of performance/achievement.

Why is that? Because if you do not like people, they don't have much reason for liking you back. If you do not truly (from their perspective) care about them, they have no compelling reason for caring about you, or about your purposes in life.

This is not a pop psychology issue. There is some logic here that you might as well accept, because you are not going to get around it.

Yet there is a twist here that leaders have to learn how to understand, but which seems to be lost to those whose minds have been colonized by the popular culture. It is that "liking" people is given in how genuinely interested you are in them, in their lives, in *their* problems and concerns. Trying to get them interested in you, in your life, in *your* problems and concerns, will not be interpreted by them as your caring about them. They have to know you care about *them* before they will join you in your cause.

Now, about caring. Most people have this all wrong. To care about another person doesn't mean that you accept that person as she is. If you want to learn how to think like a leader, *caring about others means refusing to let them default themselves.*

It means caring about the person they should *become.* It means caring about who they *ought* to be – potential realized – instead of where they are presently stalemated. This is the way the leader has to look at himself. Caring about people means looking at them in the same way. "We should love people," the German poet Goethe said, "not for who they are, but for who they ought to be." That's real caring because it is win-win. Every other form of "caring" has at least one or more losers in it.

A common complaint: "I just don't understand people." It's actually not that difficult. Our pop psychology has made it seem far more complex than it needs to be. The lesson (for leaders) is this: If you want to know how people think, watch what they do and how they do it. If you want to know what people's beliefs are, or what they are really going to do or to be in the future, don't listen to what they *say*. Watch what they *do* and how they do it.

There is no obligatory correlation between what people say and what people do.

You've had the experience. When people want to work at your place, they'll promise anything. They will offer to be the answer to your prayer. But after a few days or a few weeks, that same person may turn out to be as marginally mediocre as most of the others.

> **Leader's lesson:**
> Never mistake what people say for what they can or will actually do.

People are far more likely to talk a good story than they are to provide one. If you've been married, you already know this (but may not want to believe it). If you've ever been a boss or a subordinate, you've been exposed to it many times. Promises are far easier to offer than they are to fulfill. You may even have noted this flaw in yourself.

It's the everyday version of "walking the talk." Most people don't. Or can't. That's largely because they have never had to do so. This is the key to "understanding" people.

We'll return to that enthusiastically below. The lesson here is that you don't have to be a psychologist to understand people. In fact, the less psychological you are about all of this, the better off you will be. The lesson is that you will have a far more reliable understanding of people if you base your understanding on what people actually do than if you step into the psychological swamp of their intentions, their motivations, their test profiles, or their enthusiasms (sucking up). If you are a mind-reader, have at it. But leaders don't try to get into people's heads. For leaders, *the reality of who people are and what they are capable of lies entirely in what they actually do* – or don't do.

This is not a book about people as such. It is about how you may need to think differently about people in order to move in the direction of real achievement – personally or as a leader. So our concerns are operational, pragmatic, practical.

One of the most useful questions you can ask is this one: ***Why DO people do what they do?***

You could ask a roomful of psychologists this question and you'd get a roomful of answers. Those answers would be interesting – if you wanted to be a psychologist. But if you want to be a leader, those theories are for the most part irrelevant.

Books and articles abound about how to motivate people to do something you want them to do, or to be the someone you want them to be. Some of this is entertaining (it is meant to be). But none of it would explain very accurately what motivated those writers to write those books or deliver those seminars.

Most of what you will get in those books and articles is "pop" psychology. Consume this stuff and it will help you to think like and be like most everybody else. But it won't help you in your quest to achieve. That requires you to be different. And *that* requires you to *think* differently. You can't think differently if you feed on the same mental junk food as everyone else.

Consider *motivation*. Motivation is about causing others to do, or be, in ways consistent with your intentions. But most people can't even cause *themselves* to be different. So why would you believe you can cause in them what you can't cause in yourself? What makes you think you can motivate others to do or to be in ways they are not capable of doing or being?

Motivation is largely a myth. A very popular, and deeply ingrained, cultural myth. It is a mystical term – intended perhaps to give us the illusion of power we don't have. It is a term invented to account for why laboratory mice (literally) did what they did, and was then generalized to account for why *people* do what they do.

These lab mice were deprived of things like food or sex, and were then carefully observed under controlled conditions to measure how motivated they were to get to the one or the other. On the face of it, only a psychologist would believe that some great and profound truth had been discovered when a starving animal seemed determined to get at some food. But then it would also take a psychologist to prefer playing with mice rather than with people – under conditions that would never occur in the mouse's real world. So what was the psychologist's motives for pursuing the study of the obvious?

Motivation and incentives don't work in the long run. And they seem to work reliably only with the kind of people who have already bought into the rat race. They seem to work best with people who intend to do only as they are told, but who expect to be rewarded for even trying.

Even if they did work with extremely competent people, how many of you out there would sign up to live in a world where people performed solely for rewards provided exclusively by others? We may live in a culture where this seems natural. It is the intrinsic rewards that matter most. Not the extrinsic rewards. Over time, those destroy a person's inner life.

If psychologists are themselves performing solely for rewards (as if their theories about people included them), what exactly are those rewards? And in that world where everyone is being manipulated, what rewards motivate the motivator? Who is pulling *your* strings or pushing your buttons, without which *you* wouldn't be motivated to do what *you* do? Leaders are driven primarily by their own purposes, not by others' purposes.

So if we're not going to be psychological about it, why DO people do what they do? The best – and the most potent – answers you will ever find to this question have little to do with either "motivation" or with things like desire or intention. As a practical matter, people do what they do, first, **because they CAN.**

Simple. But powerful. You will never see a person doing something that person cannot do. If people *can* do something, they will. If they are totally incapable of doing something, then you won't see them doing it.

So leaders attend to that shortfall – that condition – first. They make it necessary for people to be competent at what they are going to be required to do. Only then can they conclude that if they don't see the performance required, the performance shortfalls are by *choice*. If you don't cover this base, you can never be certain where the shortfall lies. It will never be in the circumstances. It will be in the failure to prepare for those circumstances.

There are two useful implications here: One is that the best way of accounting for performance is not to grasp for something like motivation, or desire, or even talent. It is simply being aware that the level of performance is a reflection of the level of competence for performing in that way. The other is that being a mediocre or even a poor performer also requires competence. Poor performers are not incompetent. They are simply competent to perform in incompetent ways. If it's an everyday thing, it takes just as much practice to do something poorly as it does to do something well. It's a matter of practicing what you want to get good at.

It may be challenging to think this way. Here are some thought-prodders:

• People do not become virtuosos even at being lazy except by practice.

• People do not become adept at *not* being engaged in what they are doing except through practice. Everyone is born with his or her lights on. You have to work at turning them off.

• Leaders' rule of thumb: Don't practice what you don't want to get good at. Don't let others practice what you do not want them to get good at.

To be *competent* means that a person is fully prepared for what will occur, or for what might occur, between where they are now and successful achievement of the goal.

So one aspect of competence is **preparedness**. A person is not "competent" unless he or she is fully prepared to accomplish what needs accomplishing. To develop what it is people are capable of doing therefore requires first equipping yourself, and then those others, to be fully *prepared* to accomplish the mission from start to finish, regardless of what happens along the way.

Why do people behave as they do? Because they are competent to do so.

Why *don't* people do what they are supposed to do, or even what they say they are going to do? Because they are competent at *not* doing what they are supposed to do. Conscientiousness works both ways. Every achievement (+ or -) requires competence.

There is a **second** very practical understanding for why people do what they do. It is not that they want to. It is not that they intend to. It is not that they have a desire, or even the talent or the background, to do so. Those might contribute, in some cases.

But we are looking for a more powerful, more universal explanation. And that would lead us to this realization: People do what they do **because they *have* to**.

This doesn't mean that they were somehow "forced" to perform, because you cannot force a person to do something that person is incapable of doing. Some external "necessity" may help the process, of course. Tiger Woods' father could attest to that.

But by necessity or *have to* here, we are referring to such things as *habits*, as *competencies* (which provide their own necessity – if you're competent to do something in a certain way, it's altogether likely that you will do it in that way), as *duty*, as *interdependence* with respect to mutual survival, or even DNA. The culture you grew up in will make certain things necessary and other things irrelevant. Spouses may even provide you with certain "have-to's" in your life. The joke is that if you're not a good boy or girl (in the other's eyes), you may have to sleep on the sofa. That may provide a certain level of necessity for some people.

Necessity comes in many forms, as we will examine more carefully later on. It is enough here to think through the fact

that necessity will turn out to be a far better explanation of why
people do what they do than all of the psychological reasons
you could muster. Leaders aim to be powerful thinkers, not
conventional thinkers.

From all of the preceding, you might conclude that leaders are
inclined to think as follows:

1) There are only two kinds of people in the world:
Those who do, and those who don't.

2) And the **only** difference between those who do and
those who don't is that those who do, do, and those
who don't, don't.

This is old wisdom, of course. What it is intended to suggest
for the way we think about things is that the *only* measure of
whether or not someone accomplished something has to be found
in the accomplishment and not in the desire or the intentions of the
person involved. And certainly not in his or her words. Those are
merely promises.

It is probably also intended to suggest simply that the main
difference between the person who accomplished something and
the person who didn't is that the one did and the other didn't.
People often get involved in explaining the differences in some
other – usually psychological – way. But this will suck you right
into the psychological swamp, which is full of psychological
alligators and other dangers.

You might say, for example, that one person is "smarter"
than the other person. But what have you said here? "Smart" is as
"smart" does. And a person's "potential" is observable only in what
that person does with it. It's the same with any form of intention
to accomplish something. This seemingly
small difference in your thinking, if
you are not already there, can produce
phenomenal results. If you are already
there, you will know this.

Leader's lesson:
Actual intention can
be measured *only* by
actual accomplishment.

Some thought prodders?

- You needn't ask people why they did something they weren't supposed to do or didn't do something they were supposed to do. Unless it was consciously intentional on their part, they won't know either.
- Most words that follow the word **I** are promises, not facts. "I will do so-and-so," for example, is no more than a casual statement of intention. Whether or not a person means what she says can be determined only by what she does.
- The people who make a difference in the world – or to you – are the people who make good on their promises.
- If you want to know why people do what they do, ask a person who has done something. Don't ask a psychologist.
- If you want to know what people are *for*, ask the person who knows what real commitment requires of them.

Problems

A problem is some sort of *discrepancy* between the way things are and the way we believe things *ought* to be. So every problem depends upon how a person or a set of people see the way things are, and the way they think, imagine, or project the way things "ought" to be. What constitutes a problem for one person may not even be seen by another. What some people fret about, others may be blissfully unaware of.

The first thing that leaders learn about problems – and learn to the bone – is that a problem is **something that is had only by people**. Whether or not that is a problem worth having depends entirely on who those people are, how competent they are in their roles, and how committed they are to the mission they are engaged in or the goal(s) they are trying to achieve.

Human enterprises – like your organization or your love life – rise or fall on the basis of random events, and then on how you and every other person involved see the problems that arise in the context of those mostly uncontrollable happenings. More than that, there is not just the matter of being aware of the obstacles and opportunities on your path. Problems also have to be identified. They have to have a name.

Leaders recognize that the names people have for problems will largely determine the problems they see. What people don't have a name for they are likely to be unaware of.

- So the problems a person has are going to be primarily a function of the problems for which he or she has a name. They are going to be related to that particular person's perception of the world.
- And, thus, the problem you try to solve is the one you have named, the one you can talk about.
- How well you do all of this problem stuff will depend on the names you have handy, and the repertoires you assume you have for dealing with them.

What we're focusing in on here is that there is certain mental machinery that determines all three steps in the process: (1) what people see as constituting a problem, (2) how *those people* name that problem, for how they do that will (3) determine what they're going to do about it. The perception of the problem, the name given to it, and the solutions applied are primarily functions of the minds involved. They are interpretations constructed by those minds. They are not reality.

So *the problem we try to solve is the one we name.* And the one we name comes with a solution. This means that the chief cause of problems in an organization is solutions. How we put together an organization, and the competencies of the people we staff it with, will essentially determine the kinds of problems we are going to have – at least the kinds of problems we are going to pay attention to. It may seem perverse. But the problems people claim to have do seem to go where those people go.

You also have to consider this: every solution to every problem causes more problems. You do not simply eliminate problems in any organization. You merely replace the ones someone believed you had with others that grew out of the solution(s) employed. So leaders need to think not just, how do we solve our problems, but what kinds of problems do we want to generate out of the solutions we employ?

Problems will arise out of those solutions in any case. The right solution to the wrong problem will make the problem worse while adding some new ones. The wrong solution to the right problem will do the same. There must be a better way than merely learning some technique for problem-solving. Such techniques assume that the problem is independent of people. That is never going to happen. Such techniques also assume that anyone can see accurately what the problem is by using the correct procedure (e.g., the process for getting to root causes). Note that the procedure for determining what the problem is was itself devised by people who were solving *their* problem. A procedure for arriving at the best name for a problem may help, of course.

But the reason why the root cause rarely turns out to be incompetence on someone's part is that the problem sleuths have no solution for that. Being no more than marginally competent to perform in a given role has to be the most common cause of problems in organizations. Identifying the cause as something else must seem to people more readily fixable.

Think about it.

Some more thought-prodders for this provocative subject:
- Most people prefer a problem they can't solve to a solution they don't like – or which is not in their tool box.
- Many people mistake a solution method for a problem definition. That is, they define the problem by a known method of solution.

- The acceptability of a solution to a "tough" problem is likely to be inversely related to the time it takes to provide it.
- If you can't imagine how your understanding of the problem might be wrong, you don't really understand the problem.
- Believing that a problem named by people has only one right solution is equivalent to the mistake of believing that a problem has a single cause.

Is there a better way? Is there a way to escape the contributions people make to misnaming problems because those people imagine they have the solution? If we look carefully at the centuries of leadership wisdom and practice, yes, there seems to be a better way.

And that is to create a way forward that obviates the problem.

Problems arise out of the ways things are done. Change a procedure, change a habit, change an attitude or change a goal, and the problems you have will change. If you change the circumstances or the conditions that made a problem possible, or that nurtured it once it emerged, then you may indeed make the problem evaporate.

What would you do to make a particular problem impossible? How would you do it? That's what leaders do. The crux of the matter is not to explain the past or the present. It is to create the future out of whatever you've got or can get. That requires a far different logic, a far different mentality.

Solutions to problems, no matter how expert, always create problems in their wake. We (people) are problem-creators, not just problem-solvers. Leaders focus on the outcomes. Problem-solving procedures, no matter how popular, will reproduce the status quo.

There is always human complicity in the problems we encounter. The lesson to be learned is that the determination of what the problem *is* and what to do about it will always be more a function of the people involved than of any actual circumstances.

So what does the leader do? The leader, knowing that problems are inevitable, attempts to create the circumstances out of which will emerge the problems he or she *prefers* to have. Creating the future means picking the problems that you intend to have there, or along the way. The leader refuses to be victimized by problems. Leaders make victims of the problems and obstacles they encounter, not the other way around.

The tougher or loftier the goal, the tougher the obstacles are going to be. That goes with the territory. Most people solve this one by not having any particular goal or aim in life. Then they don't have to face tough obstacles, or being embarrassed by not overcoming them. Even this doesn't work.

The problems a person encounters in attempting to live a conventional life will be … conventional problems. They are often more onerous and more difficult to deal with, simply because they are universal and are therefore assumed to be unavoidable. This is one reason why the most common problems in conventional organizations recur and recur. Carelessness or not paying attention would be prime examples.

Another view of great value to would-be leaders comes from some ancient wisdom. It is that we are given the problems we encounter not to eliminate them, but to learn from them. We have the problems we have for a purpose. Your task is to figure out why you have the problems you do, because such problems do not come with an instruction book.

People who are never challenged to grow by figuring out a way around the problems they encounter on their quests in life are people who are not on a quest. Outstanding leaders welcome the problems that come their way, knowing that the tougher and more challenging they are, the more there is to learn, to grow on. If you have the same problems everyone else has, that means you are not different enough, or on a different enough path, to have your own. The self-help industry preys on those who want to have the most current or fashionable problems.

We've only opened the door on this subject. But here are some thought-prodders to help you take your thinking further:

- Don't ask, "What is 'the' problem?" Ask, rather, "What is **whose** problem?" (Problems always arrive at your door on two feet.)
- Don't solve problems that rightfully belong to others. One way or another, make it necessary for them to own and to deal with their own problems.
- Ownership means owning the problems one ought to own. And that means as well owning the consequences of what one does or doesn't do about them.
- Responsibility, accountability, etc. are a function of ownership – owning the consequences.
- In the valley of problem-solvers, the problem-creator is king.
- Your first obligation – to yourself, to others, to the organization – is not to be a part of the problem, because the more you are a part of the problem, the less you can be a part of the solution.
- Finally, think on this one: Can any set of people solve permanently a problem with the same mentality ~~which~~ they employed to create it in the first place?

Performance

As fundamental as this concept is to all the rest of your thinking, we can come to grips with it in short order.

Think of a continuum labeled LIFE. At one extreme are those people who are a product of whatever happens to them. At the other extreme are those people who *make* the lives they live.

The first are the people who play the role of being victimized by life. Whatever happened to them made them what they are. They have the problems or the difficulties they have because that's what life dealt them.

96

Whether life grabs a person by the throat, or a person grabs life by the throat is a matter of attitude. One can look at the world as a victim of it. Or one can look at the world as a given, simply the only place there is to work out one's destiny, one's life.

Neither way changes any actualities, or the randomness of events. What gets changed is the way one goes at life. There is a powerful way of thinking about this – the leader's way. It is that life is a performing art.

Leadership is a performing art.

What this means is that we are either given roles to play in life or we forge a role for ourselves. In either case, our lives are a function of how well we perform those roles – not how elevated that role is, but how well it is performed. There are plumbers who perform their role better than some surgeons perform theirs.

So, to develop the capacity to be a leader, you have to look at everything that people do or don't do in terms of **performance**. The leader intends to be the author of some aspect of the future – to interfere with the unfolding of history, of the story that would have been if that leader had not intervened. Leaders are measured by their performance. If they intend to be successful, they have to measure others by *their* performance.

It is how well an organization performs that counts. It is thus how well the people who comprise the organization perform their roles that counts. A healthy organization is one whose members have assumed full responsibility for shepherding their own lives in the context of the life of the organization.

The right measure of any organization is its performance. Which depends primarily on the performance of those who comprise it.

Performance is not about play-acting. It is the serious business of becoming fully and increasingly competent in one's role – individual or organizational. The real qualities of the good life come from becoming increasingly more competent at life, whether at work or elsewhere.

To be a leader, you have to perform well in a leadership role. How your organization performs depends on how the people who comprise it perform. Leaders know that the only measure of performance is performance.

Necessity

So please, put on your thinking caps. This is not going to be what you may expect.

There are two gates to the way of thinking we want to come away with here:

1. What drives performance is *necessity*.

2. And what drives extraordinary performance is extraordinary *necessity*. Not desire, not intention, not motivation or inspiration, but ... **necessity**. Not goals, not incentives, not rewards, but **necessity**.

Necessity has many sources. The most effective necessity is unseen, intangible. In general, the most potent source of necessity is internal – habits of thought and action.

What drives a person's performance is a function of the way that person is built. You can threaten and cajole, you can holler and scream, you can be gentle or you can be forceful, you can attempt to politic or to blackmail or seduce or entice. You can offer rewards or you can threaten punishments. You can offer heaven, or hell. You can do so articulately or by getting red in the face and huffing and puffing. You can be angry or sweet. You can try all of the tricks there are. But nothing you can do will work in every case. And nothing you can do will hold a candle to the drivers that are an intrinsic condition of a person.

The lesson here? Surround yourself only with people who are internally driven to perform – no need to ask why or how. But it takes one to know one. Or to cope with one. If *you* don't have the internal drivers, you won't be able to surround yourself with the people who have those drivers. Simple enough. Here's how to think about necessity:

- Competencies are bundles of habits. Whatever we are capable of doing depends upon bundles of habits over which we have no immediate control. If we are competent to do something in some way, that's what we will do and that is how we will do it. For a person to do something differently, or better, requires fundamental changes in fundamental habits, not one of which can be dealt with tangibly. The path of practice by which these habits got ingrained is something we will never know – too complex, too subtle, too out of conscious intention or control. They have to be changed in the same way we got them in the first place – by practice, practice, practice. The habits that underpin our competencies can rarely be eliminated. But they can be displaced by other habits. There is nothing we do – including our thinking and our feelings – which does not hinge upon bundles of habits that got nurtured and took root long ago and out of memory.

- So why **do** people do what they do? As we have seen, because they have to. And the core have-to's are the habits that underlie and inform our competencies. The main source of the necessity driving people's performance, for good or for ill, from the highest levels to the lowest, is the conglomeration of habits that push and pull their competencies.

- The second aspect of internal necessity worth thinking about is that of **conscience**. Some people are conscientious, some are not. Quality in an organization is a function of conscientiousness, not of some program or technique. People who are conscientious preclude the errors that lead to poor quality, whether in a product or a service. It may be a word that is in disuse in our particular culture. But it is a powerful driver. Look up this word in the dictionary. It is a concept that suggests certain people may have a strong sense of guilt if they do not do what is right. As conscience fades into disuse, so does what we call the work ethic.

- A third concept that will help you understand what accounts for level of performance is that of **duty**. A very useful concept which, unfortunately, is similarly out of fashion these days. It is useful to any person who wants to lead a worthy life. It is indispensable to the leader, both personally and for the purpose of developing an organization capable of real achievement. The idea of **duty** was central to the leadership philosophy of General Robert E. Lee. "Duty," he said, "is the sublimest word in our language. Do your duty in all things. You cannot do more; you should never wish to do less." But keep in mind that people cannot do their duty unless they are competent to do so.

- If I see myself as a person who can be depended upon, no matter what, to do my duty, to perform my role, to achieve the goals or objectives set before me, it's far more likely than not that this orientation will be a driver. If I don't have such a sense of myself, then how I perform may depend upon the circumstances, or on whether I feel like it or not. Both self-images are drivers. They just drive the person in a different direction. Another is what we sometimes refer to as peer pressure. I may perform as required because others expect me to, and if I have a sense that they may punish me in some way if I don't perform as they expect me to. Great organizations of all types depend heavily on this kind of driver. The Mafia, elite military units, sports teams, religious communities all control performance in this way – by peer pressure. Given competence, of course. Nothing can drive performance if the competence required to perform at that level is not a precondition of the person or the team. That's why you start there. That's why you go there first to assess and to develop the competencies required for the performance expected.

CHAPTER 4 • THE LEADER'S LEXICON: II

- Or it might be something very personal. I may refuse to let down another person who means much to me. A coach, perhaps. Or a parent. Or a friend. Or even a leader. I may equip myself to perform at a superb level just to have the feeling, at the end of all the pain and effort that I have not let that person down. Over time, everyone you associate with in any way has an image of you. Out of all of these images that are implicit in the way others treat you, you will create one for yourself that enables you at least to accommodate those that are important to you, or critical to your path. Some may see this as a negative, as a constraint on your freedom. But it works both ways. The more conscientious the people you have in your organization, the more conscientious will be the people you have in the future. You don't make this happen. They do.

It is the way of the manager to try to get people to perform by rules, by rewards, by threat, or by trying to micro-manage performance. It is the way of the manager to exhibit and exercise power or authority. It is the way of the *leader* to build necessity into personal and organizational performance where the internal drivers are. This is what makes performance reliable and sustainable.

This is what accounts for performance when the leader is nowhere in sight.

People who have to perform because of who they are, because that's who they **are**, do not need a policeman or a mother at work, or at play. They do the right thing, they perform at the level required, because they **have to.** That is an aspect of them, not something that the leader does *to* them.

Given a *conscientious person* who is *competent* to perform at the level required, that person will do his or her *duty*. What leaders do is take all possible ambiguity out of what that duty is. The leader puts into place first the bedrock preconditions for performance. The leader does not imagine that he or she can provide that necessity during or after the fact.

101

In a traditional society or organization, it is "tradition" that provides the necessity for performance. In a traditional society, individuals are not "committed" to anything. They are merely fulfilling expectations, since there are no alternatives. In a "modern" society or organizations – such as we have today – it is **fashion** that guides, constrains, and drives us.

Those who run organizations often do what they do out of the need to keep up with others, to be like those others are, to be up-to-date. In short, to be in step with what's fashionable. We've gone from the tyranny of tradition to the tyranny of fashion – in smaller and smaller subgroups. We're so busy chasing the fashionable ideas in leadership and organizations that we have little time left to implement one. Every few months it's something new - from "participative management" to "Six Sigma" through "Reengineering." In a traditional society, tradition reigns. In a society driven by fashion, the currently-fashionable reigns.

The real struggle is for whose proprietary ideas reign. And that changes every couple of months or so. What gets lost is whether any one of them actually provides a ROI. At the rate of 2,400 business books a year, there are more ideas about how to do it than there are people capable of doing it. Tradition required competence to DO. Fashion requires only the money and cosmetics needed to LOOK LIKE you're doing. It is my conviction that performance requires far more than appearing to be fashionable.

The less tradition-bound people are, the more fashion-bound they are likely to be. People say what is said, do what is done, and try to be as the current fashion demands. If it is fashionable to think of work as drudgery and leisure time as freedom from that drudgery, people will drudge and trudge through the hours at work just to get the paycheck to buy the (fashionable) leisure time activities and stuff they think they deserve.

People may claim to be thinking for themselves. People may claim to be individuals in their tastes, their personalities, their attitudes. But in a world like ours, it's much more likely that they are just being fashionable. They are much more concerned with what's "cool" and what's not than with any wisdom. So when people begin a sentence with the word I, what the leader hears is a report on the currently fashionable opinions of that age group or economic group. To be where it's at is more important to most people than to carry out what would actually serve one's own best self-interests. Leaders become astute at looking for the unseen but operative sources of necessity behind people's thinking, attitudes, and actions.

Advice

Thus the "advice" you get these days is more likely to be fashionable than it is to be useful.

Consider the fashionable idea of "empowerment." A person who has not made himself or herself totally responsible for his or her own destiny cannot be empowered. People can empower themselves to be the instrument of their own destiny, but you cannot empower them to be the instruments of *your* destiny.

Leaders are not seduced by buzzwords. They say what they *mean* and they *mean* what they say.

Repeating fashionable mantras is not a method that works where excellence or high performance are the aim.

Let's cut to the chase on this age-old bugbear of advice:

• If you know the difference between good advice and bad advice you don't need advice, as the saying goes. But the only way *you can* know the difference is by having a purpose or cause that you can use to distinguish what's relevant from what's not.

• Whether it's free or you pay dearly for it, people cannot tell you what you need to know. They can only tell you what *they* know. The problem of knowing what you need to know remains yours.

• The worst advice and the best advice you will ever get comes from how you advise yourself. Fix that first.

• Power attracts advice like light attracts moths. Be certain your light is powered by your own thinking.

- No advice ever offered has had any more value than the receiver made of it. In other words: No advice exceeds a person's ability to implement it.
- If you don't need to know the answer, don't ask the question. If you need to know the answer, ask just the right question of just the right source.

Commitment

If there is something that is common to all of those who are the engines of great achievements, it is the fierceness, even the fanaticism, of their commitment.

There is a HUGE difference between having a cause and **being had by** a cause. A person who merely has a cause will usually be willing to compromise. A person who is *had by* a cause will be unreasonable, relentless, and even ruthless, especially with himself or herself.

The one-time CEO of Volkswagen said, "A passion to build automobiles has me by the skin and the hair." If you intend to be a leader, you must be *had by* your cause in life in this way. You are a servant of your cause, not the other way around. It is your cause that is your destiny. You will let nothing stop you, nothing get in your way. The leader is the person who holds himself or herself to this standard with respect to what **has to** be realized, made into reality. Great leaders cannot make excuses. Nor accept them.

> "But suppose," a CEO once said to me, "I don't have that level of commitment."
> ME: "No one will know but you. If you perform your role as if you were had by your cause, and people give you that role because you are utterly convincing, two things will result:
> "One is that you **will** be had by your cause as a result of sheer and effective practice at performing that way. People judge you on your performance. They have

no direct access to your mind or your heart. What counts in the real world is performance.

"Second, the more you are **had by** your cause, the more likely it is that you will attract the kind of followers needed to make you successful in your role."

Change?

Things change. What leaders do is to *create* a world that would not have existed without them. Change is unavoidable. Changing some part of the world from the way it is to the way it ought to be is the work of leadership. Michelangelo said he saw the finished sculpture in the raw slab of marble. His task was to release it, to change it from what it was to what he envisioned. To bring about something that never existed before. That's what leaders do.

Much of all this talk about change seems to suggest simply rearranging things. Leaders do not simply rearrange things. Leaders create a future out of their vision of it. In retrospect, they may have altered the course of history, if only of themselves or of their organization. But that was a byproduct of composing something that never existed before.

• Managers change things. Leaders compose the future.
• What people want is to be relevant. Changing them does not make them relevant. Being a part of making the future does.
• The leader's relevance and influence lie there.

One last cluster of thoughts about change:
1. *If you **need** to be liked by people more than you **need** to fulfill your cause in life, or*
2. *If you have settled into your own comfort zone, or*
3. *If you prefer consensus over unpopular decisions,*
you are not likely to be very successful in a leadership role.

Change is often painful. People will not like you for making changes that affect them personally. People may enjoy talking about change. But when it comes right down to it, they would prefer the status quo. That is why, in any contest between change and the status quo, bet on the status quo. Leaders are change agents. It is their cause they serve, not the sentiments of the day.

ROA

Everyone knows about ROI – i.e., Return on Investment. But not everyone appreciates the fact that the investment we all make which has the most far-reaching returns, plus or minus, is how we invest our attention. What we pay attention to, why, for how long, to what ends: these create the wake in which everything that follows will be thought, or done.

So the key investment for any individual or for any organization is that of *attention*. We can make ROA refer to Return on *Attention*. If you get this one right, most of the other hoped-for "returns" will occur without focusing on them. If you invest in what *drives* performance, you will get the desired performance without endlessly fussing with yourself or your people about it.

Randomness, Luck, Etc.

There are ALWAYS factors over which you have no control that will bear on how things turn out. We could refer to those inevitable events as "luck" or as "randomness" or as one or more of "Murphy's Laws." It makes little difference what you call them. As we all know, the first of Murphy's Laws is really proverbial: "Whatever can happen will happen, and usually at the worst possible time."

So be it. The leader doesn't imagine that he or she has the omniscience to see what is going to happen. But leaders have learned that much of what determines the outcomes of any endeavor can't be foreseen. And that they could not control them even if they could be. What leaders have learned is how to collaborate with luck or chance happenings, how to roll with the realities, how to collaborate with the perversities of their world. They develop a sixth sense about when to raise and when to fold in the face of unbeatable forces, as Sun Tzu suggested, and as every good poker player learns quickly.

Leaders do not imagine that they have more power than the world has. They do not imagine that they could comprehend what is going on there in all of its dynamic complexity. They learn to play their hand within the context of whatever happens that is beyond their ken, beyond anyone's control.

A one-line thought-prodder, to be pondered and practiced:

Leaders *partner* with luck, with randomness.

A Brief on Time

People who are clear about their purpose or cause in life have all the time they need to plan and pursue those ends. Those who are not clear about why they are here, or what their aims in life are, will have problems managing their time.

That's because people who always have their eye on "the ball" (their purpose in life) can sort out what is relevant to their path and what is not in nanoseconds. Others, sadly, will have to carry an "organizer."

Think on these:

• If you can't figure out what is relevant, on the spot, that's likely because you have no clear purpose in your life, or at that moment. Being had by a cause requires continuous vigilance. It's not something you can schedule.

• This cannot be fixed by buying something. Real achievement is not for sale. Neither is time. Everyone has the same number of hours in a day. What make leaders different is the way they *use* time.

There are many more such thought-prodders we will meet as we go along. A word is a handle on a concept. The lesson for leaders is that the concepts you carry around with you as tools to navigate the world are the critical part of your resources. Get those right and your endeavors will be optimum. Not perfect, not always successful, just optimally so.

We all have to use the same words. But the way we conceive of those aspects of the world which those words trigger can be quite different. When we say that leaders **think** differently, that is what we mean: they are using the same words, but they understand those words differently. It is a difference that makes the difference.

We could take almost any important word in the dictionary and revise it for purposes of a Leader's Lexicon. Try it. It's **how** you think about things that matters.

Some "thought-prodders" and other questions:

- What's **necessary** is not what *you* think is necessary. It's what the person who has to act upon it believes is necessary.
- The necessity a person can't bring on herself to perform is necessity you can't place on her to perform, in most cases.
- People may do tricks for you, for money or recognition, but those will be no better than mediocre tricks.
- If it boosts your ego to imagine that you can manipulate someone, think about this: that is how they manipulate you.
- If it were necessary for you to *make* someone perform, that would measure that person's power over you.
- What leads you to believe you could make people perform beyond their inclinations, if you can't make yourself perform beyond *your* inclinations?
- Why is it that you may try to by subtle means to get the credit for another's performance if it is superior, but attribute the blame to that person if it is not?

• What is it, exactly, that *you* want from others' performance?

And a thinking test, just for fun:
• About *what* does the leader need to be a competent thinker?
• What or who makes any *leader's* exceptional performance *necessary*?
• Is it wrong to be content with being mediocre or just average?

See Ray Bennett's
The Underachiever's Manifesto

• Even so, incompetence in the service of some intended good will produce the wrong results. Incompetence *always* misleads.

POINTS TO PONDER

+ Fashions about "how to manage" are tickets to mediocrity.

+ Tools and techniques applied to compensate for marginal competence actually retard competence.

+ People who are real achievers don't talk much about their intentions.

+ People are not psychological. Only psychologists are.

+ "Motivation" is a myth.

+ It takes as much practice to be incompetent as it does to be competent.

+ Competence and preparedness are two terms for the same thing.

+ Intention is the refuge of the incompetent.

+ Owning the problem turns competent people on, turns incompetent people off.

+ How do you know that what you know is what you need to know?

+ If you are "had by" a cause, you cannot escape.

+ People perform. That's all that can be directly observed. All the rest is made up.

+ Fictitious (pop psychology) myth: "You can be whatever you want to be." The reality? You can only be what your constituents permit you to be.

PART II

Obstacles and Barriers

What makes it so hard?

No one has ever over-estimated the difficulty of great achievement. No one has ever over-estimated the difficulty of making a great – a high-performance – organization. No one has ever over-estimated the difficulty of leading people (the Moses story), or of changing the order of things (the Lincoln story). Here is what Machiavelli had to say in 1532 about the perils and difficulties of becoming an exceptional leader:

> *There is nothing more difficult to take in hand,*
> *nothing more perilous to conduct, or more uncertain*
> *in its success, than to take the lead in the introduction*
> *of a new order of things.*

Consider every phrase carefully. He does not say that improving things for the benefit of the people will be warmly welcomed and aided. Just the opposite. It is, in fact, easier to do harm to people than it is to do good for them. Think about that.

If anything has changed since those words appeared, it is that they are truer today than ever. Machiavelli was trying to coach his prince (his "leader") about how to protect and preserve the state, about how to be a successful – a great – leader.

His book is about how to be the leader you need to be in order to create a healthy, long-lived organization. One that is full of quality and growth and rich human life for all of the people involved. It is about how to make an organization that is actually good for people and for the society; an organization that enhances and enriches the humanity of all who are a part of it, or are touched by it.

Let's visit the Moses story. Moses was told what to do ("Free my people from their slavery and deliver them the life they should have.") But not how to do it. Those people did not want to be led somewhere else. Nor were they all that pleased to have as a leader a guy with a speech impediment and not a clue about where the "Promised Land" was. There were no incentives or bonuses involved. So Moses' challenge was:

> *How am I supposed to organize 600 people ... get them on an unknown path to some unspecified future ... feed them and clothe them and take care of their needs along the way ... when they don't want to go, anyway?*

A challenge is always a challenge to your thinking. In the following chapters, you will continue to provision yourself with more powerful ways of thinking about what you need to think about. We'll start by examining in depth some of the universal obstacles and barriers you will face if you undertake to introduce a new order of things. The better you anticipate these, the better prepared you will be to deal with them.

Such obstacles on the road to great achievements may be there for no reason other than that of testing how committed you are. Reason enough.

If it were easy, this undertaking, you'd be surrounded by the same people who hover around you today. Any easy path will lead to exactly where you are today.

Chapter **5** Dragons

If you grew up with picture books, television, and cinema, you will imagine that "dragons" are those loathsome fire-breathing monsters that have been the standard depiction for decades. So it may be that what I have to tell you will seem, simply ... wrong.

Centuries before there were "illustrated" books, and for millennia before there were photo- and life-like moving pictures of these fantastic creatures, humans did not have a conventional image of them. Quite the contrary, in fact. For those who lived in oral cultures (most of the humans who have ever lived), a "dragon" was not a creature that came to scare us into some heroic defense of our lives, our territory, or our lovers.

Dragons had no corporeal existence.

They were indeed believed to function as obstacles to any journey or quest undertaken, but they were not real things on the path in front of us. They were simply metaphors for those attitudes, fears, and anxieties that existed *within* people that kept them from doing what they ought to do, that kept them from undertaking the quests they perhaps should have undertaken to make their lives what they ought to be. Those dragons were the mental ghosts and goblins that kept people from venturing forth, imaginary creatures that people created to convince themselves that they should not undertake anything dangerous or risky. They were seen as obstacles to any venturesome human undertaking.

But they were not physical obstacles along our path. They were obstacles in our thinking, in our imaginations; obstacles about how treacherous it would be to attempt any change or to undertake tasks that might have a questionable outcome.

Nothing much has changed. We still have a love-hate relationship with the future. It is the unknown because we have not experienced it yet and can not look at it as we look for the answers to life in the rear-view mirror. The future is not visible in the rear-view mirror. We may want change, or even **to** change, but we are comfortable only with the "hope" we find in hindsight.

The dilemma? We have to understand life backward, but we have to live it forward. We would like to be adventurers in life. But we would prefer to deal with the risks and uncertainties involved by doing it vicariously. Enter, thus, the stories that allow us to remain in our comfort zones while pretending to undertake dangerous missions. Most of these become the favorites of today's large audiences of couch potatoes: "Mission Impossible," "OO7," "Star Wars," "Dinosaur," the "Super Bowl," "WWC," and on and on. We love "consuming" the adventure. We merely prefer it in the comfort of our familiar surroundings and security.

So we entertain ourselves with the notion that there are dragons out there – creatures that are bigger than we are, fiercer than we are, and cleverer than we are. We like to look at them and to be scared or thrilled by them. But we wouldn't really want to come face-to-face with one. So we've organized the world in such a way that we don't have to.

This misses the point. The point is that obstacles or barriers to achieving something in the future ALL belong to the person who imagines them. You can't escape the logic. What external actualities that might keep you from doing something in the future can't be known, in fact, until you pass through to that future. If there is an obstacle there, you can't *know* that until you can see it in the rear-view mirror.

It pays to be realistic. You don't have to jump to your death off the top of a mountain to determine whether or not you can fly. You can't do something in the present OR the future if no human can do that. But at one time it was thought that the four-minute mile was impossible. So was heavier-than-air flight. So was a trip to the moon.

114

What Columbus did was considered to be, at best, improbable. Fred Smith, who originated Federal Express, was told that his idea was foolish, a failure at the outset.

It was also impossible to split the atom.

Most of what we now take for granted in our lives – things like elevators and telephones – were considered fantasies. Until someone came along and made them happen. Sam Walton was told, several billion dollars ago, that what he wanted to attempt was not doable. Steven Jobs couldn't interest the major "computer" companies in what became the PC, the laptop.

The lessons of history are that most of what the experts ~~have~~ considered impossible is now commonplace. In the 1920s, it was declared that no human could perform in the Olympics beyond the records already set. What kept many athletes from trying was their belief that this was true. What made it possible for those who broke those records to do so was, at least in part, their belief that it could be done, even if most of the rest of the world thought it was not doable.

In other words, the "dragons" were internal. And those who achieved "impossible" goals simply slew those dragons, in order to achieve the unachievable.

Leaders are "dragon-slayers." They **Think about it.** first slay the dragons within themselves that might keep them from setting out for fear of what might happen along the way. Those inner dragons are often put forth for why something can't be done. In a typical meeting in a typical organization, there are always many more nay-sayers than yea-sayers. These are the people who, when the subject of what needs to be done in the future comes up, can tell you that it can't be done, and why. These are the same people who have nothing substantive to offer about what to do, but can readily tell others why this, that, or the other thing can't be done.

These people are not leaders, whatever their role. These are people who have not slain their own dragons. They are still clinging to the fear of change that could free them, and others, to talk productively about a plan for achieving the "impossible" – that is, something that they have not yet accomplished.

A leader is a person who refuses to recognize impediments to a future mission or goal. There may indeed be some. But the leader realizes that they have to be encountered along the way. They cannot be seen in any tangible way before getting underway.

What leaders bring to bear is the need to prepare to meet those obstacles, and the spirit of determination that says we will achieve our aims whatever it takes. What leaders bring to bear is the *whatever it takes* kind of determination coupled with the kinds of competencies and preparedness that will thwart most of those obstacles. Leaders bring a discipline that makes possible improvising around, over, under, or through those obstacles. Nothing worth achieving comes cheap. The more impossible the goal, the more prepared you have to be: competencies, heart, imagination, and all the rest of the tools of achievement.

It would be foolish to be "Pollyannaish" about all of this. There is a great difference between being fully prepared to carry out one's aims and being merely foolhardy. People don't bring off exceptional achievements because they want to. Or because this is their dream. Or even by being "courageous." There are always risks, no matter how well prepared you are. There are always failures, no matter how determined you are.

And yet, more success comes to those who are more determined coupled with being more prepared. Even luck, it is said, favors those who are best prepared to accomplish what they have set out to accomplish.

We are not falling for the pop psychology myth that success is a matter of heart or of desire. Heart and desire count, but not as much as competence, preparedness, and absolute determination. You will recall the old proverb: Necessity is the mother of invention. The necessity here refers to obstacles you encounter along the way to a destination you are determined to reach. People who are not committed to purposes in life have none of this kind of necessity. Their necessities might come down to getting the VCR repaired by someone else. The necessity referred to in the proverb refers to what the person on her quest has to find within herself to deal with the obstacles being confronted. And what *can be* invented is a function of who that person is, how determined that person is, and how competent and prepared to invent truly successful solutions that person is.

In other words, a person who is forever doing battle with internal "dragons" is not going to have the time, the energy, or the competencies to deal with the real obstacles that inevitably arise on the path to anywhere worthwhile. That's why most people who never leave their own comfort zone can tell you why the difficult thing you propose can't be done. It can't be done by them, so they conclude it can't be done by you. They want you to be as certain as they are that it can't be done. A prophecy is not an achievement. Nor does a prophecy make an achievement possible or impossible. It may be conventional wisdom. But to an achiever, conventional wisdom is always wrong.

It is the rare person who emerges from all of this comfortable disdain in order to actually undertake the pursuit of impossible goals. These are the leaders. They lead thought; they lead practice; they lead movements; they lead every aim or purpose that has been deemed "impossible." As Captain Piccard, of the Starship Enterprise, says, "Make it so." The time for considering the pros, the cons, and the alternatives is over. If you *think* it can't be done, you can't be a member of my crew.

Those who make it so have slain the dragons that would keep them from undertaking the "impossible." Only then is it possible for them to lead others, to lead the way toward some *collective* aim or purpose.

A leader is a person who has slain his or her own personal "dragons."

A follower is a person who wants to go with the "dragon-slayer."

And this raises two additional questions:
1. Why does the prospect of changing oneself loom larger or harder than changing the world – for most people?
2. What, then, is a *hero*?

Private dragons are usually more fearsome than the obstacles we actually meet along the path to our goals. Imagination is often more potent than actuality. There will be known obstacles, reported by those who have gone before us, or extrapolated from the past. If our past experiences have revealed obstacles faced in the pursuit of impossible goals, we will know how to prepare to deal with them. If a person has never encountered such adversity (having never undertaken to achieve impossible goals), then that person will not know how to prepare, or what personal and other provisions might be needed. She will therefore be faced for the first time with her internal dragons. If your baggage includes those internal dragons, you may freeze, go dumb, and be unable to cope. If you have no internal dragons, and if you have prepared yourself for any likely or unlikely adversity along the way, that adversity will not produce the same level of fear or helplessness, either before undertaking the journey or along the way.

For the person who is determined and prepared, obstacles are merely problems to be solved. They are a challenge to one's capabilities, an opportunity to put oneself to the test, a part of life on a worthy quest. For the person who is not prepared, those same obstacles will either preclude planning for setting-forth, or will incite retreat or despair. What you can bring to bear on actual obstacles depends upon how much you have to struggle with your internal dragons.

A hero, then, is not first a person who has achieved something notable in the world. A hero is a person who has slain his own internal dragons.

This is the greater feat. Having accomplished this, the hero may then take on the role of leading others. For good or for ill, what stands between us and our goals is … us. We can't *know* whether or not something can be accomplished until we have done it. And that requires a kind of passionate abandonment of oneself to one's cause. We cannot abandon ourselves fully to any cause unless and until we have slain those internal dragons that function to keep us from actually undertaking that cause.

That is the mother of all dragons. Most people prefer their own mediocre (at best?) lives to any cause or purpose they may imagine expressing or achieving. They will never fulfill their dreams because they are too consumed with protecting their own status quo. They will ridicule others' goals. They will be the nay-sayers because they have said "No!" to their aims by saying "Yes!" to themselves as they presently are. They will offer explanations or rationalizations. But it always comes down to their failure to exorcise their own dragons. Those dragons are to them not imaginary. They are reality.

For them, the dragons have won. When the dragons win, there is no *hero*. There can be a hero only when those dragons have been slain.

And no matter what else it may be, or where else it may be, the one that stands in our way is the one we imagine will keep us from success in the pursuit of any goal we permit ourselves to characterize as impossible.

The lessons for leaders?
- The critical prerequisite for leading others is first "conquering" yourself.
- Whatever you imagine will keep you from achieving the impossible goals you set for yourself are personal dragons. Slay those first.
- What is required is determination, competence, preparedness, and the zeal to encounter the actual adversities encountered when you are diligently on the path to your achievement.
- There is always an easier path. That path is offered by the devil to seduce you, to keep you in your comfort zone.
- It is not aims or purposes or causes that explain the difference between people who achieve greatly and those who do not. It is indifference to the effort and the challenges to be encountered.

- To abandon yourself to your worthy goals or purposes in life requires an openness to the world that comes from first slaying your own dragons.
- Extraordinary achievement requires you to be the servant of your purpose or cause in life, not the other way around.
- The best theory about how to accomplish something worthwhile is the one that works. That can be determined only by looking *back* at the accomplishment.
- Life is not in the destination. It is in the struggle to get there.
- The critical obstacles to real achievement are within. It is their own dragons that keep people from setting forth.
- Leaders slay their own personal dragons. Then they equip others and make it necessary for those others to slay *their* dragons.

No person can know that something can or cannot be done. The evidence has to come from doing it. Dragons make lives for people out of what happens *to* them. Escaping that prison requires first slaying one's own dragons.

POINTS TO PONDER

+ We "modern" people prefer to represent dragons as having corporeal existence. Why is that?

+ Even in meetings, initiatives that have uncertain outcomes invoke dragons.

+ People consume adventures vicariously, avoid them personally.

+ Leadership requires having slain one's dragons. Have you faced-off with yours?

+ People's hopes and dreams are guarded by dragons.

+ The "hero" is the dragon-slayer (Bond?), who also wins the girl. And the premise is ...?

+ A prophecy is a dragon-free environment.

+ If you say a thing can't be done, you're right.

+ A dragon is a problem to be solved.

+ For mediocre people and organizations, the mother dragon is the status quo.

+ Ever notice who believes there are fewer dragons on well-worn paths?

Chapter **6**

The Way You Think About Things

It may seem odd to consider the fact that the way you think can be the central player in the world you face. We've discussed this at some length previously. It is, in fact, the first of the building blocks of leadership: Thinking, Being, Doing. Now we need to revisit and to provide more specifics.

How you think about what needs thinking about can be your own best ally, or your own worst enemy.

Everyone has dragons. Slaying them makes any achievement seem more doable. The second set of obstacles/barriers to getting on the path toward great achievement, the path required to make a great or a high-performance organization, derives from something so common we hardly ever give it heed: the conventional managerial *mindset*. That mindset is a part of our culture. It is almost universal in most organizations. We could garner the most fashionable ideas from the most popular books. But we would still be faced with the obstacle that gets in the way of actually implementing any one of them. And that is the "managerial mindset." It is a way of thinking about things that gets in the way of any better way of thinking about those same things.

So what is it about the managerial mindset, which is assumed to be prerequisite to reaching higher levels of management in mediocre organizations, that functions as a bundle of obstacles to extraordinary performance?

Here are several aspects of that conventional managerial mindset that invariably work against the kind of thinking required to achieve high performance. Or to become the kind of leader who could preside over a great organization:

Management Is Not Leadership

Managers are not necessarily leaders. Managing is not the same thing as providing leadership. We use that term loosely and are thus misled by it. A person who has position power in an organization or an institution is not magically transformed into a leader merely by calling him one. It might be a good thing if calling people by a different name made them more competent.

But that doesn't happen. It's rare that a manager (given his or her managerial mindset) ever becomes a leader. Calling a hamburger a steak doesn't make it a steak.

Managers are appointed by their bosses. Leaders have to earn a leadership role by being endorsed by their constituents. Managers hire subordinates. Leaders have to earn their followers.

Responsibility is not the same thing as leadership. Managers think of themselves as responsible for the outcomes. Leaders think of themselves as responsible for the people who make the outcomes happen. Managers require people to do things right. Leaders lead people to do the right things. Managers devise schemes and deploy technologies to compensate for incompetencies. Leaders, as the old saying goes, do not give people fish. They teach people how to fish.

The list of differences is lengthy. But what's most to the point here is the mistaken belief that becoming a better and better manager will eventually turn that person into a leader. *This will not happen.*

What it takes to be a profit-maker is not what it takes to be a performance-maker. Leaders develop people for purposes of sustainable performance under adversity (which is the only measure of competence). Managers use people to make an acceptable "bottom line." Those who do not deeply comprehend those differences will never become leaders, no matter how good they get at managing.

A manager can be a successful manager for reasons that have nothing to do with that manager's capabilities. A leader succeeds or fails on the basis of the actual outcomes.

Managers can often explain-away their shortfalls, attributing them to someone or something else. Leaders fail themselves because it was *their* aim, *their* purpose in life that was at stake. Managers can tell you who was responsible. Leaders hold themselves accountable.

The managerial mindset takes you down a path that is contrary to the path of leadership. Under the influence of this mindset, managers do not think like leaders do. Thus managers do not make decisions or take actions like leaders do. If you want to be a leader, the managerial mindset will take you in an opposite direction from the one you need to be following.

If you are a competent manager, with timing and luck on your side, you could preside over a successful enterprise – personal or organizational. But to preside over a *high-performance organization*, you have to think like leaders think in order to grasp the world the way leaders do and thus to perform as leaders have to perform.

Managers organize for what's likely or what's possible – leaders for what is unlikely or for what is deemed at the outset to be impossible. Managers chase the possible. Leaders challenge themselves against the impossible. Leaders have a lust to experience the world of which they have a vision – beyond the possible. Managers prefer the comfort and security of working safely within conventional limits – of measuring against last year's numbers, for example.

Yet, and very important: leaders do not disdain the numbers. They understand that fiscal health is just as important as personal health to the pursuit of any mission. But they do not permit the numbers to define them or to define what's possible. They do not believe that destiny is *in* the numbers. They believe that destiny is what they can make it to be. Leaders take the measure of numbers. Numbers take the measure of managers.

It is our mindsets that lead us, that take us where *they* go. In this case, our conventional Western managerial mindset can be a serious obstacle to the kind of thinking required to pursue a great achievement. Mindsets are bundles of habits. Feelings are bundles of habits. One's identity is a bundle of habits. Our habits take us in the direction they aim, not necessarily in the direction we aim.

This is one of those things that makes the process so hard. You can't get there by conventional thinking, especially if your conventional thinking is bounded by this one bundle of habits we are referring to as the managerial mindset, or if it is entangled with addictions, as follows.

Being the Boss Is Addictive

Every person who has ever been put in the *position* of being the boss has become – more or less – *addicted* to the role.

Addicted to what?

Well, the boss has power. It may be no more than position power. But people who have not conquered themselves (remember the dragons?) easily become addicted to having power over others.

Becoming something other than the conventional boss, with the conventional power bosses have, is almost certain to provide that person with some anxiety about losing that power. You know how addictions are – very hard to give up voluntarily. A person might agree that the addiction is not healthy. But he or she would still be reluctant, even resistant, to giving it up – as managers (to the extent they are bosses) certainly are.

One thing that makes the whole process of doing the right thing so hard is that it might diminish something that the boss has become addicted to – for example, the way subordinates defer to them, or the feelings of omnipotence that can easily engender. There has been a lot of talk about "empowerment." Why is it so hard for managers to empower others? Because empowering others requires giving up some of one's power *over* them.

Like power, the sheer exercise of control over others is addictive. The more people are able to control themselves and their circumstances at work, the less control the conventional manager will have *over* them. To be addicted means wanting more and more of what you're addicted to. This is especially the case with power and control.

Money – at least the buying power of money – is also addictive. If the only way to maximize the getting of money is to be the boss over more people, then the conventional mindset leads many people to be *upwardly* ambitious. They don't necessarily want the additional responsibility. But they'll do what has to be done to get more money. They'll do what it takes to move up in the organization because that's obviously where the monetary rewards are disproportionately higher. A person who is addicted to money will either go where there is more money, or make a bigger cookie jar to which he or she has the key.

What else is addictive for the conventional mindset? Prestige. The prestige that goes with the position can easily become addictive. When you see the arrogance that often goes with position, you can see that the person is addicted. The perks that go with the position are addictive. People who are addicted to prestige will do whatever is necessary to get more of it. Are the people who have struggled and connived to feed more of their addictions ready to give up what they are addicted to – those perks? The kinds of addictions we are talking about here work like drugs. The person who is addicted needs to be sure where his or her next "fix" is coming from.

It is also the case that the sheer *dependence* of subordinates on the whims or needs of the boss is addictive. This is universally understood if not always stated. You've been the subordinate and you've been the boss. Which do you prefer? If you're the boss, it is understood that you are more important than other people. More relevant than they are, more indispensable. Having people defer to you because you are more important than they are can easily become addictive. And if you get addicted to such things, you'll want a steady supply.

Leader's lessons:
• **Get de-addicted.**
• Addiction-proof yourself.
• If you don't, you will not lead yourself or anyone else

Why are most bosses not great bosses? Because they become addicted to what comes with the position, and lose sight of what makes them truly successful – or not.

Some Additional Obstacles

If you don't want to be tripped-up or blindsided by the most common obstacles to extraordinary performance, it helps to know what they are. Here are some additional obstacles that derive from the folklore of management in our time, beliefs and myths which are themselves products of the popular culture:

1. One of the most basic of these obstacles is our compulsion for short-term thinking. And as well all of the short-term practices that result. We are a quick-fix society. That has in some instances served us well. But becoming really good at *anything* requires a commitment to whatever it takes – and that includes the investment of time and effort required. Air Jordans *will not* by themselves enable a person to jump higher. Business is not obligated to occur quarter-by-quarter. The Gregorian calendar (the one we use) was not created as an aid to measuring business. It does not encourage business. It inhibits business. More thoughts along this line:

- Why is it that we always seem to have the time required to talk about and deal with our problems after they occur, but we don't have the time to become competent enough beforehand to avoid those problems?
- Those who live by the quarterly numbers will likely die by them.

2. A similar obstacle that bars anyone's entry to world-class performance is recipe/panacea thinking. This kind of thinking culminates in your belief that somehow, just around the corner, there is a magical solution to your problems that merely has to be applied – the less effort, the better. Modern magic. Like predators, whole industries have sprung up to prey upon such gullibility. There is no painless, immediate ticket to being masterful at anything. No recipe can be better than the cook. The business press may peddle the panacea of the month. But it is only our belief that there *is* such a panacea that they prey upon. If it weren't for our belief that there is such a panacea just around the corner, they might be forced to sell us some reality. But, then, reality doesn't sell like "hope," does it? There may be no seminars about how to be mediocre. But most managers end up in that category. Where did they get their recipe for doing so?

- No snake oil salesman could sell anything to a person who isn't out there looking for a magic bullet or a cure-all tonic.
- An idea, no matter how good, is not an accomplishment. You can buy the best cookbook. But that will not transform you into a great cook. The believers, failing at real cookery, simply buy more cookbooks. Maybe they just haven't found the "right" cookbook. It couldn't be them, they're thinking. Or could it?

3. Closely related is the belief that words can be used to change people. That is, if you use just the right magic words, you can "motivate" people from being merely adequate to being truly masterful at what they do. If we ourselves buy just the right words, we will thereby – shazam! – be great. Or, if you use just the right words on others, they will thereby be transformed into great performers. A widely-held myth. But not even a shred of evidence. Why do people cling to what doesn't work, and avoid what might actually work?

This is what, in our belief in easy magic, we often mean by the term "motivation." Can you somehow simply *talk people into* being more competent, more diligent, more attentive to their work? Leaders have had to learn the difference between enthusiasm and competence. Or maybe you could buy something that magically produces the performance you hope for. You can't. But maybe it would sustain your hope.

Faust made that deal with the devil. But that didn't make him any smarter. Here are more thought-prodders along that line:

- If people come to your place because you offer them more money (or other goodies), wouldn't they leave for the same reason?
- If *bribery* hasn't made great performers out of people in their first twenty-five years of life, does it make sense to try more of the same?
- If words like responsibility and duty don't alter the attitudes or the behavior of the people you intend to "motivate" by words, what words would you need to use?
- And when you go to the bank to borrow money to pay people what they believe they deserve as a bonus for performing the role they signed up for, don't you and they both lose?
- It isn't technology or ideas that change the course of history or the destiny of any organization. It's people, and what changes *them* is a change in the way they think about things.

4. If you believe that the answer to your prayers is in some how-to recipe, then you must necessarily assume that people are interchangeable with respect to that recipe. They are not.

5. If you go with the flow – the conventional mindset – you will see the world as far more linear than it is. And you will see human behavior as far more controllable by you than it is.

To see things as more linear than they are is to attribute simple cause-and-effect explanations or predictions to a world that only rarely works that way. To see things as more controllable than they are is to attribute more reality to your observations than they could possibly provide. It would be attributing to others' words more reality than they could deliver. And you would assume that there is a one-to-one relationship between a word (or a number) and the reality it supposedly refers to. All of these would be obstacles to your ever becoming a leader, or to your success in that role if you fell into it.

Either way, it is to miss the fact that the world is far more convoluted and full of happenstance than this kind of thinking can capture. You may want to revisit our discussion of "Cause" in the lexicon chapters.

About what people say: They may not know what they mean. They may not have the words to approximate what they mean even if they do have a grasp of what they want to say. What they offer is at best no more than their interpretation. That is more likely to be an opinion, or a minor political maneuver.

At worst, the world is full of people who cannot lead you, but will inadvertently *mislead* you. People often don't mean what they say, and sometimes this is intentional. Sometimes people are speaking metaphorically. That is, their words or pictures or numbers may be intended figuratively – to provoke in you something other than a picture of any reality except their own. But there is always the possibility that they are playing upon your addictions, or your fears or anxieties.

Whatever else may be said about it, our cultural inclination to look at the world as linear, and at words as literal, are obstacles to any successful pursuit of real achievement.

6. The last of these conventional mindset obstacles we will consider here is this: Across the range of people we look to for leadership, such as the managers of our organizations, there is a significant shortfall of courage, of vision, of passion, of commitment, and of competence.

All these are required for those who would either lead themselves or others. Such shortfalls function as obstacles. Those who can't muster the courage required, the vision required, the passion required, and the competence required will neither find the path nor be able to deliver what it takes to stay on the path to any extraordinary performance.

Some potentially useful thought-prodders:

• George Bernard Shaw once said,

> *"The reasonable person adapts to the world. The unreasonable person persists in getting the world to adapt to him. Therefore, all progress depends upon the unreasonable person."*

Can that be reasonably understood?

• Most people are okay with the notion of change as long as it does not involve them personally.

• Most people are satisfied with their mediocrity. In fact, most people will work harder at preserving their mediocrity than at anything else. What "motivates" them to do this?

• People and their byproducts are *perverse*. What sort of logic, therefore, is required to provide leadership to them?

• How do *leaders* have to think about these things?

POINTS TO PONDER

+ Any way of thinking about things is an obstacle to any better way of thinking about those same things.

+ Calling a person a leader does not make her a leader.

+ Managers are not leaders, and vice versa.

+ You have to be one to know one.

+ Power, control, and status are addictive.

+ Being indispensable is the aim of the good leader.

+ The calendar, like the clock, frames everything as if all things were equal.

+ Hope sells. Reality doesn't.

+ The "fix" you buy is always independent of who you are.

+ Leaders have the magic power to change people.

+ Leaders are perverse.

7

The Drivers,
Right or Wrong

What makes it so hard? What are the obstacles that impede the few who try, or discourage the many from even setting forth?

Here are five usually unseen but potent drivers of wimpy behavior, of mediocrity, of tunnel vision, of lack of heart, of reluctance to change – even for the better:

Habits

The biggie, as we have seen, is habits. People essentially see the world, think the world, feel the world, and behave in the world, according to their habits. You are never free in the sense that you can see or feel or act in the world according to the way the world actually *is*. You are the prisoner of your habits. They take you where they would go, not where you would go. If you want to predict your, or anyone else's, destiny, observe their everyday habits. If you do, you will see that she is the person she is because this is the person her habits make possible, and also make necessary. We live our habits, and they live us.

Your habits will serve either to enable you to accomplish your aims in life, or as obstacles to moving in that direction. They make your life possible without your conscious effort. But they serve at the same time to make any other life impossible. If you've wondered where the bulk of all of that resistance to change we hear so much about comes from, this is where to look. Once formed, your habits will then persist as drivers of your thoughts and your actions forever. Some are hard to come by. Have you tried learning a foreign language? But they are even harder to change or dislodge. They are not just habits. They are who you *are*, a bundle of interwoven routines, from the smallest to the largest. Changing them means you can no longer be who you are. Not many sign up for this kind of adventure voluntarily. Leaders do. Because leaders are adventurers, understanding deeply that leading the way to getting to where they intend to go may require them to change – sometimes to change even their most basic drivers.

Displacing habits would be a better concept. Your present habits will take you where they have to go. If you want to go a different direction, you have to displace them with the habits that will take you there. You can't simply add on habits that are inconsistent with your present bundle. Not smoking doesn't have immediate appeal to a smoker. Scary stuff. This is where everyone's basic set of obstacles will always be found. If you can't destroy the habits that inhibit your future and replace them with habits that enable your chosen future, you will never be the maker of that envisioned future – you will never be a leader.

For your rightful or intended destiny, the wrong habits are dragons.

And if you haven't figured out how to replace the wrong drivers with the right drivers in your own thinking, attitudes, and behavior, you haven't much of a hope of helping others make those changes in themselves. To summarize and extend:

- Leaders are "driven."
- We are all "driven."
- The difference is that most people are victimized by their drivers. Leaders choose the drivers that work for them and their purposes, rather than being merely victims of them.

Routines

Habits grow into routines. A routine is best described as the way a person thinks, or, in an organization, the way things get done – essentially "how we do things around here." Routines are habits made tangible, public. The way people or a group of people habitually do things is a *routine*.

When two or more people are involved, those routines are a part of the subculture to which those two people belong. It may be as small as a marriage or a boss-subordinate relationship, or as large as a civilization. What makes routines so resistant to change is that they become part of a culture that is larger than the individuals involved. They are then no longer subject to change by you unilaterally. A spouse, for example, may want to change some routine in the marriage that seems not to contribute in a positive direction. But the routine belongs to the relationship, and therefore cannot be changed at will by either person unilaterally. A thoughtful person in an organization may see a way to improve a process. But that might put in jeopardy a routine that involves other people. Even though the change may obviously be for the better, there will be resistance to it. This is not intentional. It is that those other people have a vested interest in the status quo.

So, a routine, like a habit, is a barrier to changing things – whether in the best self-interests of the people involved or not. Leaders understand this. Those who think like managers may take the resistance personally, or believe the resistance to originate with the individuals involved. They would be wrong. People will struggle to maintain a way of doing things even if they see a personal advantage in the change. This is because they have a vested interest in the way things are being done now.

It gets worse. People develop a rationale – explanations – for why they do things the way they do. Unintentionally, they create mythologies that justify their current routines, making those ways of doing things more or less sacrosanct – unchangeable by people because they are a part of the mythology which those people take as givens in their world. Think of it this way: there are people who starve to death looking right at cattle. Why? Because their beliefs – their mythologies – make the cattle untouchable for the purpose of human consumption. Routines in organizations are like those "sacred cows."

There is another very important aspect of routines. It is that a routine enables a person to function on "auto-pilot." That is, they can function without really being engaged mentally or emotionally in what they are doing. Routines thus have the byproduct of disengaging people from their work. Once routinized, you can do much or most of your work without thinking, or with no feeling. There are two dangers here: one is that, in certain occupations, like driving a car, operating a machine, or flying a plane, safety may be endangered. The other is that those who are not vitally engaged with their work are not going to be the ones who see or implement ways of improving the processes by which they do their work.

Ideas like "continuous improvement" depend upon people being engaged in what they are doing. The more routinized their work, the less engaged they are with it and in it. Where Toyota automobiles were manufactured some years ago, more than 5,000 process improvement ideas were *implemented* every day. This required people who were engaged in what they were doing, not a "Suggestion Box." The workers initiated the improvements because they were thoroughly engaged in what they were doing as that related to the desired outcomes.

Having people in every role who are fully engaged in what they are doing is what leaders think through and make happen. They do this by making it impossible for routines to take root and thus become a part of the culture. They do this by making *engagement* with the work every person is doing *necessary*.

More thought-prodders:
- People frequently read what they read routinely. They are not really engaged in what they are reading. Thus the return on their investment in reading is negligible.
- Lovers routinize their thoughts, their feelings, and their actions, and love disappears.
- People at work aim to get on auto-pilot, so that they do not have to think about what they are doing. The day gets longer, their performance gets poorer.
- Routinization displaces life. The more routinized one's life, the less life there is in what people do.

Bureaucratization

Big word. Big subject.

HUGE barrier to any extraordinary performance.

138

In a bureaucracy – as small as a marriage, as large as the largest corporation or government agency – the rules for how to do things take precedence over the accomplishment. In a small community or a small organization, the rules are imbedded in the practices, the routines, that have evolved by trial and error over time. They are a part of the culture. But in large organizations, with more people coming and going all the time, managers decided that the way to achieve reliability and consistency was to have a formal set of rules for how to do things, called "Policies and Procedures."

The problematic is how to control things so they turn out the way they are supposed to turn out even though the manager may be some distance away. They are substitutes for direct supervision.

Maybe a necessary evil. Until the rules become ends in themselves. People get rewarded – or punished – not for achieving a goal, where the rules are the only correct means to that end, but for following – or not following – the rules. In a bureaucracy, not violating a rule, or following a rule to the letter, is more important than what was supposed to be accomplished. Or even in spite of the harm that might have been done. How often do you hear "It's our policy"? A customer, for example, does not dictate how she or he wants to be dealt with. It is the large company's bureaucracy that decides how things are to be done.

I was once told, "That's not how we do business, Dr. Thayer."

My reply, in lieu of telling this company where to go was, simply, "Well, that's the way *I* do business."

It was like baying at the moon.

But isn't it interesting how easily bureaucracy gets in the way of any real customer service, in spite of how vocal these same companies are about "customer service"? They haven't learned after all these years that following a rule is not the same thing as accomplishing what needs accomplishing.

It isn't that rules are not useful and sometimes even necessary. We couldn't keep all of those aircraft in the skies away from each other if there weren't rules with serious consequences for violations. The leadership issue is whether or not you have

your sights set on what is to be accomplished – not on slavishly
following the rules. Here are some thoughts that may help make
these points:

- If you have formal rules about performing sex, you've
  lost what you were trying to gain, full engagement
  and creativity.
- If you think you can wow customers with the rules
  you devise to control your own incompetent people,
  you would be … wrong.
- The less say your people have in how they do what
  needs to be done, the less likely it is that they will
  experience much "satisfaction" in their dealings with you.
- Again … what are rules *for*? And what are the trade-offs?

Comfort Zone

We all have one. It refers to certain habitual, comfortable,
familiar ways of thinking, feeling, seeing, acting and reacting.
It refers to the fact that we are who we are because we think the
way we do, see the way we do, feel the way we do, and act the
way we do. If these work, even marginally, we'll settle into our
"comfort zone."

Why is this an obstacle? Did you ever try to rock yourself out
of your own comfort zone? Ever try to see the world from some
alien point of view? Ever try to think thoughts you never even
imagined before? Ever tried to make the opposite out of some really
strong feelings you had, and for which you felt justified? Ever tried
to act or react so differently that others didn't recognize you? That's
what our comfort zones protect us from.

Why is *this* an obstacle? Well, if your comfort zone is going
to provide the infrastructure for real achievement, no problem.
But not even superior athletes imagine they can compete unless
they suffer the pain of staying in condition or competition. If your
competitor is better prepared, in better shape, more competent, and
better informed than you are, it may be that your enemy is not
your competitor, but your own comfort zone is.

140

It is *dissatisfaction* with the status quo that energizes leaders. And the status quo they have to deal with first is their own comfort zone. All of our dragons live and flourish in our personal comfort zones. They would keep us as we are – or worse. With comfort comes arrogance. From the point of view of our comfort zones, we can see that there is truth – those who agree with us – and untruth – those who disagree with us. From our comfort zones, we judge others and everything else. We see any change as a threat to who we are. We are like pit vipers around anyone who tries to better us. If your comfort zone is at stake, you will indeed bite the hand that might advantage you. Or maybe dismiss it simply as wrong.

We are *driven* by the need to stay within our zone of comfort. We automatically attempt to ignore or disagree with anything that would rock our boat.

Leaders have had to learn how powerful a driver their own comfort zones are.

And this serves them as a constant reminder of what they face if they appear to be a threat to anyone else's comfort zone. They know what kind of fierce obstacle this is. They lead others out of their comfort zones in the same way they had to lead themselves out of theirs. Think, then, on these things:

- Whether or not you have what it takes to lead yourself depends upon how dissatisfied you are with yourself.
- Whether or not you can provide significant leadership at work or in the world depends upon how dissatisfied you are with the status quo.
- If you crave or pursue comfort, you are on the wrong path.
- The more maintenance you require from others, the less likely it is that you can become an achiever.
- The reason why most people can't think out of the box is that their box *is* their comfort zone.
- Why would anyone want to leave the comfort of his or her comfort zone?

The Knowing Mode

Yes, that is an awkward term. But we don't seem to have a word to refer to the fact that most adults are in the knowing mode. When we were infants, our driver was an insatiable curiosity, an often out-of-control need to learn about everything around us. We were in the learning mode – the opposite of the knowing mode. As we became older, we little by little left the learning mode and entered into the knowing mode. We either knew the answer to everything we considered important, or we sought an acceptable answer. We no longer lived in wonder or awe. We were no longer the active instrument of our learning. We no longer asked questions – silently or not – about everything we came in contact with.

We lined our comfort zones with the bits and pieces of what we knew, and began to fuss with the world if it did not fit our understandings of it. We began to get into all sorts of contests with others about right and wrong, good and bad, or how something in the past really happened. We wore our particular understandings like armor. And we fought with any weapon we could find in our petty stash of knowledge to dismiss or destroy others who seemed to disagree with something we happened to know (and then fell in love with – our beliefs). We stopped asking and started telling.

Here and there we might have added a bit of information that seemed to fit with what we already knew. But if it didn't fit with what we already knew, it had to be wrong and therefore never found its way into our thinking, and thus never changed us in any significant way. We stopped asking and started telling – the beginnings of the cancer-like growth of the knowing mode.

Obviously we have to know a lot of stuff about all kinds of things in order to get around in our complex world. But we lost sight of the great advantage, which is considering everything we know as *provisional* – that is, as subject to revision or elimination when something better or more useful comes along. We became strange and paradoxical archivists: we wanted to store and preserve all of the knowledge that preceded us. But we wanted to learn only from our own experiences.

New knowledge was always useful for cocktail parties and for verbal parrying to one-up others. But we were unlikely to internalize any of it for our own use if it didn't fit what we already knew, i.e., the current folklore we shared with others.

You may recall Siddhartha's dictum:

"Wisdom is not communicable."

For a person to receive wisdom, past or present, that person would have to be wise enough to see it for what it is. What we pass around to each other is not wisdom but mere folklore. It is gossip, hearsay, common knowledge. To most of those in the knowing mode, a good conversation is one that never touches upon anything relevant to the lives that the conversationalists have. I tell you what I know. You tell me what you know. Most of it is irrelevant to anything vital to our lives. And that is what makes it so inconsequential.

That is a partial definition of the knowing mode. Is there another useful term for all that?

The knowing mode, thus described, is the primary driver for most people. That is, what drives your knowing is what you already know. What drives your feelings are the feelings you have in your repertoire, the ones that belong to you. What drives your observations of others or of the world are the limited mental models you can bring to bear. What drives your interpretations and explanations are the ones that seemed to have worked for you previously. Their future is a product of what you know. What drives your life is the way you were yesterday.

To be in the "learning mode" means living toward the other end of that continuum. It means being curious. It means being open to contrary ideas or beliefs. *It means asking rather than telling.* It means growing rather than withering on the vine. It means taking the position that the world will forever be more complex than you can ever be, and thus always beyond your reach.

Our belief, fed by our faith in pop science and pop psychology, is that one day we will know everything there is to know about ourselves and the world in which we live. Well, perhaps. But if that did come to pass, we would no longer exist as humans (as we understand that concept now), for what would we have to do *then,* since everyone would automatically know all there is to know? Is there anyone who actually believes that sex is better to the extent we know more about the physiology of it? Are the humans and animals who don't know everything about it without feelings for it? On the other hand, don't those products of the learning mode – the art and the poetry and the music we have about living and doing – have the potential of elevating our *sense* of the wonder of it all? Is "Bolero" merely a tune? Is the Mona Lisa's smile intended for you?

You get the point – it's this: what you know is always an obstacle to what you *could* know. Or, even more critically, to what you *need* to know. The lesson here is certainly not to try to know everything. It is that one of the indispensable skills for leadership lies in the virtuosity one can muster for asking just the right question. The purpose of knowing stuff is not to play social or educational games. It is to enable you to ask sharper and better questions. The ones that light the way to your purposes. The ones that enable you to invent a solution to an intractable problem. The ones that give you the rush of learning something that would not have occurred if you had not asked that particular question. The ones that reveal to you (or me) our wrong-headedness or stupidity about something.

One thinker suggested that something is meaningful to us to the extent we could formulate the question to which that something is the answer. The quality of life rests on the meaningfulness of the world. And that meaningfulness is spun out the questions we can put to ourselves about it, and about ourselves.

A competent organization, like a competent person, is the one that asks the better questions.

How does this provide some invaluable foundation for real achievement? Maybe that rides on the question, "What does real achievement mean to *you*?" This is probably the best predictor there is for assessing your potential for leadership.

Some thought-prodders?

• Questions are life-giving. Answers diminish life.

- When you are in the knowing mode, you are part of the problem and cannot, therefore, be a part of the solution, whether in personal or organizational life.
- It is better, as the old proverb has it, to ask a question and appear to be stupid for the moment, than to never ask a question and be stupid forever.
- What is the one question which you could ask of yourself that would make it impossible for you to continue on as who you are?
- What you know – your habits of thought – are your drivers. Masterful questions are a way of getting better drivers.

These are some of the obstacles and barriers to getting on the path that leads to real achievement – to perhaps becoming the best. There are others, of course. But this will get you started.

Knowing that what you know can be an obstacle to what you want to accomplish may not be the conventional wisdom on the street or in your own thinking. If you intend to be a leader, you can't get hung-up on what you know. You would, rather, pursue with zeal and abandon what you *need* to know. How can you do that without asking the questions that are going to illuminate your path for getting there? How can you do that without shaking yourself out of – or being shaken out of – your comfort zone?

We like to prove to others that we know stuff. So we pretend that we already know the stuff we need to know. Learning is hard. Thinking is hard. Leadership is harder still. That's because it hinges on those two prerequisites.

You can't *know* how to be a leader. You can only *learn* how. If you want to know how, you're in the wrong place. If you want to learn how, you are in the right place.

There are, ultimately, no obstacles to your journey but your personal ones. How you think makes all the difference at square one. What you learned here is not given in what's here. It can only be measured by what you *do* with what's here.

POINTS TO PONDER

+ The best predictors of future performance are desire and talent.

+ Change your habits, change your life.

+ People have a vested interest not in their futures but in the way things are.

+ Being in your comfort zone eliminates the need for thinking.

+ The more predictable life is, the less engaged people will be.

+ In any contest between common sense and bureaucracy, bureaucracy usually wins.

+ What ARE rules for?

+ It is dissatisfaction that energizes leaders and other achievers.

+ The knowing mode is a form of walking death.

+ If the learning mode engenders life, why do most people try to avoid it?

+ Leaders are certain of one thing: what they need to know always outpaces what they already know.

Chapter 8 Under-empowerment

It may be the case that empowerment adds to the prowess and the performance of people. If so, then "under-empowerment," which is the standard in modern America, is an obstacle for the individual or the organization where there is a serious commitment to extraordinary achievement.

I should first caution you about the use of a buzzword like "empowerment." As a synonym for "motivating" people, empowering people has the same flaws. People may or may not be capable of motivating themselves, or of empowering themselves. There are two fundamental reasons for being skeptical of these loosely used terms. One is that people have no need to be motivated or to be empowered if they are not up to something worthy and long-term.

It makes little sense to be a self-starter if you have nowhere to go once you're started. So the need for being motivated or empowered lies in the significance of the purpose which that motivation or empowerment is supposed to serve. Trivial pursuits don't require much in the way of being motivated to achieve them. The pursuit of real achievement – of great performance – does. So if a person is not committed to great ends, there is not much needed in the way of motivation or empowerment.

The other reason for skepticism is that it doesn't make much sense to be motivated to do something you do not have the skills to do. And it becomes dangerous for people to be empowered to make decisions or to take actions they are not competent to carry out. It may sound good, this popular myth of empowering people. But you cannot empower people to do something they cannot do. You cannot empower people to do well what they are incapable of doing well.

The issue is not empowering people. It is helping them, and making it necessary for them, to become *competent*. It is *competence that is empowering*, not a management technique.

The obstacle is under-empowerment. This obstacle is a shortfall of competence – or of a purpose in life, or at least of compelling conscientiousness.

Empowerment?

The fashionable how-to press has taken us down the wrong path on this one. Empowerment is not kissing up to employees. Empowerment is not a trick to make employees *feel like* they now have a say in things – and, since they think they have a say in things, would therefore feel some ownership for the performance of the organization.

The buzzword empowerment may have grown out of an earlier fashionable buzzword, "participative management." Although there were some sincere attempts in this direction, most of those who picked up on it as a panacea put on a show of involving employees in strategic and tactical decisions, but it was mainly pretense.

The managers who tried this technique for elevating performance and solving some perennial people problems may have fooled themselves. But there were not many employees who were fooled. After years of trickery in the name of finding a short-term solution for a long-term problem (like competence), employees are increasingly not much taken in by the managerial buzzwords of the month.

Empowerment is not a fringe benefit (some have tried making it so). It is not a way of providing a feel-good atmosphere for employees in an otherwise indifferent organization. It is about responsibility.

A person who has even a vague notion of what she intends to be when she grows up has some small beachhead of responsibility for her own destiny. So the basic fact about empowerment is that people can empower themselves. But they cannot be empowered by others, any more than they can be motivated by your words. If they have assumed some significant level of responsibility for their own destinies, they have "empowered" themselves. It is obvious that this is not something that can be done *to* them?

A person who believes that winning a gold medal at the Olympics is his chosen destiny and who is dedicated to doing whatever it takes to get there, is empowered. A person who is simply told she can be "anything she wants to be" is not.

People who are thus under-empowered are dangerous – to themselves, to their organizations or communities, to the society. They are dangerous because they have to be dealt with as children – that is, as *dependent on their parents, their bosses, and/or their peers for their own destinies*. They do not own the problems of their own lives, and thus do not see themselves as responsible either for what they do or what they fail to do, for you or for the organization.

Getting on the path to real achievement personally requires *ownership* of the problems of one's destiny – and thus of everything that happens between here and there. Getting on the path to outstanding performance as an organization requires at least a critical mass of people who are no longer children – people who have assumed an adequate level of responsibility for themselves and for how well they perform the role they are in. This is the dilemma of corporate "welfare." Yes, people sometimes need help, and we should help them. But, we should be helping them to help themselves, not nurturing their continued dependence. If all we provide them with is a safety net that keeps them comfortably but minimally functional, they become dependent upon that help, forever needing more of it.

At its worst, empowerment is deployed as if it were a form of corporate welfare, of which we already have a surfeit. If attempts to empower people make them more dependent, then it does them and the organization harm. Here's a review:

- You cannot "empower" people who have not already "empowered" themselves.
- If you could "empower" another, or others, you would then have less power yourself *over* them. Most conventional managers struggled and politicked to gain power. They are not likely to want to give it away.
- Like other panaceas, simply professing it doesn't work.

Empowerment Isn't Competence

Empowerment and competence are two quite different things. While it is the case that increased competence empowers people directly, it is impossible to increase competence directly by offering people empowerment. It might spark their enthusiasm or their superficial appreciation – that is, they might pretend to like you more. But, as we have seen, a lesson every leader must learn is how to distinguish enthusiasm from competence.

If you have a worthy goal or destiny that is more important to you than your present comfort or your comfortable routines, then you have empowered yourself.

If you *have* to get there, and can develop the discipline and the competencies required to get there, then you have empowered your mind and your feelings and your actions.

The idea of empowerment apart from competence just doesn't make sense. If you can't do something, you can't do it, no matter how empowered you feel, or how empowered you are told you are.

Some thought-prodders:

- There is a book about every trick so far created for getting to real achievement without having the necessary competencies for doing so.
- We have many, many recipes, secrets, etc., and new ones are being invented monthly, because none of the existing ones can function as panaceas across the board.

- Are *you* an empowered reader? Think about this one. *How* you understand something will always be a function of your competence as a reader.

More Empowerment

People who are (self-) empowered (in the real world, there is no other kind) are people who are accomplishment-driven, not event-driven. We have visited this before, and will visit it again, because it is such a central and potent concept.

Most people, and thus most organizations, are *event-driven.* What this means is that their day, then their days, then their lives, are determined by what happens to them, the happenings of the day they give their attention to or happen to get involved in. Since they have no particular destination or purpose of their own, their destination has to be wherever the events of the day take them.

Those who do have a purpose or chosen aims in life look at the same events of the day, but interpret them – their importance, their urgency, their value – *in terms of* how they might bear on the short-term or long-term goals to be accomplished. Same events – different interpretations.

The event-driven person (or organization) becomes a hapless victim of the events of the day. The accomplishment-driven person (or organization) *either* uses those events to pursue self-chosen goals, or pays them no more heed than they deserve as random (non-controllable) events. People either use events for their own purposes, or they get "used" *by* those events.

Ponder these:

- Events are relevant only as they bear upon someone's goals. If there are no specific goals to be served, then what happens makes little, if any, difference.
- Most people's lives (and the lives of most organizations) are determined by what happens to them along the way, willy-nilly. To have a specific aim or purpose in life

means making certain events happen, rather than being *made by* the events that arbitrarily happen.

- To choose to have no purpose or mission in life is to choose to be a victim of whatever happens.
- To be empowered means to have some power over the events that occur.
- Whether an individual or an organization, being under-empowered in this sense will function as an obstacle to getting on or staying on the path to extraordinary performance.

Measuring Empowerment

To be empowered means that you know in great detail what constitutes performance in your role. It means that you can measure your performance in that role not only in terms of your growth in competence from month to month and year to year, but you can measure your performance against both the standard level of performance for that role *and* the best performance in that role there has ever been, anywhere, by anyone. It means as well that you know with great awareness what bears upon your performance in that role from within or outside your organization, and what your performance in that role bears upon elsewhere in your organization or in the world.

If that seems like what you mean by empowerment then you are on the right track. If that seems like what the people in your organization or your peers mean by that term, then you're on the right track. If not, then you may be falling into a trap.

How empowered people are can be measured directly by how well they are performing the role they are currently in, and by the rate of growth in their competencies in that role. We are repeating here: but to be empowered is to be fully competent in your role. The more competent the person is, the more empowered that person is. More?

- Empowerment is a function of competence, not the other way around.

- To measure empowerment, measure competence.
- All this provides some clues about how awesome an obstacle under-empowerment is.
- Most useful clue? You cannot talk your way out of patently poor performance, either personally or as a leader of others.

Under-developed Conscience

We have to come back to this. Conscience is the great unseen regulator. It lays down the law internally for individuals about what is right and what is wrong, what is good and what is bad, what is useful and what is not, what contributes to chosen purposes and aims and what does not.

We are not born with a conscience. And it cannot be bought, borrowed, or shared. It either got developed or not. The more developed it is, the more empowered the person is. People who are under-empowered have a distinctly immature or under-developed conscience. As a practical matter, this is where poor quality comes from. This is where mistakes and errors and injuries come from. This is where poor customer service comes from. This is where the costs of fixing errors and mistakes come from. This is where waste comes from, and indifference, and inattention. If the devil is in the details, as the old saying goes, then the devil emerges in all of those under-developed *consciences* there are in your organization. From the standpoint of your aims in life, this is the devil's playground and it will stretch widely and extensively as a persistent obstacle along the path you need to take.

In a typical organization (or for the typical person), problems will arise on top of those that have been fixed or solved … forever. The reason is that the root cause – the absence or under-development of conscience – continues on unabated.

There is no competence without conscience. Even then, the level of competence will always be limited by the level of conscience. A person may know the difference between right and wrong. But it is only a powerful *conscience* that will make it necessary to DO the right thing. A person who is not competent to do the right thing even if he or she knows the right thing to do – will not be able to carry it out. It takes both. One without the other will diminish performance. Here's a summary that may provoke more thinking:

- A person who is not competent, *or* a person who does not have an adequate conscience, will not be an exceptional performer – will not be a dependable achiever.
- That person is under-empowered.
- Under-empowerment will always be an obstacle to the achievement of any worthy goal.

The *Bricoleur*

Let us latch onto a different kind of concept. It is useful. It is powerful.

A *bricoleur* is a person who accomplishes what has to be accomplished, when it has to be accomplished, with the tools and resources at hand. This means that when you invest in bricoleurs, you get a full return on your investment. Otherwise your investment has to be discounted. A bricoleur is a fully empowered person.

It's interesting that we do not have an English term for this concept. And it is interesting that we do not regularly use such a concept. Is that because a part of our management folklore is that to accomplish something we have to throw money or personnel or capital equipment at it? We seem to assume that people must be aided or supported to accomplish something they have already agreed to accomplish. Is that why we buy the most prestigious, highly-advertised paraphernalia for our kids: on the assumption that these amateurs will turn into achieving professionals if we just buy them the best shoes or tennis rackets or ski boots available? Is it that we assume that it is easier to buy people more tools or resources than it is to equip those same people to be more resourceful themselves? Is it that we find it too hard to

Something to think about.

elevate people's competencies, so we buy them mental or process prostheses instead?

If clerks cannot add or subtract, do we need to buy them a cash register that will do it for them? Or, if they cannot think, do we need to send them to a seminar on time management?

Or, if they are not accomplishers, do we need to reward them for simply trying? Or, if we have despaired of making them truly competent and conscientious, do we devise incentive and bonus schemes to get them to do what they have already signed up to do? Or, if we have a laptop on every lap, does that mean the organization will perform smarter?

It's fairly obvious that we do not believe that there are people who can accomplish what they said they would, with the tools and the resources available to them. And that, over the years, we have made this a self-fulfilling prophecy. By assuming that there aren't such people, and proceeding as if people will accomplish what they have agreed to accomplish only with additional tools or support (or "incentives"), we have made our belief come true. There may not be many bricoleurs because we have precluded the necessity for having them.

And that may be why this is not a familiar term for you.

But if you had an organization of bricoleurs, you would be doing things at far less cost than your competitors, faster, and better. And you wouldn't be spending an inordinate amount of time most days on "people problems." And if you did make capital investments for tools or other resources, you would be getting the full return on your investment. That is, much of that investment would not be going to *compensate* for people's incompetence. *The return will always be related to the level of competence in which you have invested* – them *or* you.

It could be time or money. It takes more time to fix stupid errors than would have been required to preclude those errors through competence/conscientiousness to begin with. It takes more money, more time, more involvement to get the same level of productivity out of marginally competent people (the average employee).

To believe that you could ever be the best requires that you become a bricoleur. It requires that you have the level of discipline and of mastery that enables you to *improvise*, to invent a way to your accomplishment when the path you are on seems to have insurmountable obstacles. How well you have mastered your role, and the tools required to perform it, can only be measured by how well you perform under adversity. It is the bricoleur who smashes through adversity.

It is the bricoleur who finds a way through, or around, or over or under, obstacles that stand in the way. All great achievers are bricoleurs. All great bricoleurs are the pushers and pullers of achievement. In other words ...

- What can be accomplished with the tools and resources at hand is a measure of how robust is the competence of the individual, or the capabilities of any organization.
- A great tool or a great resource is of *full value* only to those who do not need them in order to accomplish what needs to be accomplished.
- Being under-empowered leads to an "Open Sesame!" magic belief in more or different tools or recipes or resources, not in oneself.
- *Somebody* has to pay for the paucity of bricoleurs. Will that be you?

Consider, then, these overall thought-prodders:
- People who don't know what they want to be when they grow up usually never do.
- People who don't know what they *ought to be* when they grow up believe that it is solely a matter of finding something they "like" to do.
- People who don't own the problems of their own destiny will never understand what it would mean to assume some ownership of the problems of the destiny of the organization (or the team or the society).
- People who are not bricoleurs will never really understand ROI.

POINTS TO PONDER

+ Empowering people raises their performance.

+ Taking ownership for one's own destiny is real empowerment.

+ You cannot "empower" people.

+ Most managers are averse to having empowered subordinates.

+ You can buy many "secrets" for getting real achievement without the prerequisite competence.

+ Are YOU an empowered student of high-performance organizations?

+ To be empowered takes away any "victim" excuse.

+ Under-empowerment is an obstacle to growth in performance.

+ There is no competence without conscience.

+ Being the best requires being a *bricoleur*.

+ There is a good reason why so many people never "grow up."

Chapter 9

"Dumb" Systems

The world in which we live – both internally and externally – is comprised of *systems*. As a practical matter, what this means is that everything is more or less connected to everything else. In your thinking, for example, everything is connected in some direct or indirect way. In the world outside of us, everything is loosely or tightly connected to everything else.

Why is this important? Because looking at the world this way takes us out of our cause-and-effect, linear mode of thinking, which rarely fits actuality. It is also useful to see the world this way because it forces us to recognize that we can rarely ever change one thing without affecting the other things to which it is related. If you change a procedure, it may well make another procedure, keyed to the old way of doing things, fail to operate. People are related to each other. Attempting to change one may be difficult or impossible because of the way that person is related to all of the others. Providing customer service may not be easy if the customer has had bad experiences in the past. The present is always related to the past in some way. And the future to the present, since one thing leads to another. Even a revolution requires some status quo that someone thinks needs revolutionizing. But you can't have the one without the other.

Trying to change yourself, for example, is difficult not only because of your own habits, but because who you are is due largely to the image others have of you, and they may be disinclined to change their image of you. You are a part of a whole set of systems – consisting of people, ideas, communication channels, relationships, habits, routines, things, devices, and happenings. So is everyone else. You are who you are because of your *roles* in those systems.

Systems both *enable* and *constrain*. What can be done depends upon what those systems enable – that is, what they make possible, and what they make necessary. What can be changed depends upon what those constraints will permit. Leaders know, for example, that how they can deal with people depends upon the *relationship* they have with those people individually and collectively. And leaders know that people are different people depending upon what other people they are with.

We all do it. When with others, we are in different systems and will perform roughly in accordance with the system we find ourselves in. You typically will not tell people to their face, for example, what you might say about them to others. You will always behave in keeping with the system you're in. Emailing a person usually brings out a persona that is different from who you are when you are face to face with that person.

When with your boss, you will behave differently than when you are with a subordinate.

The *system* in which you are operating will always provide both enablers and constraints on your aims and purposes. In order to see them for what they are, you have to look at the *system* and not the component parts of that system. Thinking psychologically leads you to focus only on the people and your past relationships with them. Thinking technologically leads you to focus on the modes of information exchange. Thinking rationally leads you to attribute more rationality to the event or the persons involved than is ever there. And so on. You will see the parts but not the whole (the system), and how that *system* works.

For example, you might try to "fix" yourself or another person when it may actually be the system in which you are embedded with them that is faulty. Marriages are often this way. There's nothing wrong with the people, but the way the system is put together is dysfunctional. It helps to keep in mind that organizations as well as every other human institution in our modern world are *always* more or less dysfunctional.

Probably more rather than less.

Most systems are "dumb" systems. That's because the output of the *system* is dumb. Interpersonal relationships do not always produce the kinds of outcomes we had hoped for. A bad relationship with a customer clouds perceptions on both sides. It may not be the people who are bad. It is that the relationship (the system) shared by both parties is flawed. It is the relationship (the system in which these people are operating) that needs to be fixed.

Poor performance may be a function of a dumb system, and may not reflect the capabilities or the competencies of the person or the people involved. Here is an initial test: If you put extremely competent people in a dumb system, the output of the system will be at best mediocre. (Extremely competent people can and will fix the system in order to avoid this depreciation of their competencies.)

Yet if you put average performers in a "smart" system, the output of that system will rarely be better than average. A "smart" system produces outcomes that are close to what was intended. A "dumb" system produces dumb, inadequate, or unintended outcomes. What happens in many conventional organizations is that marginally competent people are required to function in dumb systems. The output of that system is going to be unreliable, and always less than marginally competent. The performance of any set of interdependent people will vary with how smart or how dumb the system is. A smart system will make anyone appear to be smarter than they actually are. Dumb systems will make even competent people appear to be dumber than they actually are. Flight attendants do their work in the context of extremely dumb systems. That's why they so often appear to be without souls. Or brains.

The universal product of most conventional organizations is the careless emergence of dumb systems. Marginally competent people in dumb systems try to fix the *people* involved because they don't "see" the system they are in. The prognosis is not good.

Most human systems – including our organizations and institutions – were not designed to be smart. They simply emerged over time, according to the fashions of the day, and therefore became routinized with very little thought given to their architecture, their functioning, or the criteria by which they were to be measured. Paying people to carry out the activities that are listed on their job descriptions is an example of a dumb system. It isn't their activities that are of value. It is only their accomplishments that might be.

Most compensation systems are dumb systems. They pay whether or not the person actually makes a contribution to the health or the growth of an organization. They even pay people for being sick, which seems not an altogether intelligent thing to encourage in people. CEOs can arrange a contract in such a way that they make more money by getting fired than they could by making the organization more successful. Celebrities are frequently paid not for what they do (or even how well they do it), but for how much money their names can attract. So we have singers who can't sing performing for people who wouldn't know the difference. The money wins. Everybody else loses. Is that a smart system for purposes of the culture we say we want to live in?

The business press has a vested interest in keeping you dumb, so you continue needing more and more of their stuff. If you were actually getting smarter yourself, you wouldn't need more of their stuff. That may be a smart system for the business press, but for you and the world in which we live, isn't that a dumb system? A politician with principles is an oxymoron. Is *that* a smart system? Crime has to increase to justify more police, more laws, more cells. Is that a smart system? More people have to have more illnesses in order for the medical industry to grow and prosper. Is that a smart system? Similarly, for the educational enterprise to grow and prosper, there has to be an increase in ignorance and incapability. Smart system? The U.S. government subsidizes tobacco growing while paying for anti-smoking campaigns. Is that a smart system?

Before you begin to feel above it all, take a look. You will have in your organization more dumb systems than smart ones. But you get the point. The point is that smart systems have outcomes that elevate the performance of competent people. Dumb systems are great levelers. Their output is dumb, making everyone who functions in them look incompetent.

Smart systems contribute to the outcomes intended or required. Dumb systems produce outcomes other than the ones intended or required. You may say to someone, "This is what has to be accomplished." Clear enough. But if that person is not capable of accomplishing what you intended, then the conversation is itself dumb. The system can't be much smarter than the people who comprise it.

That's why competence is always the critical criterion at every position in any organization. You can compensate to a degree for the marginal competence of the people involved in a system of work by designing an impersonal system that controls their actions and requires them not to think.

But that's always a trade-off. Non-human data systems are ultimately dumb because they can only do what they are designed to do. Yet, if you need thinking humans in the system, those humans could make poor judgments, even with all of the data those systems provide. The ideal is coupling very competent people with smart systems. Every other way is sub-optimum.

Predictability vs. Adaptation

This is the perennial dilemma. A robotic system is a purely rule-following system. As long as everything occurs routinely and no thought is required, robotic systems maximize the predictability of the system. (Not necessarily the efficacy of the outcomes.) Not necessarily even the efficiency of the system. In this case you want reliability/predictability. You want to know that the output is going to be what was intended. McDonald's kitchen systems (by the numbers) would be an example.

But it's actually very rare that things go as assumed. You want some form of human intelligence in there to adapt to the unexpected happenings, to the glitches that inevitably occur. You'll recall that

Henry Ford wanted to hire *hands* to do the work involved when there was a rationalized division of labor. Things were supposed to go like clockwork. The problem he faced ("Do I have to get their minds when I only want to hire their hands?") is, in a dynamic, ever-changing context, the only possible solution.

You can rationalize the systems involved to an optimum degree. But none of the robotic systems involved in the Apollo 13 return flight would have figured out how to save it. That would have been, for that particular software, impossible. Humans were required to think about a problem never before encountered (which of course never guarantees a happy ending, even though it did so in this instance).

If the problem that arises is not anticipated by the rule-following robotic system, then human competence is required. A robotic system applied to a unique set of circumstances will be a dumb system. Creative people working on a routine problem will create a dumb system. A rule-following organization will produce certain kinds of problems (customer complaints, for example). But an organization with few constraints would produce other kinds of problems (communication problems, for example). So you can rationalize a system only to the extent that it repeats an invariant routine.

It takes both. You rationalize what is fairly routine, although this has to be designed by extremely competent people. Otherwise, the rationalized system is as dumb as its designers. And yet the more freedom there is for people to follow their own interests and inclinations, the more chaos there will be. Either extreme fails at some point.

You have to leave open to human adaptation those problems that emerge uniquely from the sheer dynamics of the human/organizational/economic world. A smart robotic system can tell you how to optimize your shelf space. But it can't tell you what product mix should be there to maximize sales, especially when customer demands fluctuate unpredictably.

Since most systems are combinations of data infrastructure and of human input, what's clear – and worth thinking about – is that *both* have to be extremely competent for the system to be optimum. A good way to think about this is to be alert to how your performance varies with the systems in which you operate. That might be a relationship with a trusted lieutenant, a meeting, your reading list, the ways in which you deploy yourself, or a source of advice or intelligence. When are you smarter? When are you dumber?

How much of that is you? How much of that is attributable to the system? In terms of the operant systems at work, when are you at your best? What does it take to overcome a dumb system? Smart systems cannot always compensate for incompetent humans. But dumb systems will always make people appear to be poorer performers than they might otherwise be. To think about:

- How would you design the systems in which you are embedded if you wanted to optimize your performance?
- What would that require of you?
- What would that require of the system?
- Why are the two so cussedly interdependent?
- If you can't put in place smart systems for yourself, you will have great frustrations trying to do so for your organization's communication system.

"Communication"

We'll sneak this back in here. You can make it a big word or a small one. You can talk about it endlessly or you can pretend it is no part of the problem.

But the underlying logic has always been there. It is as follows:

1. Communication is the universal and indispensable component of any system that involves people.

2. Even robotic systems are, at the core, communication systems.

3. Communication guarantees outcomes or consequences. But communication is a neutral process. It doesn't care whether the consequences are good for us or bad for us.

4. As we communicate, we will create the problems that confront us. But it's the only means we have for trying to solve those problems. So we can't actually have "communication" problems. We search endlessly for the external causes of our problems. But they are typically internal – our own stupidity or incompetence.

Competence begins and ends with mastery of the communication process, first for oneself, and then for the complex interdependencies you find yourself in.

This is especially so for people who are joined together in a partially robotic system (e.g., wherever there is a rule-following data-based infrastructure).

No IT system can compensate for human incompetencies. The more competent people are, the more they can neutralize the effects of dumb information systems.

It is only when they are both fully competent, and fully competent in their interactions, that there is efficacy in the system.

Here are some thought-prodders:
- Those who cannot design efficacious systems for their own lives will be unlikely to be able to do so for an organization. If you want to know how competent an IT person is, examine the consequences of the systems they have designed for themselves.
- Great achievers first put in place smart systems for themselves.
- Leadership – like all performance – depends upon smart systems.

Identifying Dumb or "Sick" Systems

A dumb system is a system that is dysfunctional, to use a fashionable term. That simply means that
a) it contributes to outcomes other than those desired or intended; and
b) it functions as an obstacle to anything worthwhile you may want to accomplish.

So here are some tips about identifying them for what they are:

- A dumb system is a system that accommodates inferior performance. It impedes rather than contributes.

- A dumb system encourages mediocrity, absorbs profits, permits indifference and/or inattention.

- A dumb system inhibits real performance and produces problems that engage people endlessly, but misleads them from identifying it as the underlying problem.

- A dumb system is one that rewards "**A**" while you were hoping for "**B**."

- A dumb system, once accommodated, will be preferred over a smart system by mediocre performers.

- A dumb system is one that is more resistant to change than is a smart system.

- A dumb system is one in which the persons who ought to own the problem don't, and the people who ought not own the problem do.

- Every adversarial system is a "sick" system. An adversarial labor-management relationship is an example.

- The tendency for every system is to become, over time, a dumb system. What used to work may no longer work. For example, customer relationships seem to deteriorate when the honeymoon period is over.

- People who are in the knowing mode will always support the dumb systems they are accustomed to.

- Any system you cannot make smart will be dumb.

POINTS TO PONDER

+ In a system, you can't change just one thing.

+ If you are "right," then someone else has to be "wrong."

+ A compensation system can be designed solely to encourage performance.

+ The business press has to keep you feeling needful/minimally not up-to-date. A "dumb" system?

+ "Smart" systems don't make the people in it any smarter.

+ Why are most systems dumb systems?

+ Systems and the people embedded in them are critically interdependent.

+ The logic of systems is never the logic the people in them are likely to use.

+ The logic of systems is never the same as the logic of the real world in which they must operate.

+ Mediocre performers prefer the systems they are embedded in, no matter how "dumb" they may be.

+ Dumb systems are those in which the ownership of problems is misallocated.

Chapter 10   Pop Culture

It may seem strange to identify the larger popular culture as an obstacle or barrier to real achievement. But it seems clear that some cultures have been more prone to facilitate higher levels of performance, and others to inhibit that kind of thinking. In our own (American) civilization, there are orientations and beliefs having their source in the pop culture that actually run contrary to commitment or competence, or even diligence in support of a chosen, worthy goal in life. We like our celebrities. But we prefer to attribute their success to something other than choice and hard work. If we did attribute their success to choice and hard work, that would leave the rest of us no-talent people with no excuse. There are negative epithets for anyone who takes work or achievement seriously.

There has never been a human culture or civilization that both encouraged and facilitated excellence. Perhaps some of the Native American Indian cultures were an exception. They had very few possible roles, and there was no option to demonstrating virtuosity in those roles. Our own contemporary culture is a mixed bag: we seem to have a penchant for heroics, and we love to consume sports and other competitive excellence in books, magazines, and television programs. And yet we are inclined to attribute superiority (which we dislike) to "talent," to "luck," or to "knowing the right people" or "kissing-up" at the right time in the right place. We seem to be disinterested in the fact that even those with talent have to work hard, discipline themselves, make social and personal sacrifices, and practice, practice, practice. We may dote on the finished product, but we don't want to hear about what it takes to get there.

There are two lessons to be learned about all this:

1. One is that, at least in our own culture, we prefer the idea of achieving greatness as a sort of immaculate conception – that is, those who achieve greatly got there because they couldn't help it – it's just the way things happened. In order to get ourselves off the hook, we attribute the great achievements of others to everything and anything other than the effort and discipline and commitment that was required to get there – whatever advantage they may have had at the outset. So the notion that an ordinary person could re-engineer herself to achieve extraordinary goals *on purpose* is not something that makes sense to most Americans. Ours is a culture that may promote excellence, but we mystify and denigrate any on-purpose way of getting there. It's as if achieving some on-purpose goal is a little bit like winning the lottery. It's a matter of luck or happenstance, so it is not something you might actually work at. If you *do* work at it, you are likely to be laughed at or put down by others. So, yes, there is a fundamental obstacle right there.

2. Second, there has never been a culture that made the process easy. So what makes the process so difficult? Other people. The culture itself. We may be our own worst enemy. At the same time, we are not likely to be aided and abetted by our peers, our communities, or our fellow workers in any such endeavor toward greatness. The closest we can get to the work and the effort and the years of practice required to become a top athlete, for example, is "Just Do It!" Wouldn't it be a wonderful world if that was all that was required? We'll take our heroes wrapped in a myth.

170

It is not that others always *directly* oppose your efforts or your dream. The more immersed other people are in the pop culture, the more likely they are to react to your commitment in one of two ways: (1) by ridiculing you behind your back, or (2) by actively humoring you. It's not an easy environment for would-be achievers.

So what *are* some of those aspects of the pop culture that function to preclude an orientation to real achievement?

Victimization As A Way Of Life

There was a time when parents and communities largely determined the values and beliefs of succeeding generations. But the more people surrender their consciousness to the pop culture – via peers and the media – and the more there are who do this, the dominant players in our values and beliefs have become the themes and ideologies explicit or implicit in media fare. In that world, MDs are "sexier" than CEOs. It's better to be "hot" than to be competent. Style is far more important than substance. And so on.

There are many pop culture beliefs we could choose from. In the aggregate, they define who we are as a people. But let's focus in on those that function as major obstacles and barriers to real achievement or great performance, the targets of this book. They would thus be crucial to how you think.

Perhaps the most ubiquitous pop culture belief is that of victimization. Because the media (and our peers) are saturated with what we might call pop-psychology, we are increasingly a civilization of victims. This is simple enough in its origins. To appear to be scientific, all of the popular branches of psychology assume that whatever happens is caused by something beyond a person's control.

There are acceptable ways of performing being depressed. We are victimized by our parents, by our teachers and the physical conditions of our lives, by our friends, and by the organizations we work for. People who want to know how they have been victimized can tune into a talk show like "Oprah" to discover any number of new ways never thought of before.

It isn't how all of this works that is of interest to us here. What is of interest and of value to your thinking is how this and other orientations end up changing the laws and regulations, and increasing the availability of "helping" institutions of all kinds. We noted previously that a student's inability to learn led to an army of special education teachers and programs. The child is taught – reinforced by peers and the media – that any shortfall on her part is not her fault. She's merely a "victim" and the rest of the world is responsible for protecting her and somehow compensating her for not being able to learn. She may indeed be handicapped. But she might also be a "victim" of those who make money off of people who can convincingly perform being mentally handicapped. The supply seems to expand to fill the resources for amelioration.

From the pop-psych point of view, smoking-related illnesses are no fault of the person. Smokers are said to be victimized by the manufacturers; million dollar settlements in court have said so. If you spill hot coffee on yourself, you're not to blame. The restaurant is. Obesity is a "disease" for which a pill-shaped "cure" is needed. You have been victimized. From this perspective, stupidity is a disease to be treated. In the meantime, you can be "mentally disadvantaged." You are denied *choice*. You are caused by forces beyond your control – and beyond your ken.

A person who works at your place, and who is militantly incompetent, can sue you for saying so, or doing anything about it. Those who can't or won't are merely victims. They must be protected by government regulation. According to the popular press, women are predominantly the only victims of sexual harassment. But, seemingly, never by other women. Sexual harassment is the pop-psych term for what used to be called "flirting." The government intervenes on the assumption that someone is being *victimized*. In the German version of "Little Red Riding Hood," there is no "victim." Red, being a farm girl, very cleverly does the wolf in herself. She needed no woodsman to save her. People these days want to be *free*, but still be saved from their complicity if they become *victims*. That runs contrary to the way leaders have to think.

You're the one responsible for the ineptitudes of anyone on your payroll. There are laws protecting them from you, but not you from them. That's the way it is.

Try *The Excuse Factory* by Walter Olson if you haven't yet lost at this game of protectionism.

Summing up and extending these thoughts:
- The point is that people are victims of forces beyond their control. They are not responsible for what happens to them.
- Therefore, you are.
- That's what they learn from their peers and the media. That's the obstacle. That orientation never made a great anything. The leader has to invent a way of overcoming it.
- Real achievement can't be pursued with a victim mentality.
- To your peers, you may be a fool for simply trying to do your job well, or to pretend to own your own destiny.
- If you achieve through no fault of your own, you may be okay. Getting something for nothing, in school or in life, makes you a local hero.

If you intend to pursue real achievement, you have to be crazy enough, and committed enough, to crash through all of that. Or be impervious to it. If you can't, those obstacles will bring you down to where everybody else lives and thinks.

About this pop-psych mentality:
- If something or someone denies your right to choose, and if something or someone else has the right to explain your emotions and decisions, you are a victim.
- And, a propos the previous chapter, when you take away from people their *ownership* of their own problems, you typically create sick systems. The problems that emerge in such sick systems will be essentially insoluble.

Where Life Is

Pop culture includes popular songs, however distributed, whether by CDs, concerts, radio, or television. It includes popular images (for style), whatever their source or means of distribution (e.g., magazines, commercial advertising, how your friends dress and comport themselves). It includes popular ideas and ideologies, popular understandings, feelings, explanations, etc., however they circulate. And in a modern culture, they *will* circulate, since much depends on being in fashion, keeping up with the fads of the day.

So the instructions for how to be, how to do, what to think, what to have, and what to say (and how) will be explicit or implicit there.

Let's consider one of the most relevant examples. Most Americans have a job. For most, this job is not an essential part of who they are or how they live. It is incidental. Often no more than a means to an end. A job is what a person does to earn the money required to buy what they feel they deserve. Or what they feel they need in order to create or maintain an identity they desire.

Work is not a central aspect of life in our civilization. Life is what can be *bought* with what you *earn* at work. Most people work because they *have to*. Their lives are mainly what they can *buy* with what they earn at work. What leaders face in their organizations, as the saying goes, is that people don't live to work, they work to live. What this means is that:

- Most people will not be interested in your (or anyone else's) ideas about any great achievements. They will be interested in the paychecks and other benefits you provide them. But if they can't get their quasi-welfare at your place, they'll get it someplace else. That's the leader's challenge.

- Work is something they *have to* do; play or leisure is something they *get to* do. Thus life is pursued mainly in leisure activities. Observe carefully the bulk of TV advertising.

In order for anyone to pursue a goal such as being "the best" at anything, that pursuit has to be the driving force of their lives. It cannot be a hobby or an avocation. It has to be the core, the very trajectory, of their lives. In other words, if the role one has at work is not a vital part of one's life, there are two terrible consequences to think about. One is that the person has to accommodate to the fact that he or she is simply blowing off the major part of his or her life. They put in their time. They go to idle while waiting for their real lives to begin. The quality of their lives thereby suffers. The media advertisers offer the solace of buying something – a vacation, some cosmetics, some booze, some drugs for whatever ails them, better sex, more stuff, etc. And this is what people are offered in exchange for selling the bulk of their waking hours for the years of their lives.

Faust sold his soul. Many people sell their time. But isn't it the same thing?

The second consequence is that the organization for which such normal people work can never be the best no matter what the top person buys to try to make this happen. The reason is that you cannot make a robust, prepared, extremely virtuosic organization when many are just putting in their time at work. People at work who are not wholly awake or engaged will not contribute to causes that are larger than they are.

This circumstance stands as a formidable obstacle to any attempt to make a great organization, or to pursue any real achievement.

Think on these:

- It isn't until one's work is a vital and central part of one's life that a person has a twenty-four hour quality of life.
- It isn't until people have a life at work that they willingly put their lives into … that they become fully awake human beings. How to do this is but one of the many challenges of leadership.
- When life begins after work, as the beer commercial has it, the hours at work are merely thrown away, doing whatever is supposed to be done, without anyone's heart in it.

Me-ism

Let us not overlook the fact that the media and the pop culture that provides its content do not *cause* people to be the way they are. They merely refract the kinds of trends and movements in the most popular ways of doing, being, saying, having, and knowing. It will always be the case that a seducer requires a seducee.

We now live in a me-first (last and always) culture. A culture of radical individualism. Meaning essentially that my concerns and interests come first. And maybe there are no others that concern me at all. Spoiled children who complain about their families apparently have never learned that if they want a great family, it is their responsibility to make it so by sometimes putting the collective interests of the family before their own. Most Native Americans learned that the tribe comes before individual interests before they learned how to talk. Our contemporary "me-ism" and the ferocity with which many of today's children (of any age) pursue their own immediate gratification may seem natural to them because that's all they have ever known: self-indulgence. If this interests you (which perhaps it should since it relates to the difficulty of getting people into a common cause), take a look at Lasch's *The Culture of Narcissism*.

But this is not a book of social criticism. It's a book about leadership thinking. And what leaders have to be able to think about is how to mold a set of interdependent people out of a bunch of radical individualists.

With the popular culture came the focus on self. And with affluence came the means of gratifying every self-need. We live in a therapeutic environment, where much of what goes on in the culture is geared to providing solace and therapy to the individual selves who pay for it or can find a third-party payer. As the commercial has it, "You deserve it." Apparently, we believe we deserve whatever we want or need at the moment. And, as long as we have the means, we'll buy it because there will be enterprises of all sorts stumbling over each other to minister to our momentary needs and interests.

It has to be the other way around in a high-performance *organization* (whether that is a community, a family, a team, or a civilization). A leader who can't turn that "me-first" orientation around will never be able to pursue any real achievement.

Relativism

You may have noticed that many young people believe deeply that there is no authority higher than themselves. It's an orientation (attitude) that is widely and deeply nurtured by the pop culture.

Derived from some popularized theories in physics, this is basically the notion that any perception, any opinion, any explanation is as good as any other. Just because someone is far better informed, or is wiser, or is in a position of higher authority doesn't make that person's judgments any better than your own.

One corollary to think about: A consequence of this pervasive attitude of "relativism" is that of making everyone and every idea equal. Just because you're the boss (or the parent, or the teacher) doesn't make your opinions (even in math class) any better than mine. It's a way of raising my voice above yours by lowering yours below mine.

It's subtle. But it's powerful. A leader who cannot neutralize or co-opt this attitude will fail. The contrary, of course, is not necessarily true. Parents and teachers and bosses can be as stupid as they are sometimes accused. But a failure to establish and abide by *some* standard of right and wrong makes losers of us all. Here's more to think about:

- The best standard for leaders is the fact that different interpretations have different (better or worse) *outcomes*. People may have a right to overeat their way to obesity. But we'll all have to pay for their right to self-destruction. We will (via taxes). And they will (via jeopardizing their health).
- If such "rights" don't end where a person's obligations begin, it's merely a slide to the lowest common denominator. There was never a great organization or a great achievement that came from there.

Nonresponsibility

There are exceptions. There have always been exceptions. There will always be exceptions. But what we're trying to capture here are some deep tectonics in our culture (which is, indeed, the "pop" culture). Trends – growing and spreading inclinations.

Like an epidemic. It's not as bad as the worst-case scenario. But, without changes of direction, it will be. They are what future leaders will, increasingly, be faced with. Increasingly, people are into personal freedom. They don't want to be committed to anything that might seem to reduce their absolute freedom to do whatever they want to do whenever they want to do it. Everything that reduces this leads to the recognition of responsibility as a quaint notion that could possibly reduce their freedom, whether that responsibility is to themselves or to something or someone else. That attitude might be characterized thus: Don't tell me what my "responsibilities" are. Let's talk about my "entitlements," my privileges, my "rights." After all, those are owed to me. And I don't owe anybody anything.

Those who share this kind of attitude are aided and abetted by certain political ideologies. And ideologies always have ideologues – people, in this case politicians, though it might also be CEOs – who confirm the correctness of the attitude and cater to it. Witness the growing tentacles of the well-intentioned Environmental Education Outreach Program (EEOP).

Young people, who are the heaviest consumers of the pop culture and its styles, seem to understand the concept of freedom as freedom from any constraints. And perhaps even more insidious, freedom *from* any responsibility for their actions (or their failures to act). Thus "non-responsibility." More and more people simply refuse any responsibility for anything, in order to keep their freedom.

This is seldom merely a passive attitude. Those who are seriously infected will be actively and even aggressively anti-accountability. Where they are concerned, they want no measures of performance but their own. They scoff at the idea of accountability. Duty is not even in their lexicon.

Maybe all of that is a bad thing. Maybe it's okay. It is what is occurring. The point is not to pass judgment on them, or even of the pop culture where they nourish and justify themselves. It is simply and emphatically that there is no real (intended) achievement without accountability. There is no high performance without responsibility; at minimum, responsibility to something bigger and better than oneself.

To claim certain "rights," but to disown any ownership of the consequences of exercising those rights describes a very sick system. You cannot build on it. More thought-prodders?

- A person who has no particular purpose in life (except to avoid having one) will never understand why you have one.
- Being non-responsible is the ultimate self-indulgence. It gets you off the hook, no matter the circumstances.
- Pop culture sells envy as the prime "motive," and consumerism as the answer to everything.
- In this kind of culture, those who do not cater to your whims are undesirables, to be avoided when denigration is not possible.
- The consequence of non-responsibility is victimization. And the answer to being victimized is to be actively irresponsible. Nice "catch."
- If you don't own the outcome, you can see no connection between what you do (or don't do) and how things turn out.
- Advertisers know how to target these people. Can a leader afford to be less competent as a persuader?

Protectionism

If people are to be protected from those who would prey upon them, who will protect us from our protectors?

Good intentions have consequences that are not necessarily good for those who are supposed to be helped by government regulations, by unions, by therapists, by friends who try to bring them down to their level, by any who would save us from ourselves.

Seeing the world as adversarial makes one adversarial.

The good leader takes the position that the measure of his or her leadership lies in how well people are able to lead themselves. Do we have enough protectionism in place to make that impossible – in *your* place?

Think on these things:

• A mediocre performer at work potentially jeopardizes the present and future well-being of every fellow-worker. Who protects *them* from his or her incompetence?

• Protectionism encourages victimization. The victim is presumed to innocent. Communication never works without complicity.

• Where leadership is most needed, it is probably most constrained.

• Competence is more in need of protection in our culture than is incompetence. Will the weeds protect the flower?

Entertainment

All of this probably brings to mind a long list of the obstacles to real achievement that are recycled and elaborated endlessly by the popular culture. Many books have been written about them.

Here we might consider one more, knowing that you can, and will, extrapolate, bringing into your own thinking the obstacles from the popular culture that bear most directly or most heavily in your situation.

It is that the pop culture is mainly devoted to entertainment. Nothing wrong with that. Until it becomes the predominant mind-candy. Then a strange thing happens. The more one lives in the pure entertainment world, the less one is able to think for herself. The reasons are obvious: the images, the plots, and the themes are all built from one formula or another, with only minor variations. For example, all commercial advertising works because the premises hit their consumers' hot buttons. So the premise that whiter teeth will lead to a richer, surer romantic life is easy to swallow (pun intended). Or that you drink to have fun with your friends. Or that buying Air Jordans will enable you to jump higher. You get the point. If you comprehend any commercial ad, it is because its premise works for you.

You don't have to think about this. All the thinking required has already been done for you. Entertainment is a consumer sport. Ultimately, it eats away at whatever capability you had for thinking on your own. Again, without passing judgment on whether this is a good thing or a bad thing, but is just the way things are, what all of this means is that the people who may need to be able to think at your place may not be able to do so. It isn't that they don't want to. Or don't claim to. It is that they *can't.*

Something to think about:

- People who can't think can readily be replaced by an impersonal system that can't think either, but is not nearly so high maintenance.
- The inability to think is not a "psychological" problem. It is a basic shortfall in simple but needed competence.
- How long does it take for a person to lose that capacity to such a degree that it cannot be rekindled?
- Investing time in people who can't or won't think is a waste of time. The ROI in people is the leader's most critical decision.
- Beginning with the leader. If you are one of them, how can you lead them?

The journey to real achievement is a way of life, not a destination. Those who have a contrary way of life have made the obstacles and barriers to real achievement into a way of life. The struggle for the hearts and minds of people is universal. In our pop culture, as a leader you are up against some formidable opponents in this struggle, including the people themselves, along with their habits and their penchant for remaining marginally competent for the rest of their lives, and the dumb systems into which we pitch them, along with, of course, your and their … dragons.

But that was the lesson from the story of Moses, wasn't it? If you have overcome such obstacles as we have considered here in yourself, you might then be able to figure out how to help others to overcome them.

The journey to real achievement is the best journey they could ever take. Taking that journey with *you* is the best win-win they – and you – will ever encounter.

POINTS TO PONDER

+ How many people in your organization believe that achievers are either born (not made), or are just "lucky"?

+ If you have lofty goals, people will swarm to help you achieve them.

+ Employees (including you) check their pop psychology mentality at the door when they come to work.

+ Most people prefer to be victims rather than achievers.

+ In the pop culture, stupidity is a disease that confers protected status.

+ People having a victim mentality will never be good leaders (or parents?).

+ A sick system is a dumb system.

+ "A job" is something people need, often don't "want."

+ Competence precedes full engagement with one's work.

+ "It's about ME!" could be our national anthem.

+ People have a right to self-destruct (by overeating, smoking, laziness, etc.).

+ Protectionism promotes victimization.

+ The more "rights" people demand, the less responsibility they assume.

Chapter 11

Perversity

Perversity is an obstacle to real achievement? That may seem perverse to you at the moment. But when you have finished with this chapter, you may be wondering why you wouldn't consider perversity as the toughest of all the obstacles you will have to deal with.

If you look it up in the dictionary, you will find that perversity refers to the illogic of what goes on in the world. Best interpretation: it refers to the common experience of living in a world that frequently does not coincide with your expectations about it.

It is what actually happens rather than what you had hoped or expected was going to happen.

It refers to the fact that people are inconsistent, always improvising, changing their minds, putting a spin here and there on what they heard or what they saw. It refers to the fact that you apply your hypotheses about the world in that world as if there were some necessary connection between actuality and how you perceive it or expect it to be.

It refers to the obvious: that in the real world things are forever evolving – not randomly, in a technical sense, but with no predictable pattern. Our imaginations about the future are as flawed as our recollections of the past.

So "perversity" arises in the disconnect between outcomes we believe will occur, and the realities that do occur. Our perceptions may be full of wishful thinking. Our predictions, even more so. What we call perversity derives from the fact that the actualities of the world – past, present, or future – are not obligated to be consistent with our hopes, our fears, or our mental models of the way they should be.

Perversity is what can be said to be at work behind every situation where your reaction is, "I can't understand how that happened!" It has three fundamental sources:

1. Neither the people nor the world you co-habit with them is obligated to be the way you think they are, or to behave in the way you expect them to. Your mind is not reality. It is only your take on reality.

2. The way other people see the world and think about it, and the way other people make decisions and take actions in the world, is something you can neither control nor predict with much accuracy. That's because those people have minds of their own and, like yours, those minds are flawed. But, they are beyond your control. The short version? People are perverse *because* they are always doing stuff, whether they think about what they do before or after they do it. The aggregate outcomes are complex beyond anyone's ability to predict.

3. The world you live in with lots of other people is forever generating happenings and outcomes and effects other than what you intended. The three or four volumes of "Murphy's Laws" capture some of the perversity you will encounter. Add the electronics and other information and communication devices, and you'll have a surfeit of "perversity."

People Are Incompetent And People Lie

There can be very little news for you there.

The catch you may not have thought of is that people lie to themselves all the time – about their competence. And will therefore lie to you. Intentional lies can sometimes be detected.

But the lies people tell themselves about themselves come into the mix masquerading as facts. That kind of perversity is deep-rooted. Fixing it requires fixing the person's interpretations of who he thinks he is and what he "knows." If these habits of self-deception are long-standing, they may not be fixable.

A person who is *barely competent* to do what has to be done will not have what it takes to even *imagine* what is in their own best self-interest. So large numbers of people pursue ways of being and doing that are not in their own best self-interests.

A variation on an ancient Greek adage would be, "You cannot confer a benefit on a person who is incompetent to see the benefit in it, or to do anything about it even if they did." Now *there's* a leadership challenge, since leading people toward their own best self-interests is *the* dilemma for any good leader. The story of how Moses struggled to lead people for their own benefit is, again, a good example of this almost universal dilemma.

Most People ...

If you have to deal with people (and who doesn't?), there is another fundamental dilemma. Most people are enough like other people that they can be put in the category of "people." But every person is different. The challenge is to know when to apply the "most people" category, and when to look for what makes a particular person an exception. For reasons of what we would today call limited bandwidth, we use the category of "people."

About people, there are some generalizations that hold reasonably well:

- Most people prefer a problem they can't solve to a solution they don't like. Many problems recur in organizations because the people who have them prefer them to any solution. Incompetence is a good example. Most people prefer the problems that occur as a result of their incompetence to the effort and changes required to become competent.

- Most people will promise you future performance, if they imagine they can gain something by doing so. Leaders make this impossible by measuring performance solely by performance. As Harold Geneen put it, "...words are words, explanations are explanations, promises are promises – but only performance is reality."
- Most people will end up being like and thinking like most people. They didn't set out to be *average*. But that's where their comfort zone is. That's why most people are scornful of those few who try to be *better* than they are.
- Most people do not want to hold themselves accountable or to be held accountable by others for the consequences of their actions or inactions. They'll give up their responsibilities to anyone who will take responsibility for them.
- Most people don't know what their best self-interests are. That's because they have no cause or aim in life. So they'll take immediate gratification over their own best self-interests anytime.
- Most people know some stuff. Most people assume that what they know is what they need to know. If they have no aim or purpose in life, that will seem to them good enough.
- Most people don't want what they need. They want what they want, whether that is good for them or not.
- Most people will prove to you any given day that in any conflict between emotion and intellect, emotion will win.
- Most people in large, bureaucratic organizations will behave in a way that confirms the proposition that no good deed will go unpunished.
- Most people can't understand something if their paycheck depends upon their *not* understanding it.

Leaders don't take any of this personally. It's just that most people are just that way. People may be perverse. But their perversity is also the leader's reality.

If you want to have an understanding of what most people are like, you have to listen to the people-watchers. The more intelligent and the more insightful, the better. You need to pick your intelligence sources very carefully, because there is no possibility you will ever get your own arms around most people, simply because you never know *most* people. You have to be a student of those people-watchers who have figured out what is common to large numbers of people, and what is more individual. Scott Adams ("Dilbert") would be a good example. P. J. O'Rourke would be another.

However, if you want to understand a particular individual, then it's up to you. You have to ask the right questions, make the right observations, and collect the evidence yourself. And how you understand another person as an individual will depend upon the *relationship* you have with her or him. How that person thinks, talks, or behaves for you will depend upon who *you* are. Keep in mind that we are who we are in relationship to others. You are not someone independently of the others you associate with, or the role(s) they perceive you to be in. Neither are they.

So when you are taking the measure of someone else, you need to remember that what you see there is as much a function of who *you* are as it is of who the other person is pretending to be. That's why leaders take the caveat of "Know Thyself" seriously. They have to know what part of what they see is them, and what part belongs to the other person. This is a competency greatly underrated by mediocre executives and their coaches.

Is there perversity even there? For sure. The other person may listen to you. But not to what you meant by what you said. They listen to what *they* meant by what you said.

Most people don't do what they *should* do. You need to be able to recognize the person who is an exception to this rule. Most people who buy lottery tickets don't seem to know that they are more likely to be struck by lightning than to win the lottery. If you come across a person who seems to play by the real probabilities rather than her own faulty take on the world, you know you may have a "keeper." If this person wants to know what you *mean* by what you say, there's an exception that may turn out to be very valuable. Most people are perverse in common ways. A person who is individually perverse may be more challenging to get along with. But it may indicate that the person has a mind of her own – a rather remarkable characteristic these days.

Most people are not as perverse as pop psychologists are. And then there are individuals who are not as perverse as pop psychologists because they aren't regular consumers. It may seem to be easier to deal with most people because of their herd behavior. But you can't pursue real achievement if you are a part of the herd.

Here are some thinking challenges:

- Social movements – like unionization – don't originate in bad times. They originate when things are good and getting better. That's perverse. But is there a lesson for leaders here?

- Why do most people avoid living until they are told the end is in sight? Perverse, for sure. As the leader, how would you enhance people's lives at work, given this?

- Your *rational* arguments are not going to move people who waste their lives, marry the wrong person, have work they don't like, etc. What will?

Coping With Perversity

You may meet a person or two who believes you can cope with perversity by this or that cookie-cutter strategy, all being very rational in construction. Well, they would be wrong.

The logic of perversity is unlike any logic used by mathematics or by science or even economics. It is the logic of everyday life, which emerges out of our personal and collective perversities. Computer programmers, who are themselves often very perverse, write code that is for the most part thoroughly linear and rational. For them, the occupational hazard is putting their minds to work in a logical way that is alien to the logic of the human and social worlds. This may be why they are frequently not very good at human and social relationships. And if they are, then they may for that reason not be as good at programming as other programmers are.

How to cope with perversity? You may not like the answer.

The more conventional your thinking is, the more you will be victimized by all of the perversity that emerges from conventional thinkers as they engage each other in everyday life. People say what people say, and people do what people do, not because they are saying or doing what *you* think they should. But because they are saying and doing what *they* think they should – if they have even thought about it at all. What's *perverse* is what you do not, cannot, control. Perversity, once again, lies in a disconnect between what happens and what you thought would happen, or should happen. Perversity thrives in how people deal with themselves, and with each other. You are, I am, one of those people.

In the beginning, we are told, God created humans. That god instructed the first humans not to eat of "the fruit of the tree of knowledge." In the version I have of that story (which exists primarily as a teaching-learning instrument), that's exactly what the two humans did. Never mind that there was some encouragement from the serpent. That will always be the case. Failures to perform as instructed or as promised can always be rationalized. The two human residents of Eden did precisely what they were instructed *not* to do.

That's perversity. You would think, wouldn't you, that if you didn't want people to do something, it would be easy and far cleverer to make their doing it impossible? Maybe by putting the tree (or the humans) somewhere else. But if God can't get something done by instruction, having actually created the humans involved, how likely are you to be able to avoid such perversity?

Back to that other point. If you are absolutely "had" by a purpose in life, you'll be looked upon as not normal. But mainly it would be your blindness to being so perverse as to have a calling in life that would produce followers. All great leaders have been perverse. This is why other people follow them. Without *their* perversity, there would be no followers.

What's reasonable is what makes sense to you. What is
unreasonable to you is something that doesn't make sense to you.
So where do historical change and progress come from? This is
how George Bernard Shaw put it:

> *"The reasonable man adapts to the world.*
> *The unreasonable man persists in getting*
> *the world to adapt to him."*

Therefore, Shaw continues, "all progress is due to the
unreasonable man." Man or woman, it is the unreasonable person
who makes a difference. That's what leaders do. If the level of your
commitment to your vision does not appear perverse to the average
person, then you don't have the level of commitment required to be
a leader.

Perversity yields only to superior perversity. It is not rational,
and therefore does not yield to rational argument.

When faced with stupidity, the best leadership strategy may be
to respond with something that will appear to those other people
as really stupid. You can't win by being reasonable, rational. That
doesn't compute.

Stupid people are not moved by intelligent argument or action.
How often have you tried it and failed? The problem with stupid
people, as has often been observed, is that they don't think of
themselves as being stupid. You might bring a taste of reality, but
that isn't what they are hungry for.

Perhaps the most potent perversity of all is that of not
understanding something, or of misunderstanding it. The mistake
that many managers make is taking the position that they
understand everything. You can't fight perversity by feeding
your ego. That only increases it. There are things that you will
legitimately not understand.

Push your non-understanding. It will minimally help others to
clarify what they are saying (or doing). But you may need to do
more than this. You may need to *not* understand what people say to
you or what you observe going on. Randomly, unless you can figure
out just the right tactical maneuvers for this, you may need to *not*

understand. Or even to misunderstand. This forces other people to be less perverse.

It's all perverse. But perversity yields only to superior perversity. You have to be capable of that superior perversity, as Sun Tzu and Machiavelli said long ago. If you're not, you will be victimized by the perversity of others.

- Meet ignorance with ignorance.
- Meet intelligence with intelligence, strategy with counter-strategy.
- Meet indifference with indifference.
- Meet emotional arguments with emotional arguments that trump them.
- The world is not obligated to be like you see it. Or to function according to your needs or intentions.

To the leader there is no real perversity. There is only the reality that challenges his or her competencies every step of the way. No time for frustration or commiseration. What the leader learns is how to outwit the unexpected – that is, how to be the most perverse element of all.

Paying Heed

It's old, old wisdom. But if there is something you must achieve, then there are things that happen that deserve no attention. There are other things that require some minimal attention. There are still others that deserve your fiercest attention and the unreasonableness (or ruthlessness) with which you must deal with them. It is those you must prepare for.

The Most Perverse Person ...

The most perverse person in the world ... is you.

Your life has to be relevant to your cause. Your cause has to be relevant to the people in the world who are capable of achieving your cause. That's why the order of things for leaders is *thinking, being, doing.*

If you can't overcome your own perversities, you cannot lead others out of theirs, no matter what recipe you use.

Most people don't know what their own best self-interests are. They may not even care. That's why there is a role for leaders. Leaders provide people with a glimpse (at least) of what their own best self-interests are. People will resist this. *But leaders make it necessary.* If you think in the conventional mainstream, if you *are* a part of the mainstream, then that's the only place you could lead people to. Leading them out of their perversities will require superior perversities. If you made something contrary, then it required your superior perversities. Even a habit will win unless you can attack it with overwhelming perversity.

So, some thought-prodders to pull us on?
- If you are not capable of meeting the perversity of the world you live in with superior perversity, you will be a victim of that world.
- In order to make that world a *victim* of the best self-interests of the people in it, their leader has to be more powerfully perverse than it is.

Or, for fun, some variations on Murphy's Laws?
- When you are served a meal aboard an aircraft, the aircraft will encounter turbulence.
- Everything takes longer than it should, except sex.
- You cannot tell for certain ahead of time which side of the bread to put the butter on, in order to keep that side from hitting the floor first.
- Any change you impose will bite you back.
- If there is a wrong way to do something, then someone will do it.
- "Gwen's Law:" Do not join encounter groups. If you enjoy being made to feel inadequate, call your mother.

Or, perhaps, by openly challenging a real achiever.

Meet ignorance with ignorance. Meet intelligence with intelligence. The leader invests time and effort wisely. The leader's cause is usually so precarious that there is little margin for wasted effort or wasted time. There are things that deserve no notice at all. There are other things that deserve some modicum of interest and attention. There are still other things that deserve the fiercest attention that can be brought to bear. Leaders do not fight battles they cannot win. Leaders do not take on adversaries who offer nothing for defeating them. Not every comment deserves a response. The leader wastes neither words, nor persons.

These are critical judgment calls. They can be made well only if the leader is *had* by a cause that can be satisfied only by achieving it.

The strategies and tactics needed can **Leader's lesson** be *seen* only through the lens of total commitment to the intended outcome. They must be thinkable by that particular leader. And they must be performable by that particular leader. This is what is meant by the proposition that it is not what leaders *do*. It is who they *are* – that is, what kind of thinking and what kind of performance they are capable of. The strategies and tactics required to lead are not to be found in a "how-to" book. They have to be a part of that particular leader. They arrive *there* only as a result of the extreme focus, discipline, and dedication that enables ingenious improvisation.

Now, there's a … perverse thought.

And, Being The Most Peverse Person …

The most perverse person in the world is you. It is not until you have "conquered" or overcome your own perversities that you can begin the journey of becoming capable of taking on the perversities of others, and of the world.

Most people are perverse, as we have seen, because they are incapable of thinking for themselves, or of pursuing their own best self-interests. They have abdicated their sovereignty over their own destinies in order to fit into the crowd.

They have learned how to think like others do, to feel like others do, to do what others do, and to have what others have. This is the modern version of selling their souls for the comfort of being an indistinguishable face in the crowd – their crowd, their group, their subculture.

What's lost here is *relevance*. These modern people are no longer relevant to themselves. They are no longer relevant to anything which is bigger than they are.

This is the great modern epidemic – irrelevance. People suffer mightily in body, mind, and spirit because they have traded their relevance to something worthy for what they can buy, trade, or pimp for in the midst of others doing little else but the same thing. They are not rebels without a cause. They are persons without a reason for being.

They have traded relevance for buying power (both economic and social) for so many years they no longer have any real grasp of what is relevant and what is not. They are consumers. They wait for someone to tell them what their interests are – or depend on "reality TV" to tell them who they are and how they should think. This is the hold that consumerism, cults, and fashions have over them.

What *is* in people's best self-interests? Competence, for two reasons. One is that there is a rough correlation between competence and standard of living. People who want a higher standard of living can best move in that direction by developing the kinds of competencies that are of value to those who are the gate-keepers of standard of living. The other is that there is a distinct correlation between increasing competencies and enriched quality of life. For people who desire a higher quality of life, there is no better or more certain path to take than increasing competency. And yet ... and yet, most people will resist any effort made by others to increase their competencies.

And they will avoid moving in the direction of being the *best* at what they do with the ingenuity of self-deception: they simply refuse to see what is in their own best self-interests. Being the recipient of parental, government, or corporate welfare is not in the best self-interests of people who might otherwise want to be real people.

So a leader cannot address the best self-interests of the majority of people, simply because those people can no longer imagine that they have any. Or, if they can imagine that they do (usually provided by the popular culture), it is *those* and not theirs that they want served.

The perversity is that you cannot lead by addressing people's best self-interests. They have none. You have to address the interests that they imagine they have because their membership in the subcultures of fashion to which they belong dictates their thinking, being, and doing.

And they do *belong* to subcultures. They have to think the way those others think, they have to feel the way those others feel, they have to do what others do, go where others go, and have what those others have. Observe teenagers "hanging out" in the mall if you want to see this first-hand.

Leading people who can think only in processed and prepackaged forms – only in clichés – is a significant challenge to any contemporary leader. Add to this the fact that they are basically unwilling to move in the direction of their own best self-interests, and therein lies a major obstacle to compelling leadership.

A person at the head of any organization who can think only in clichés – only in processed and prepackaged forms – will be as harmful to that organization as any enemy or competitor could be. There are many such. The challenge to leaders? Keeping those kinds of people from any position of power. In a "free" society, that's as troublesome and insoluble a problem as irresponsible or incompetent parenting.

- In order to serve another's best self-interests, you may have to do this without his or her complicity, or foreknowledge.

197

- Their aims are those that are fashionable (for them). Even if, in serving *those* interests they endanger their own lives. Teenage sex might be an example, affluence another.
- Thus the person who would lead others in the direction of those others' best self-interests has to do so without their permission and without their help. Perversely.

Perversity Abounds

Then there are **systems** of perversity. When one perverse person hooks up with another perverse person, there is a perverse **system**. The French refer to this as *folie a deux*: the madness of two. The peers of a person who is committed to making an organization that is good for people, for example, will probably consider that person an odd-ball when it comes time to do their conventional socializing. They would consider that person perverse. But it is they and their floating effortlessly in their collective delusions that is more perverse.

Most organizations are made up of people who typically do not know what their own best self-interests are. Organizations are thus perverse systems. That's what they are made of. The leader counters that by what he or she is made of. The other side of it is how infrequently people will put the good of the whole above their own interests. It is the leader who sews these together.

If you cannot muster the kind of counter-perversity that would neutralize the conventional and often massive perversity that you will be up against in this world, you will not succeed as a leader.

Here is a worthy ponderable: In order to make the organization a victim of her own cause and the best self-interests of the people who comprise it, any leader would have to be more powerfully perverse than it is.

A powerfully perverse paradox. But the one that constitutes present reality for any leader. Not all of the obstacles that stand in the way of being the best are the ones that are the most obvious. *Perversity*, for example, which rarely declares itself for what it is.

198

If you need more to convince you that the world (and most of the people in it) are far more perverse than we typically believe, try these:

- In any collection of data, the figure that is most obviously correct – beyond all need of checking – is the mistake.
- If there is a wrong way to do something, then someone will do it.
- Or, as a variation on Machiavelli: Any change will cause more problems than you could possibly have imagined.

How many times over all of human history have the facts taken precedence over belief, emotions, political ideologies, indifference, lust, stupidity, etc.? What makes you think that trying to do good for people is something they would welcome with open arms? Are *you* moved by arguments by others about what the right thing for you might be?

If such visits and revisits to the land of perversity (ours) doesn't do it for you, curl up with a good book like *America's Stupidest Business Decisions* by Bill Adler Jr. Or, if you become a serious student of the real world (as contrasted with the one we'd like to believe we're in), try *The Logic of Failure* by Dietrich Dorner, Rita Kimber, and Robert Kimber. I might also recommend my own perverse book, *How Executives Fail: 25 Surefire Recipes for Sabotaging Your Career*. But only if you want a glimpse of the true perversity of reality.

When **you** begin to see your complicity in the perversity that you encounter in life, then there begins to be the possibility that you might provide others with some much-needed leadership. That's the lesson for leaders.

POINTS TO PONDER

+ The old "telephone game" is a good example of perversity.

+ Children (or managers) who assume that the world is somehow obligated to be the way they think it should be are ... perverse.

+ The sheer complexity of the social world is perverse.

+ If you cannot confer a benefit on an unwilling person, where's the benefit.

+ A social movement like "freedom" originates where people have the most freedom, not where they have the least. The lesson for leaders?

+ People rationalize their own perversity.

+ If "progress" is a cultural canon, and if all progress depends on unreasonable people, how perverse is that?

+ The less relevant people are, the more perverse they are likely to be.

+ Putting the good of the whole above self-interest is perverse.

+ A solution to a problem creates more unanticipated problems.

+ People have a vested interest in any problem in which they are complicit.

PART III

How It's Done

That was a lonnnggg wind-up. But a necessary one. It is not your understanding of something that counts when your leadership is called for. It is the depth of your understanding. It is your habits of thought that take over when the heat's on. So all of the preceding is intended to provide you with some habits of thought, and some ways of thinking about certain key factors that will add to your mental horsepower and thus your performance as a leader.

All of this wind-up may have strained your patience. But far better that than being in a critical leadership situation and unable to call upon the mental resources you need. The better you can think about the things that need thinking about out of habit, the more compelling your leadership performance will be.

If you're mentally provisioned, we want to move on. What we want to get immersed in now are the strategies and tactics for real achievement. If you want to achieve something really worthwhile, or if you want to lead the making of a high-performance organization, you will need all of the leadership you can muster. What's just ahead is a clear description of what's required: of the tools you will need if you are to become a compelling leader, and if those you lead (including yourself) are to be successful in the pursuit of real achievement.

When you are standing there one day in the future, your leadership called for, and all around you are people waiting for you to provide the needed leadership, it's too late to consult the instructions. What you have not previously made a fundamental part of your thinking can play no part in your performance when your time to perform has come.

What follows will be optimally useful to you if you have seriously and with effort thought through the foundations offered up in the pages that have preceded this. Your capacity to understand and to use the tools that follow depend upon it. That's why that came first and what follows can be fully usable only now.

The next two chapters – sort of the heart of this guidebook – are about what it takes to successfully pursue a mission, a great achievement, or a high-performance organization. You won't get far without what it takes. So equip yourself with what it takes. Or locate the problem where it exists – in any shortfall you may have with respect to what it takes.

Chapter 12 What It Takes

Here's a rather remarkable fact that may deserve your attention:

Those who have most frequently risen to the top ranks of leadership in past history have done so without a current recipe book to guide them.

Neither Genghis Khan nor Tecumseh ever attended a Maxwell seminar or read a Tom Peters article on the subject of leadership. How was it possible for them, and hundreds of others like them, to provide the kind of leadership they did without our present store of knowledge?

At the same time, there seems to be little evidence that those who take courses and attend seminars or read books on the subject of leadership ever gain much of a reputation for having changed the course of history – in large *or* small ways.

What's the lesson here? That those who made their mark didn't have the disadvantage of our 10,000 or so books on the subject but did so anyway? That those who have available the world's accumulated "wisdom" about leadership don't seem to be able to make much of a difference even *with* all of that hyped advantage? If we really know so much about leadership after all these millennia of practicing it, why do we need so many books, so many articles, and so many seminars about it?

How can we understand this? People who never knew what we presume to know about this subject excelled as leaders. Most of those who have 10,000 books on management and leadership available to them don't seem to deliver that much more or that much better leadership for all of the time and money spent on acquiring the "secrets" of how to do it.

The lesson may be this: If you're standing at the site (in the middle of the circumstances that require a leader), and there is either no one else to do it – or perhaps the others seem less qualified – you're it.

There are two prerequisites. One is that there has to be an opportunity for the kind of leadership you could uniquely provide. The other, that all of the other possible candidates for the role would have to be viewed by potential followers as less desirable than you are. In the opinion of the followers, the person chosen to be the "leader" is the least-worst candidate. That's the reality.

Leader's lesson

Leadership is a role, not a person. You have to be chosen, first by the circumstances, then by your followers.

What's important here? You will not be chosen as a result of how much you want to be the leader. Or as a result of how many leadership books you've read. If there is a need, and there is no better choice than you, you might get the role.

Then it's a matter of how good a job you do in the eyes of your followers or your constituents, given their interests (as they understand them). If this is not crystal clear to you, you may want to revisit the story of Moses. Or of Churchill.

There is more to consider here. Most of the people who are in charge of other people are appointed. They are not selected by the people they have authority over. These people are therefore not leaders. They may never be. They are at most heads of some hierarchical arrangement which puts them at the top and others "below" them. They get there for many reasons having little to do with their competencies. They may have subordinates, depending upon whether or not those subordinates want to play that game. But followers are not appointed. They are earned. And a superior who does not have followers is not, by definition, a leader.

Being placed in a position of authority does not guarantee anyone's ability to provide leadership. In fact, the ways in which people get to those positions guarantees that a great many of them will fail as heads of whatever they are heads. They fail for the reason that when their leadership was required, they didn't have what it took to provide the leadership needed.

Chief executives conventionally give themselves too much credit for their successes, and not enough for their failures. A lofty position does not qualify you or anyone else as a *leader*. A desire to achieve something cannot underwrite your getting there. You have to have *what it takes* when the time to perform arrives.

With that in mind, let's move on to consider what it takes.

Luck And Preparation

Strange bedfellows those two, right? You can't really prepare for luck. And you can't depend on luck to substitute for preparation. But you're probably not going to like this anyway.

You've been exposed to gargantuan doses of fluff and folklore and "new think" about leadership. A little reality may not go down as easily as some of that fairy dust. But this small dose of reality will serve your purposes far better when the chips are down and it's time to perform.

Consider, first, the fact that you have to get lucky to be needed as a leader. Churchill was a fairly mediocre government functionary, and never had great success as a politician. But it's hard to imagine that anyone else could have carried the Brits through the early part of WW2 the way he did. Consider too the fact that we can never know if someone else could have provided far better – or far worse – leadership.

That is always determined from historical retrospective. There is never a test in advance of what the outcome might have been with different leadership.

So he was "lucky" that the second world war came along when it did. Otherwise, he would have been a minor government administrator, hardly even remembered.

A lot of things had to fall into place for him just to have the opportunity to provide his unique brand of leadership. A lot of things which he had absolutely no control over. That's one aspect of the luck part.

General Swartzkopf might well have retired unknown to the American public had not the Gulf War occurred when it did. So it will be obvious to you that the circumstances and the timing have to conspire for there to be any historical leader known to us? Somewhat like Caesar, Napoleon was a great field general, but a lousy politician. For every composer whose influence led music off in a different direction, and for every artist whose influence led art off in a different direction, there were countless composers and artists who are mostly unknown to us today. There have undoubtedly been better business leaders than Jack Welch.

But they did not serve as CEO at GE during the same period of time that he did. They may have lived and died when their unique capacities for leadership were either unneeded or, more likely, unrecognized.

Going by history, this means that if you intend to be a great leader, you have to be in the right place at the right time. You have to have "the right stuff" (what is needed by the situation and by the people in that situation). And you have to be recognized by the observers, the pundits, and the historians as a leader who made a difference. The point is that you have to be lucky in all three ways at the same time.

Even though it is frequently pitched to you that way, there is no such thing as generic leadership. There is not some set of secrets that will enable you to be *the* leader no matter the timing, the circumstances, or a widely-enough recognized need for your leadership. Leadership is a *role* that emerges from a need for your brand of leadership that is widely recognized by those who would be your constituents.

This changes the whole idea of preparation, doesn't it?

In our time, in our culture, you've been led to believe that you can have far more control over outcomes than you do. It's been made easy for you to believe that if you read about the "seven secrets" or "22 laws" of leadership, you'll thereby be able to make things turn out the way you want them to. That's nonsensical. Believe it or not, the world does not conspire to make you successful just because you paid money to be privy to certain secrets or rules that are going to make you successful no matter

206

what happens in the real world. Every investment guru has had a theory about the stock market. Sooner or later, they were all wrong. So are the secrets-of-success mongers.

Every leader has been who he or she *was*. Sheer luck has to get the credit when a person is simply playing out who he or she is on the world's stage. The *preparation* part of it occurs when you undertake to make yourself into the kind of person who is going to be needed by a particular group of people, by a particular situation, at a particular time. The leadership provided will always be unique.

Abraham Lincoln wrote:

> *"I will study and get ready,*
> *and some day my chance will come."*

A person in any leadership role is not interchangeable with other persons. The circumstances are never the same elsewhere, or at a later date. Followers never seem to want the same characteristics in their leaders as they did last year.

What you prepare for is the emergence of the need for the kind of leadership you can equip yourself to provide. In an organization, you can *help* this along – immensely. But you cannot *force* people to follow you.

Knowing you as you do, would *you* follow you? Not perfect, but still a good litmus test. If you wouldn't, why would they?

You have to be prepared *if* you are called. This book is about how to prepare yourself to answer the call to leadership. There is no such thing as leadership apart from the role. This will become more and more obvious to you as we move on.

Sorry. I said you might not like this reality check. You can go on believing the hype, or you can get real. And, just so you will know, no significant leader in history ever bought the hype about leadership. They understood that the only test of leadership is the reality test – the outcomes of your performance in a leadership *role*.

Being "Had By" Your Cause

On the list of *what it takes*, the second most challenging for leaders is this: It isn't having a vision or a mission that is compelling to followers. It is your being *had by* a vision, mission, or goal that is compelling to those would-be followers.

Joan of Arc would be a good example. As would Bill Gates. Or Shaka Zulu. Or any other of our great historical examples.

There is a significant difference between merely "having" a purpose and being *had by* a purpose. Most people abandon their espoused purposes in life. Talk is cheap. If the road is a tough one, and if it requires real effort or sacrifice, most people won't walk the talk. They'll talk a good story, but they won't walk one. The more you are had *by* your cause, the more *necessity* there is for you to see it through. A follower has to determine two things: Is this the person we need? Does this person have *what it takes* to get us where he or she intends to go? Much of what it takes comes from being in the thrall of a purpose or cause that is more important to you than is your own life. You are compelling to others because they cannot imagine you could escape your duty to your own cause.

So if you are not had *by* a cause or purpose which is bigger than you are, what can you do? You can do what leaders have always done: *perform* it. It is your performance that matters, not your intentions and not your feelings. It is only your performance that others can see. They will infer all the rest from your performance. Everyone wins.

If you turn in a convincing performance of being had by a cause that is bigger than you are, you will be had by the cause of continuing to turn in that convincing and compelling performance.

To think about:

- A professed purpose is nothing but a tenuous promise.
- People have been taken in by promises before. Why would they believe *you*?
- If you're willing to stake your life on your cause because you believe you have no choice, others may be willing to follow you.
- Being had *by* your cause is part of what it takes.

Enthusiasm

Unflagging enthusiasm for your cause and your path and your days of struggle with your followers. Absolutely required.

Leadership is not a rational enterprise. It changes the status quo, which is where rationality has its stranglehold. So, rational enthusiasm is not going to capture people's hearts. Irrational enthusiasm for your cause – no matter what the present circumstances – is what's required. If you haven't got it, perform it until you do.

Thinking about enthusiasm:

• Enthusiasm begets enthusiasm.

• Have you ever come across a great leader who expressed to his or her followers doubts about their mutual cause?

• If you are totally had by your cause, you will be enthusiastic about all the right things.

• Enthusiasm: attack, attack, attack!

• What you are not incorrigibly enthusiastic about won't gather much enthusiasm.

Who's Going To Make It Happen?

About this you have to be perfectly clear. And your clarity and single-mindedness about this must be consistently obvious to everyone else.

The distance between your vision and future reality is the greatest distance there is. If you think that you are the one who is going to make it happen, that you are single-handedly going to make your cause a reality, you have just punched the ticket that guarantees your failure. It is your disciples, your followers, who have to make it happen.

With your leadership, of course. But leadership doesn't do anything in the world. Leadership is about people, about causes that people can put their hearts and their minds into. Unless your enterprise is entirely dependent on you (as an individual competitor in the Olympics, for example, or a world-class poker player), it is everyone else around you who have to make it happen. Actually, even in that situation, it is how capable you are of leading yourself that counts.

Some requisite perspectives:

- If you are competent to attract, select, and cast the people who can and will make it happen, it can happen.
- Even the Lone Ranger needed Tonto to make it happen.
- Patton never won a single battle by himself. The leader's work is not fighting the battle. It is casting the right people in the right roles.
- The leader's work consists of surrounding herself or himself with the people who are capable of, and totally committed to, making it happen.
- What it takes is, ultimately, whatever it takes.

The Four Covenants

Between you and these key people, there have to be in place four covenants – four agreements that are indispensable to what it takes.

1. The first of these is that each of those key persons has to be dedicated to being the best there is at what they do. This means that they study their role and its context, and that they improve their performance in their role every day … forever.

This has to be necessary for them – either because that's the way they're built, or because they are given no option by you, their leader. If that person is not on the path to becoming the best there is in that person's role, it has to be because they are not *competent* enough to get to that level. Or because there simply was not enough *necessity* to do so, by internal habit or imposed.

Leadership lesson? There can be no other reason for shortfall. It was either not possible for them (as in shortfalls of competence), or it was not necessary for them (internally or externally).

2. The second covenant is that they are committed to learning how to provide compelling leadership to others. They do this by the surest route there is – by being the best followers there have ever been. The best leaders will almost always come from the ranks of the best followers.

   The critical *followership* lessons? Learning when to follow, when to lead, and when to get out of the way. And, making your boss successful – no matter what. These require impeccable competence in your role.

3. The third covenant is that each of those key persons must function at all times as the *chief steward* of the organization's mission. This means that each of those persons owns 100% of the responsibility for making it happen. No finger-pointing. If there are five such key people, each does not own 20% of the responsibility. Each owns 100% of the responsibility. If someone drops the ball, another picks it up and runs with it. There is no time for editorializing. There is no one in the bleachers or the press box. They are all on the field, and they're either playing the game to accomplish what needs to be accomplished or they are not. The only judgment that counts is the one they make of their own performance. And then what they do about *that*.

   There is no way to build a team when each does not own 100% of the responsibility not only for her own performance, but for the achievement of the whole.

   • This is not about delegation. This is about *ownership*.

   • If they don't own the outcomes, you do. And *you* can't.

   • It isn't your reality that is going to make it happen. It is theirs. If they haven't got what it takes, it isn't going to happen.

   • Max De Pree refers to this as "abandoning yourself to the strength of others." As if you had any choice.

211

THAYER • LEADERSHIP: THINKING, BEING, DOING

- Your task: to make sure they are the people who have what it takes.

4. The fourth covenant is this – each of those persons who has a role in making it happen has to equip and prepare himself to take on a role like yours and perform it better than you do. That might be in your organization. But you should never get into the maneuvering involved if they're after your job. The issue is whether or not they equip themselves to outperform you. In order to do this, they have to see your world as you do. They have to see your world well enough to make you successful in that world.

This is how people develop themselves. They look for the best role models in the world and go to school there. If that is not you, it should be. But if you're not the best there is in your role, and they use you as their role model, the future of your organization is already in doubt.

You want them to *compete* with you in terms of preparing themselves. You do not want them climbing *your* ladder. You want them to compete with you as one of the best there is in your role anywhere. To do this, you have to be one of the best there is in your role. Those pushes and pulls are all a part of what it takes.

Some additional thought-prodders:

- What you can't teach, you can't learn.
- You will know how capable your people are of keeping their covenant with you by the quality of the questions they ask – of themselves, of each other, and of the best there have ever been.
- How well they keep this covenant with you will be a measure of how well they are going to make covenants with their own people.

The aim is the performance of the organization. You cannot get that without the multiplier produced by this way of doing things.

And If You Don't Have ...

If you don't have or can't muster these prerequisites of what it takes, here is how you should assess the problem:

- That you were not capable of recruiting, selecting, casting, or seducing people into the joint pursuit of the organization's cause.
- If you have to abandon your cause for want of competence to make it happen, you should move aside and put someone in your role who has those competencies.
- If your people are not capable of fulfilling their roles in the pursuit of your cause, that's probably because you are not capable in yours.
- For people who don't have the heart for real achievement, there must be some way and some level of necessity for getting there anyway. That applies to you first. And then to them.
- And if they finally can't or won't, get someone who will.

Much of this is about **commitment**.

Leader's lessons:
- In reality, there is only one measure of commitment. And that is *performance*.
- In reality, that is the only measure of any promise – *performance*.

This is a brief look at part of what it takes. Unlike other books you may have read, these requirements are not merely helpful things to *do*. If you don't put in place these conditions, it's likely you won't have what it takes.

And never forget this: *hope is not a method.*

POINTS TO PONDER

+ Interest in leadership has grown with the growth of advice about it.

+ Why is it that those who attend the most seminars on leadership will be the least likely to become leaders?

+ Some people simply have superior leadership traits.

+ Leadership is as leadership does.

+ To be chosen by history as a "leader," you have to be prepared, but you also have to get lucky.

+ Leadership is a performing art.

+ There is no way of measuring leadership comparatively.

+ "Having" a purpose is a promise, being "had by" a purpose makes it a necessity.

+ Patton never won a single battle.

+ If the four covenants are not "covenants," what should they be called?

+ If you can't teach it, you haven't learned it.

+ There is only one measure of commitment.

+ Why would anyone follow YOU?

Chapter 13

More of
What It Takes

You've been told over and over again how easy it is. All you have to do is buy this book or take that seminar, and it's a done deal. A few "steps," a few "secrets," and you're practically there. But you may have noticed that there are very few people (or organizations) *seriously* committed to becoming the best (one perspective on what we're up to here). And fewer still who have stayed the course.

We've examined some reasons for this – all of the misleading myths and panaceas peddled by those who prey on our (your?) wishful thinking. If it were all that easy to become "the best," you would already be there.

It might take 20 years for an apprentice to really learn his craft, and that's working at *learning* it every day. Concert pianists have not read a book on "learning to play the piano like a virtuoso in 24 hours." It's hard work. It requires diligence, total engagement, and awesome focus and effort. And what we're talking about here is far more complex and dynamic than being a concert pianist or a basketball star.

Look at the best at doing anything in the world. Then multiply what was required of them to be the best by a factor of ten or more. That's what is required of you, just to have a shot at it.

It takes courage and commitment. You have to slay dragons; you have to be focused, you have to *work*, day by day, to develop what it takes to perform with the best. No one has ever overestimated the difficulty of what has to be done, of what it takes. You're not going to be told how difficult it is by the celebrities.

Difficult beyond imagination doesn't sell books. "Easy" does. "Leadership for Dummies": would you buy that? Remember, if you put a spin on reality, it's no longer reality.

So here we are, looking at more of the indispensable aspects of what it takes. Reality bytes.

Reprise

What have we unpacked so far?

- The need for a leadership *role*, and the possibility that you might fit it. You have to be at the right place, at the right time, with the right stuff.
- Putting together (including yourself) the competent and passionately committed people who can and will make it happen.
- A compelling cause that has them all in its thrall. They are "had by" the cause to which they are dedicated.
- If you have the four covenants working throughout your organization, it will perform well in any posture: bottom-up, top-down, side-to-side.
- There is no fairy dust...that works.
- If you imagine you are interchangeable with anyone else who might take up the current panacea, you probably are.
- On the other hand, if you think you already know it all, you probably don't yet know what you *need* to know.
- *Methods don't do anything.* In the same way that "Talk does not cook rice."
- Your success will not be determined by how much people like you.

Moving on ...

A Robust Plan

What else does it take? It takes a robust plan. Not a financial forecast. Not a plan for the next quarter's (or the next year's) numbers. But a plan for how you and your followers are going to get from where you are to where you have to get to.

So what does that mean – a *robust* plan? This is what it means:

- It means you must have a clear and comprehensive understanding of exactly what it's going to be like when people begin to get where you're leading them.
- It means that you must be able (might as well do it) to write the story (in detail) of how you got from where you were to the path that is taking you where you want to go.
- In doing this, you will have identified the key roles that were required to make it happen.
- And in doing *that*, you will have identified the competencies and other qualifications required to carry out those roles, which ultimately make the story turn out the way it does.
- This story, with the people, the circumstances, and the plot and themes that accounted for how you got from where you were to where you had to get to, constitutes the bare bones of your robust plan.
- You flesh it out by putting in place the business plan that is going to pay for and otherwise underwrite your pursuit of real achievement – a high-performance organization.

Merely being successful (more or less the making money part of it) is a conventional aim that goes nowhere. It isn't until you have a unique destination that you put yourself on the path of real achievement. You differentiate yourself by competing with and outperforming the best organizations there have ever been. If that is not your aim, then you don't need a plan. All you have to do is ride the currents like everyone else.

A "robust" plan means that every person and every system in your organization is healthy, competent, capable, and prepared for what is expected and for what is not expected. In terms of competence, it means that you have excess capacity at every position in your organization. It means that you actually believe in continuous improvement, which can be sustained only if every person, every system, and every process performs better today than it did yesterday. At any age, in any role, it means that if there is not significant learning today, you will be falling behind tomorrow. It means, simply, that every day is a dress rehearsal, practicing and preparing for a more excellent performance tomorrow.

It means that everyone knows what the plan is, what part of it they own, and why their fulfillment of their role is necessary. Otherwise, they have to get off the bus and make room for someone who can and will fulfill that role.

In a robust plan, there is no place for an irrelevant or unnecessary role. And there is no place for mediocrity.

Your plan has to seem to your people like *the* plan that is actually going to get you from where you are to where you are going. And, as we have seen, *you* have to be seen by your people as the only person who could pull this off – as their *leader*.

- Canned plans, no matter how expensive they are, don't (and can't) work.
- You have to *invent* the plan that fits your story, that fits you, that fits those who are going to make it happen, and that fits the only world in which it has to happen – the real world.
- A robust plan is one people have to invent for their circumstances, which they can then improvise on to keep the story going in the right direction.
- What you can't imagine you can't realize. The plan is what has to happen to get you from today's realities to the realization of your vision.

Your plan is part of *what it takes*. You will be no more successful than your plan is robust.

On Telling The Story

People have to *experience* (vicariously, at the outset) what this place you want to take them looks like and feels like. That requires a story. *Star Trek* takes you where no one has gone before. So, for most people, does your journey.

Your story has to be at least as compelling as the *Star Trek* episodes. And you have to be as compelling as Captain Pickard (who, as you know, hand-picked all of his senior officers).

What enables truly great leaders is their ability to tell the story of how something that has not yet happened – is going to happen. A compelling story of how remarkably challenging and gratifying it is going to be for everyone who makes the journey. The story of how – together – you and they are going to bring this off.

Chamberlain's talk to the "mutineers" near the beginning of the film *Gettysburg* is an example. Columbus's speech to his men aboard ship when they intend to take over the ships and turn back is another (the film is *1492*). Jack Welch was a story-teller, but was probably outdone in the long-run by Nucor's Ken Iverson.

If you are had by a great and worthy cause, people want to be a part of your story. And they want to be responsible for bringing it off by "telling" their part of the story of your journey together to greatness.

So, telling the story over and over again is a part of what it takes:

- Stories are powerful stuff.
- We live by them – you, me, and all of the other people.
- Everything depends upon whose story we are in.
- Stories are compelling if they are told by compelling leaders. A compelling leader is the one who is expected to make the story come true, *whatever it takes*.
- These people you need will either be in your story or some one else's. If it is to their benefit and the benefit of your cause, it should be yours.

Power

You gotta have power.

No matter how much charisma you may have or persuasiveness you can muster, it is not enough. You have to have the prerogative to say what will be, and who the players will be. You have to have the power to organize the place – the people and the processes – as you deem necessary. You have to have the power to change things – according to you as the primary author.

Of course people may – and will – have their say. And the more competent they are, the more you need to pay heed to what they say. The bat-boys see the game from a different perspective than do the fans or the manager. Every perspective is relevant *if* it emanates from real competence in role. Making it all move together requires that.

There can be only one leader. If that's not you, then you don't have one. Other people must be capable of leading themselves, and of leading those who are going to make their part of it happen. But they don't want to follow a person who will automatically defer to them in order to be liked – as may be the case in so-called participative management. They want to follow someone who is more passionately determined to achieve than they are at the outset. They want your strength, your certainty, your dedication, your decisiveness, and your relentless determination. They want to go, not with the person who can *see* the future, but the person who is going to **make** the future. Paradoxically, they want to follow the person who has the power – and the will – to include them or exclude them. The person who knows what roles are needed to make it happen, and who possesses the judgment and the power to cast the right people in them.

Making it happen requires power.

How will they know you are the right choice for them? By whether or not you exercise the kind of power that makes a difference – first of all, over yourself. This is what they sense they lack. When they see it in another, they are ready to follow. If you are the one with the loftiest and most worthy cause, this is what they need to see in you. Otherwise, they will follow a loser.

Nothing guarantees your success. The best you can do is to surround yourself with the people who are competent enough, and determined enough, to provide *whatever it takes* to carry out your cause.

Power comes from these ...

• Being *had by* a great and worthy cause empowers you.

• Demonstrating invariant self-leadership to seduce others to your cause.

• Developing a robust plan that lends power to followers - over themselves and their destiny. Competence is what empowers people. It is never your power *over them that makes them an indispensable part of the process.*

• Having the best leaders – who have almost always come from the ranks of the best followers. And having the best followers, who are at their best only when following the best leaders.

Staying The Path

Making change is easy. Making the right changes, sustained over time, is far more difficult. Ask those many who have failed. Or, those few who have succeeded.

Basically, what's required is that the people who are going to make it happen have to *own* the problem(s) of making it happen. They have to *own* the accomplishment, not just the activities. If they don't own the outcome(s), the effort will not be sustained, and those outcome(s) will not be maintained.

To stay the path, the problems encountered there, and the outcomes of how they are dealt with, have to be owned by the people who are making it happen.

Leadership is not owning the problem of the achievement. Leadership is owning the problem of casting in the right roles the people who then have to own that problem.

That's what your power is for. Not to wallow in. But to enable you to become a wise and prudent radical decentralizer. That is, making sure that the person or the people who ought to own the problem do, in fact, own it.

Perseverance

If you don't persevere, you will never know what could have been accomplished. All of your explanations of why it didn't happen are as fanciful as they are irrelevant. The only measure is what you accomplished. If you let yourself off the hook, others will follow your lead. If you have an explanation which is better than real achievement, you are not a candidate for the kind of leadership we're talking about here.

Leader's lesson:
If you're shooting yourself in the foot because you've got the wrong target in your scope, don't persevere.

I once met a CEO who was convinced that his whim of the day was a good enough plan. Well, it was. It was good enough to make his organization the worst performer in the industry. Of course he blamed his people.

Perseverance without the other prerequisites is dangerous. What we're talking about here is setting the right course, and then staying that course, no matter what.

Communication

It may sound like a ho-hum subject. But it turns out to be the core subject, the one that is *always* involved. Here's why:

- The way your mind works determines how you think.
- How you think determines who you *are*.
- Who you are determines what you will do, and how you will do it.
- And how you communicate determines the way your mind works.

That covers it well. But some more detail may be useful:

• There is something about the way your mind works that leads you to pay attention to certain things, and to ignore others. What you pay attention to, and how you interpret those things, will constitute your picture of reality. Your eyes and your ears work for your mind. Not the other way around.

• Or, you may seek to gather certain information about that reality by asking questions or by inquiring into things that do not come running to you. Via superb questioning and critical (of yourself) observations, you may elicit some intelligence that reconfigures your understanding of what's going on.

• Both are forms of communication – the critical factors in how you communicate. You will never be better informed than your routine strategies enable you to be. Your picture and your assessment of the reality around you will be a function of how well you have architected yourself, your own mind.

• On this side of things, a great communicator is one who continuously restructures his mind to fit the real world rather than trying to restructure the world to fit his minding of it. Great leaders partner with that reality better than most others. But they also see the world not as it is, but as it should be. And it is getting people on *that* path that constitutes their leadership.

• It matters whose *ideas* you expose yourself to, and it matters even more whose ideas you fall in love with. These will be the primary architectural framework for the way your mind works.

That's merely the input side. Not only does how you think direct you to what to pay attention to. The way you think also determines how you interpret everything you observe or everything you hear or read. Shortfalls of performance are always ultimately traceable to inadequate or faulty thinking. What determines the kind of leadership you might be able to provide is how you think about the things that need thinking about.

How you think is a cumulative consequence of how you have communicated in the past. Your ability to think in the future will be a cumulative consequence of how you communicate today. That should make communication your core subject.

We create our destinies one conversation at a time.

In spite of all the flap-flap that we engage in every hour of every day, most communication – at least most of the communication that makes a real difference – is what goes on when you talk to yourself. (Keep in mind that most people pay more attention to what they say to themselves than they do of what you or others say *to* them.)

People will protect with all the defenses they can muster their view of reality. Their view of reality is not your view of reality. Productive communication is what goes on when you're asking just the right questions to figure out what the differences are and why your own view of reality may be wrong. Intelligence lies in knowing what other people view as reality, not what you view as reality.

It's a matter of persuasion or influence. Many people think that's what communication is mainly about – persuading or influencing someone else, or trying to convince them that what you know is what *they* ought to know. It's far more about how well you discern who, or what, you need to be influenced by. And to what end.

There is, of course, always that other side of things – trying to sway other people in the direction of their own best self-interests, whether they know what those are or not, or even whether they care or not. But the ability to persuade others, to influence others, to take up a just cause the results of which are in their own best self-interests, can be readily dealt with, as follows:

• Your heart must belong to your cause.
• Your words must come from your heart, whether you are talking to other people or to yourself.

Since communication is always an issue, it will appear again and again in these pages. But let us consider here two further ways you may want to be able to think about communication.

One is the simple fact that *what you can't understand, you won't understand.* What this means is that the limits of your mind are the limits of your world.

Each of us has to understand the world the way our own mind makes possible and necessary. The world is what it is. What happens is what happens. People are who they are, and they do what they do. All of this we have to see or hear or read about. But our individual understanding of all these things comes down to the interpretations we make. You will always and inescapably function as you interpret the world, not as the world really is.

That's why the leader's primary instrument of leadership is his, or her, own mind. The more capable your mind, the more successful your leadership. It is made of communication. It comes down to how good you are at informing yourself, how good you are at acquiring the intelligence and the interpretations you need to underwrite your success.

The other is the flip side. What other people can't understand, they won't understand. That's always square one. Their interpretations of what you say are enabled and constrained by *their* minds. Being able to influence others requires you to start with the workings of those minds on which your words will fall. What you cannot ask of others' minds will produce no answer useful to you.

We all have two enemies. One is the way our own minds work. The other is the way other people's minds work. They're either working for you or against you. There is no neutral ground on which to stand.

Some thought-prodders:

• Here's an old saw. You must say what you mean and you must mean what you say.

• That requires you to understand what you mean – not in terms of the words, but in terms of what the consequences are supposed to be.

225

- And that requires a tacit understanding on your part, and the part of others, that there are significant consequences for any failure to accomplish what is explicit or implicit.
- Communication doesn't *do* anything. It should never, ever be taken as an end in itself. It is the consequences or the outcomes that matter. Not the words. Not the agreements or the disagreements. But the consequences.
- Leaders focus on the outcomes, the accomplishment, not the words, not the chatter.
- If people don't say what they mean, or if they do not mean what they say, they cannot be a part of your endeavor. Beginning with you.
- If you want to know something, you may have to ask the person who knows, and who has a great and worthy purpose that absolutely depends on knowing that.
- What people mean by what they say is what they *do*. Begin developing this habit so it is invariant for you. Then you can hold others to it.
- Every human enterprise has to be conducted by communication.
- Verbiage is verbiage. The reality is in the consequences, the measurable outcomes.
- A mind is an ongoing product of communication.
- Words that do not come from your heart will never engage the hearts of others.
- If you are not a servant of your cause, you will be a victim of whatever words are aimed at you.
- A person's mind and the way a person communicates are two aspects of the same thing. Consider what this means to you.
- Choose your mental diet carefully. That's who you will be.

In communication, there are two basic maneuvers: making a statement or posing a question. Asking the right questions will take you further – and with more compatriots – than will telling, no matter how much you know.

A question permits you to try again to figure out what you want to say. A statement closes everything down, except for explanations and arguments about who is right or wrong.

Sometimes words are more or less adequately *referential*. But words – and every other mode of communication – are always *consequential*. Leaders are after the required or desired consequences. Never for the opportunity to play yawp-yawp with people who do not have their eye on the consequences.

The conditions of real achievement always come down to matters of communication; your competence at gathering the intelligence you need to pursue your aims; your competence at processing that intelligence (your ability to think about what needs thinking about), and your competence to draw others to the level of performance necessary to achieve your mission. If you don't seem to be getting to where you need to go, check first how good you are at those three things. You can't fix the world. You can't fix other people. But you can fix your own shortfalls. For example, if you need to have a meeting, what's caused the problem is most likely some failure or incompetence in communication. Can you fix that in a meeting? Or does that have to be fixed in some other way?

There are many paths to success. But there is only one way to be the best at what you do. And that is – by an unwavering commitment to becoming the best.

And by having what it takes to stay the path of getting there.

For those who pursue real achievement, what it takes is whatever it takes, beginning with the ability to *think* precisely about what it takes, and then to *be* what it takes, so as to be able to *do* what it takes. It seems that the only thing that holds us back is not having what it takes.

What leaders know: The meaning of anything whatever – a thought, an idea, a question – can be accurately deduced only from the consequences. Only what people *did* about what was said. If you want to know what people (including you) mean by what they say, look to the consequences. Communication takes us where it goes. Better to be the master rather than the victim.

POINTS TO PONDER

+ If there are two or more people involved, who is going to make it happen?

+ What is the robust plan you have for your life?

+ How many characters are needed to make a story? Which ones?

+ If you can't tell the story, your story won't be told.

+ What hasn't been practiced won't be performed very well.

+ A plan for becoming requires people who are becoming.

+ What kind of story do your people want to be cast in?

+ If people are not in your story, they'll be in someone else's.

+ If you have sufficient charisma, you don't need power.

+ The best followers will seek you out in order to follow you.

+ There is never a time not to persevere.

+ You will never be better informed than your own mind makes possible – and necessary.

+ Leadership requires a leader's mind.

+ If you want to know what people mean by what they say, ask them.

PART IV

Some Tools for Making It Happen

The two indispensable tools for making it happen we have dwelt on at length in the preceding pages are:

1. How you think. If you can't think the way you need to think in order to put together all of the pieces of this puzzle, you'll never it put together in a way that will actually get you where you want to go.

2. Who you are. Who you are is the second most necessary tool you have available to you. If who you are isn't the kind of tool you need to make it happen, you need to change that first.

Most people skip over these soft issues as if they weren't very important. That's one of the reasons why most people fail at this. These two – how you think and who you are – hold up all the rest of it. These are the master tools. If they are not right, you cannot make any of the other tools work like they need to work. No tool is any better than the person who wields it.

Too many people are eager to begin with what to do, and the tools and techniques to do it with. But no tool or technique is optimally effective without the right master tools – how you think and who you are.

The Right Tool for the Right Task

A Phillips screwdriver won't work on a slot-head screw. It's tough to drive a staple with a hammer. A master carpenter has a tool for every purpose. An amateur has a few standard tools and tries to make them work for every purpose.

So it is with amateur managers. They pick up a few tools from their limited experience, or from a casual reading of a business magazine, or from attending a seminar, and try to force them to fit every new situation they encounter. If dentists did their work the way amateur mangers do theirs, they'd have a couple of all purpose drills and maybe a pair of pliers.

Amateur managers define the problem in terms of the tools they have personally but accidentally acquired in the past. Whether a tool or a technique will work in a present situation is not guaranteed by the fact that it worked in some situation in the past. The amateur manager looks for why the present situation looks like a previous one. Leaders look for why the present situation is different – unique.

Leaders acquire or invent the tools they need to fit the circumstances. They let the situation or the problem define the tools or techniques needed, rather than defining the problem by the tools they happen to have available. They look at problems as an opportunity to learn something, rather than merely as an opportunity to apply something they already know.

So a leader is a tool-finder as well as a tool-maker. She realizes that unconventional situations require unconventional tools. Unlike amateur managers, who let the tools they happen to have define the situation, leaders let the situations define the tools required.

A virtuoso at what he or she does is enabled by virtuoso tools and vice-versa. A tool does not make a person competent. A tool is the right tool only in the right hands. A master carpenter and the tool he is using are interdependent. They each enable the other. That's the way it needs to be with leaders.

There is this sense of seamlessness with their tools. The aim is not to use the tool properly, but to accomplish something that would be difficult or impossible for the amateur by bringing together the right tool with the right person. When you are witnessing virtuoso performers, you cannot separate the dancer from the dance. And they make it look easy because it is … for them. Trying to gain wisdom from amateurs would be a bit like trying to climb a mountain by walking downhill.

By itself, a hammer does nothing it was designed to do. In the hands of an amateur, expect damage. In the hands of a master craftsman, expect superior results. No tool or technique – including high-tech gadgets like computers – can compensate for the inadequacies of their users. We are led – easily on our part – to believe that we can buy smarts, or at least buy something that would compensate for our own or others' incompetencies. You cannot. I cannot. No one can.

The right person is the person who is fully capacitated – fully competent – to combine with that tool or technique what can be achieved when each is "right." So the potent tools and techniques that follow will range from "don't work" to downright dangerous if deployed by semi-competent persons. Powerful if deployed by masterful leaders.

Think on these, and then move on to meet them:

- A poor tool in the hands of a fully competent person will produce results far superior to a magnificent tool in the hands of an incompetent person.
- Who is the "right" person? The one who is fully competent to make use of the right tool.
- Any shortfall in competence lessens the value of the tool.
- Computerization has contributed little to productivity. Why?

Chapter 14

The Basic Tools

Wherever and whenever performance matters, there are fundamentally two kinds of tools:

- Those that contribute to making that level of performance **possible**;

    and

- Those that contribute to making the required performance **necessary**.

The main reason people don't perform as required (or desired) is that they *can't*. They are not competent to accomplish what needs to be accomplished. Given the "people" problems that absorb excessive amounts of time and attention daily, it seems that we need to be reminded of this simple fact repeatedly.

You will recall the second reason why people don't perform as required (or desired). It is simply that they *don't have to*. They didn't come with the necessary "fire" in their bellies that might drive their extraordinary performance. They may have loved adolescent irresponsibility, since that was the only life they had known, and wanted to stay in their comfort zone. It was never necessary for them to set goals and then be accountable for achieving them. In short, they never learned how to perform because they never had to.

If so, then some of the necessity that drives outstanding performance would have to be imposed by others, by a performance culture, or by systems that make the required performance possible, and also necessary. Nucor would be a good example. As would the U. S. Marines or Special Forces or the University of Connecticut women's basketball program.

The more difficult the goal, the tougher the preparation for pursuing it has to be. Young people escape the necessity of this logic by having easy goals in life – or none at all. But if you have a real aim in life, you have to equip yourself (and your organization) with the necessity for achieving it. Here's the bottom line:

- What drives exceptional performance is *necessity*.
- What drives mediocre performance is the absence of the level and kind of *necessity* required for exceptional performance.

Preparedness/Readiness

So the indispensable or essential tool is **preparedness,** or **readiness**. Pilots do this *before* they get into the cockpit. Surgeons do this *before* they enter the operating room. Warriors do this *before* they enter the arena. The best organizations do this *before* they are confronted by the need to perform at extraordinary levels.

"Prepared?"… for what? Well, for one thing, if you don't know or care exactly where you're going, you're simply going to end up where you're headed. No need to prepare for that. No way even *to* prepare for that.

But if you have a cause or a mission, you have to prepare yourself to carry it out. You have to prepare yourself for what you are likely to encounter on the path from here to there. You have to prepare yourself for what you may possibly encounter in your efforts to get from here to there. And you have to prepare yourself for all of the unexpected obstacles you will encounter along the way.

If the telephone rings in Customer Service, the person who answers doesn't know in advance what the problem or the inquiry

234

will be, yet ideally (and in terms of high-performance) has to be prepared for it whatever it is. You don't actually know how or what that customer is going to present you with when there has been tough competition for a complex sale. But you have to be prepared, regardless. You don't know what kinds of strange turns the economy is going to take. But you'd better be prepared for an up year or a down year, anyway.

Being prepared is, simply ... being prepared. You have to be prepared for the unexpected. If you are not, you will be victimized by those unexpected happenings.

This is one of those master tools.

It requires planning. It requires the ability to improvise and keep things on track. It requires great competence – not just being good at what you do, but in seducing others to go where you want to go. It requires the kind of intelligence you can use to strategize no matter the ongoing action. And it requires the resilience and the forethought to win in spite of losing. Without this master tool, you may end up being at sea without a paddle.

Some thought-prodders:

• What you don't prepare for, you can't be ready for.
• A mission does not exist in a statement about it. It is what you and everyone else involved have to be prepared to achieve, whatever it takes.
• You cannot intelligently prepare for a journey you are not committed to take.
• A purpose is the tool for setting direction and maintaining course.
• If a purpose has no starting power, it is worthless. If it has no finishing power, it is just idle talk.
• What you are not prepared to understand, you will not understand.
• What you are not prepared to accomplish, you will not accomplish.

Accountability

In any organization, any problem or failure on the part of the organization can be traced to a shortfall of competence in one or more roles. The consequences usually suck in the time and attention and effort of other people – people above, below, and on all sides. Probably more than 75% of all meetings are called to solve a problem which can be traced to shortfalls in competence. The consequences for the organization of these shortfalls of competence are the largest single cause of *waste* in an organization.

We seem to have time to talk endlessly and get involved in these consequences. But never seem to have the time – or the will? – to preclude them by fully capacitating every person in every role. And, by designing every system to be a smart system, and every process to be a smart process.

Talk is not an accomplishment. It is typically what people do in lieu of an accomplishment. The more accomplishment-minded people in an organization are, the less they have to talk about. In other words,

- The less people achieve, the more need they feel to talk about it.
- Communication fills the void left by having no clear purpose, or by failing to accomplish what needed to be accomplished.
- Much if not most communication in organizations is in lieu of accomplishment. Or it may simply be as irrelevant as are the people who engage in it as a substitute for purposeful performance.

Accountability means owning the outcome. Not the talk. The person who is regularly involved in an exercise program has little to say about it. The person who talks endlessly about his or her need for it is (you can bet) not doing it. This is not always the case, but it is extremely useful to your thinking.

Besides, it is *always* the case that the more people talk about stuff, the less time they have just to *do* it.

Accountability requires the competencies required to accomplish what needs accomplishing, and for avoiding those consequences that ought not to occur. Many people these days won't understand what you mean by accountability. That's because they've never been required to be accountable to anyone or anything, including themselves.

Accountability may strike many marginally-competent or incompetent people as being somehow alien. You are challenging their reality. But to develop a high-performance organization, you will have to wield this tool. You are, and the people in your organization are ...

- Accountable for statements made. If those mislead, the person who made the statement – if only to herself – is accountable.
- Accountable for the promises that were made to anyone inside or outside the organization.
- Accountable for an implicit promise whenever they cash their paychecks – that there is no one else who could perform their role better than they do, or for less pay.
- Accountable for every accomplishment you sign on to, explicitly or implicitly, and for the ramifications of whatever occurs as a result of your failure to perform.
- Accountable for developing all of the *competencies required* to accomplish what you have signed on to accomplish – your role and all of the performance goals or assignments that you take on.

There is no accountability where there are no *consequences* for failing to accomplish what was agreed to (even if the agreement is with oneself). An excuse is the opposite of accountability. If people are pretty good at lying to themselves (which is what a well-worn excuse is) they will feel no compunction about lying to others: to you, to your customers, to their fellow-members. People who do not have personal integrity (accountability to themselves) will diminish the health and the performance capabilities of your organization from the inside out.

Every hour of every day there are "Moments of Truth" in every organization, as Jan Carlzon (then head of SAS) wrote some years back. Every transaction that occurs within the organization or with customers or suppliers is a "moment of truth." Add all of those together at the end of the day and that will provide you with a picture of the state of the organization. In the outcomes of those moments of truth, there is either accountability or there is not. Making it necessary for people to be accountable is simply indispensable to making a high-performance organization.

Think about it.

There's hardly a person I know who is pleased with his or her treatment by airline personnel. "Have a nice day" is a statement made in lieu of real performance. **Shouldn't** *those airlines be in bankruptcy? Isn't it about time for a comeuppance?*

If you were to add up the performance of every person and every piece of the organization at the end of the day, as Carlzon said, you would have a picture of that person's or that organization's destiny. That's where accountability counts.

Here are some thoughts to ponder:

- What *cannot* be done *will not* be done.
- Outcomes that are not *necessary* will occur only as a matter of chance or of good or bad luck.
- Becoming the best at anything on purpose has nothing to do with luck.
- It has to do with competence and necessity – with accountability.

Capacitation

By this point, you have noted that there are two concepts that pervade everything else. They are *competence* and *necessity*. People simply have to be *competent* to perform at the level (or in the way) required. If they are not, it isn't going to happen.

And it has to be *necessary* for them to perform at the level required. That necessity may be internal (the best kind), external, or some combination. People may be competent and very conscientious. But unless they *have to* perform to an extraordinary level, they won't. Occasionally, you could be surprised. But it's better to be surprised than it is to fail.

Another concept (and all concepts are tools) is *capacitation*. This concept is perhaps more encompassing than competence. You take the measure of competence on persons. A person is either fully competent to accomplish something or he/she is not.

Capacitation refers to designing or equipping a team of people or a work system involving several processes so that the larger system can accomplish what needs accomplishing.

IT, for example, doesn't increase anyone's competence in the short-term. But if the system designer thinks in terms of *capacitating* the whole system, the performance of the whole could be improved. Capacitation refers to what might be needed by any component of the overall system, or by the way the components function together.

People can be more or less competent. A team or a work system or an organization can be more or less capacitated. For example, no one person controls the outcomes of an organization's performance in the real world. But everything that an organization contributes to that outcome can be reasonably controlled, by design and by capacitation. The way an organization is put together (given the outside conditions) can either capacitate it to perform, or incapacitate its performance.

It is reported that Southwest Airlines hires only one out of fifty applicants. They are looking for the one that adds – doesn't subtract – from the already successful capacitation of the organization. A person is likely either to fit into the existing culture or not. If GE eliminates the bottom fifteen percent of middle managers every year, it's because they don't want to invest in people if there is unlikely to be much in the way of payoff.

For the leader, both are indispensable tools: competence *and* capacitation.

239

Inescapable Logic

One of the most reliable of ancient wisdoms is this: Don't challenge the inevitable. If there is an infrastructure logic to something, go with it. Don't go up against it. Inherent in most situations, from those involving the machinations of the organization to those involving the machinations of the marketplace, there is such an underlying logic.

You can use it as a tool for your purposes by recognizing and acquiescing to it. Otherwise, you will simply be a victim of it.

Organizations may succeed for many different reasons. But many organizations fail for one reason: they did not adapt to the logic of the situations in which they found themselves. The logic of situations, from the interpersonal to larger economy, is always implicit – hidden, tacit. You have to figure it out without having the code book in your hand. It changes, never asking your permission. If one of your lieutenants is gung-ho for your mission, and another expresses overt hostility to it, the logics of the two situations are quite different. If you play them the same, you may lose both ways.

Consider poker or bridge. Each game has a certain logic to it. If you can read it better than your opponents, you might win. It is the same for every competitor in every marketplace. The logic of the situation will always win. It pays to be on the side of the forces that are going to win.

Three ponderables:

- How good you are at what you do is revealed solely by how well you perform *under adversity*. Make the logic of adversity your ally.

- What doesn't make you the best at what you do makes you ordinary. What makes you ordinary can never make you the best. You can't beat that logic. People have been trying to do that for years.

- There is no necessary correlation between what people say and what people do. That's the logic. You can play it the other way. If you do, you will lose.

Casting

The most important decision you ever make as head of an organization is who to hire. This is the person who is going to make you successful. Or not. The higher your aim, the more critical the decision.

Every organization has a history that is its story. The people who have roles in that story make it turn out the way it does. If you want that story to turn out as you intend, then you have no choice but to create the roles that are indispensable to that story, and then to find and put in place the right people to perform those roles. They are accountable for performing up to or beyond those roles, as we will consider in more detail ahead.

You need to have just the right roles to make the story of your organization turn out the way you intend. And you need to cast just the right people in those roles – and, when they don't, you must hold their feet to the fire. Casting, whether for a movie or a symphony orchestra or an NFL team, is crucial to the outcome. It is even more so for an organization dedicated to a cause, to real achievement, to extraordinary performance.

We've been here before and we'll be here again. But let's take another look at one of the fundamental obstacles.

People think of what they do in organizations as "work." Work has a negative connotation for most people. People do not come to your place primarily to develop their competencies in the role they're in. They come to your place for *their* reasons, not yours.

Before they arrive at your place, it's likely they were looking for "a job." A job to them is an arrangement that enables them to obtain the money to pay for the things they want to buy (or assume they deserve). They want to be at your place as a sort of reward or recognition either for past accomplishments, or just for being willing to put up with you and your organization's silliness. They are there to get some "bread" (AKA $$). They are there to carry out, less or more conscientiously, the *activities* vaguely described in a "job description." They typically expect you to be responsible for their capabilities, their safety and security, and their "job satisfaction."

The problems of the organization, even if they cause them, are usually not matters of much interest to them, except as a way of spending the day. They expect you to be responsible for their performance, and to be generously grateful to them for being willing to spend that much time at your place, engaged in activities that they perform more or less adequately, depending on how they feel at the moment.

Is that cynical, or merely realistic?

The bottom line: Most people do not come to your place with any longer-range ambitions than today (or perhaps payday). They do not sign on with you with the intention of being world-class at what they do. Only those who are compelling leaders, or who have the right stuff to prepare themselves as leaders, can change those circumstances. And only the very courageous, very ingenious, leader of an organization who is able and willing to go up against those seemingly overwhelming counter-forces can seriously expect to make an organization that has worthy and lofty aims.

What has to be altered is obvious. Mere work has to be made as richly challenging and as richly rewarding as any other aspect of life. People who are enervated have to be awakened and brought back to life. Having "a job" won't do it. People have to have a relevant role in some worthy quest. The answer to getting a life is finding the right role and becoming forever better at it. You now know this. They probably do not. Of necessity, leaders lead people to a higher quality of life, even though those people may resist it every step of the way. It is a unique role performed superbly in the context of a larger cause that provides people with a real sense of life. That's what high-performance organizations provide, and that's what leaders make possible – and necessary.

These need your best thinking:

- If you intend to pursue real achievement, like a high-performance organization, you have to take a different path.
- You have to have some tools for being different.

242

Tools For Being Different

To be able to use the tools for being different (like being the best), you have to be different yourself. In the following ways (as we have seen):

IF you are had by a great and worthy purpose ... and

IF you have a potent and compelling strategy for getting from here to there ... and

IF you can tell the story of getting from here to there in a way that seduces others ... and

IF you have the right roles to make that story come true, and the right people cast in those right roles ...

THEN you may be the right person to wield these tools for being different.

If you aren't, these tools will under-perform. There is no tool that can be better than the person who uses it. Make sure that you can optimize these tools. Make sure that any person who intends to use them in your organization has the above qualifications at his or her level.

Role Descriptions

The first of these basic tools we want to deal with here is that of *role descriptions*. A role description is **not** another name for a "job description." In fact, it is how different they are that you want to come away with.

A job description describes, more or less ambiguously, the *activities* that a person carries out in her job. Using job descriptions almost guarantees that the status quo will be maintained. That the organization will recycle itself on a daily basis, becoming more and more like it is. And that its destiny is given in the *activities of the day*.

A role description, by contrast, describes unambiguously what a *virtuoso* in that role would be able to accomplish regardless of any adversity. A role description does not describe a person nor the activities that person might engage in. A role description is a description of a role to be performed with great mastery in order for the organization to fulfill its intended destiny. A role is one of several indispensable functions for making that story turn out as intended. The people are players and they have a role to perform to make the story unfold as envisioned. A role description describes what the incumbent of that role has to *accomplish* in order for the whole to evolve as intended.

A job description lists *activities*. A role description sets forth the *accomplishments* the incumbent has agreed to become capable of delivering under adversity.

The significant and very consequential difference is that job descriptions generate the present out of what worked in the past for a particular person. A role description, by contrast, outlines the contributions required of that role for the organization to fulfill its cause or mission in the future (its story). The incumbent of a role description develops the competencies to perform that *role*, not relying on the skills or experiences they happen to bring to it. People act out themselves in job descriptions. A role description requires them to play, not themselves, but the performance demanded by the role.

The envisioned organization doesn't yet exist. It is the right people performing extraordinarily in the right roles that bring it into being. Most people have not lived under the influence of a cause or mission in life, and therefore never had – because they never needed – a role description designed to get them there.

Every person at every moment of the day is performing a role. But for most people most of the time, they are not conscious of what it is. They may have thought fleetingly about the future but didn't like thinking about the role description required to get them there. (Too demanding, too much accountability.) And most of the time their roles are in the default setting – meaning that their old habits and other people are pulling their strings.

It's a waste of time to get involved in designing role descriptions into which people are to be cast if those roles do not have "teeth" in them. If failure to live up to a role description has no serious consequences, it's all an exercise in futility. A violinist who can't perform up to the level of his or her role in a world-class symphony orchestra won't get, or won't be retained, in that role. It's simple. It's powerful. But if the CEO can't or won't live up to *his/her* role, there is likely to be loosey-goosey acceptance of mediocrity throughout the organization.

For all of these reasons, learning how to think about and craft role descriptions is a capability few people have. Yet it is a basic tool, having many of the pushes and pulls in them that are required to elevate performance continuously.

There are no neutral roles. Roles either contribute positively to the outcomes as intended for the organization, or they contribute negatively. If you and the incumbent do not perceive any role as being as important as every other role in pulling the organization into its intended future, eliminate it. It's waste. And waste is trouble. Broaden the roles required, both laterally and vertically, to the fewest roles required to carry the organization to its cause. This is not the new "lean." This is old, old wisdom.

Increase the requirements of the role to have fewer roles with more requirements, not more roles with fewer requirements. This is the only way everyone wins. **Enrich the role.** Don't impoverish it just because the present incumbent can't or won't perform as the role requires.

Start at the top. It's a perspective that helps to see how the pieces should fit together. Keep in mind that this is a key tool only if you intend to pursue real achievement – like a high-performance organization.

Begin with these kinds of questions:

- What is this organization *for*? Why does it exist? What is its rightful destiny? What is its legacy to be?
- What is its role vis-à-vis its stakeholders: employees, customers, suppliers, owners, the industry, the community, the economy, the nation and its cultural environment, history itself?

- What part of the larger architecture of economic, political, human life will it occupy? How will it adapt to the world? How will it need to make the world adapt to it?
- How will it *do* all of this?

It is the organization's *role* in the world (not its mission, myopic and inadequate) that reveals what is important and what is not important, and for what the organization itself is to be held accountable. If the criteria for its accountability are not clear, it becomes impossible to make anything else about the organization clear to people – inside or outside the organization. *If the CEO doesn't understand what the organization's role is, his own role will be ambiguous, fuzzy, without real accountability.*

Clear, comprehensive answers to the questions above establish the core criteria for the CEO's role description. And that's the way it has to work from the top to the bottom of the organization. What needs to be accomplished at every position is what is required by the level above that one. So, given the comprehensive answers to those questions, the CEO has his (or her) basic role description. Then the question is, what roles are needed to carry out those accomplishments, and what are the criteria for those roles – the accomplishments required by those roles to achieve what is specified by the organization's role in the world.

We'll see what that might look like. But first, more caveats:

- Given the real achievement envisioned, you are free to put into the role description what, in your wildest dreams, would make your dreams come true. It doesn't have to fit a person. It has to provide a set of accomplishments for a person to equip herself to carry out in that role.
- Always think in terms of accomplishments (not activities) in the long-term, and always objectively measurable. (This means that any reasonably intelligent person could measure the accomplishments.)
- Every part of the organization should have a role description – every department, every unit, team, work group, project, person. Whatever or whoever is critical

and relevant to the pursuit and accomplishment of the organization's role needs a sub-role to play, spelled out by a role description.

• Every role description is provisional, meaning that it could be improved upon tomorrow. Its purpose, collaborative or not, is that of *aligning* everyone and everything to the organization's chosen destiny. The words are important only to help the leader and subordinate involved explore together what the words of a role description *mean*, so that the incumbent can devise a plan to fulfill every required accomplishment and both can track progress on the plan toward every accomplishment.

• The more conventional the title and the description, the more likely the outcomes will be mediocre. They are for the purpose of creating an organization that does not yet exist. They have to be at least creative enough to light the way to that happening.

• You want everyone to be in the same business – to be as much as possible on the same page. To do this, every role description needs to have the same first line.

There's more to the design and construction of this core tool than that. But here's an example that shows how to accommodate all of these provisos. Here's a very generic role description for an "Executive Assistant," just to give you an idea of how it's done:

Role Description: Administrative/Executive Assistant (CEO Enabler?)

My role: To make XYZ Corp the best in the business by any measure, by –

1. Developing my competencies to ensure that the events that ought to happen, happen, and those that ought not to happen, don't.

2. Enhancing the performance of anyone who needs (whether they know it or not), requests, or expects my resourceful support.

3. Knowing the who, what, when, and where that others need to know to fulfill their roles superbly.

4. Achieving all performance goals with zero errors, and in increasingly less time and others' involvement.

5. Making certain that all aspects of my goals are fulfilled whether I am physically present or not.

6. Establishing and maintaining a world-class, always current, repository of the intelligence required for every process and every request.

7. Being the spiritual leader of this organization's mission.

8. Routinely improving the administrative infrastructure of this organization through my innovativeness and by continuous improvement.

9. Becoming the key source of intelligence about what is going on, what ought to be going on, and what ought not to be going on, in this organization.

10. Distilling and distributing that intelligence in order to create the most well-informed executive team in this or any other industry.

11. Providing real-time monitoring of specified performance data with variance analysis and projections.

12. Adding measurably to the performance of the CEO.

Not perfect. Never is. But as a way of grounding an ongoing dialogue between the executive and this assistant, this tool can be made to do its job. You can see the posture. The people involved must agree about how each accomplishment is to be tracked and measured, about what's missing from a complete description of what a real virtuoso would accomplish in this role, and about the incumbent's plan for raising her/his competencies to the level required. If a person could walk in and fulfill the role, the description is not demanding enough. The role description needs to reveal how the incumbent would have to develop herself/himself over the long-term. It is also a grounded blueprint for the capabilities that have yet to be acquired.

The CEO? That one might begin this way:

Role Description: CEO (Chief Steward of the Organization's Destiny?)

My role: To make this organization the best in the business by any measure, by –

1. Designing the organizational architecture needed to carry out our mission, identifying the roles required for our story to be told as envisioned, and casting the people in those roles who can and will make it happen …

You see how this tool gets constructed. But tools as such don't accomplish anything. If the role incumbent can't or won't pursue the accomplishments expressed and implied, he or she needs to make room for someone who can, and will.

How about these?

• If role descriptions don't have teeth in them, they are little more than bureaucratic exercises. Real achievement that isn't necessary won't happen.

• A plan for every entry makes the accomplishments *possible.*

• But if they aren't *necessary*, the time involved is wasted. This applies throughout. But the leader is the model.

• A tool that is not going to be used for the purpose for which it was designed, by a person who knows how to use it, won't do much good. Can do some harm.

• Great role descriptions make explicit *who* owns *what* problems required for the organization to pursue real achievement.

POINTS TO PONDER

+ Making it possible, but also necessary, are the leader's key tools.

+ Inadequate necessity promotes mediocre performance.

+ If the phone rings, be prepared. If it doesn't, be prepared.

+ Having a mission is not the same as being prepared to achieve it.

+ Much communication is a substitute for accomplishment.

+ For what is an organization's member accountable?

+ Outcomes that are not necessary will occur at random.

+ How does your organization need to be capacitated?

+ The logic of the real world is the logic to be accommodated.

+ There are people's promises. And then there are people.

+ The leader's tools are like the artist's tools.

+ A role description for a reader of this book would look like what?

+ Virtuosity is measurable only under adversity.

+ Being accountable requires being competent. Being competent assumes being accountable.

Chapter 15

More Tools

More tools. Even though we have to deal with them sequentially, they are all equally important. Different circumstances call for different tools, the right one for those circumstances being, for that purpose, the most important one. What is most important is that you have the right tools in your toolbox.

A role description has three parts: (1) the Role Description proper, which describes as best as possible what a virtuoso in that role would be able to accomplish under adversity; (2) a provisional set of Performance Goals, which sets forth short-term and mid-term performance objectives, objectively measurable, and on a time-line; and (3) a Learning Plan, which addresses the incumbent's shortfalls with respect to the achievement either of the Role Description or one or more of the Performance Goals.

Performance Goals

Every role in the organization has to have a set of performance goals; from that of the organization itself through to every division, department, team, project, and individual. Where do these P/Gs come from?

1. From the needs and interests of the organization.
Real achievement – like making a high-performance organization – requires that the organization out-perform the best, especially competitors. This is not bench-marking. Doing that assures that you will be more or less average, since everyone else is using that as a standard. Instead, knowing what and where the best performances

have ever been, and beating those in significant ways, is what you need. This means that the organization has to be better than any other(s) at everything that matters (contrary to Crawford & Mathews, *The Myth of Excellence*).

These, translated and divvied-up, will provide the minimum set of P/Gs for the various parts of the organization. These need to be distributed appropriately and strategically to one or another of the organization's operating entities. If each role delivers to the P/Gs thus distributed, the organization will then achieve its overall P/Gs. Added up, the performance goals of each part and each person in the organization will produce the P/Gs of the whole organization. Every player on a football team has a specific role to play, with specific P/Gs. If they all deliver, that play will be run successfully.

P/Gs may be mildly financial, just because that's the easiest thing to measure. But they work best when the *drivers* of the bottom line are identified and used as the locus of performance measurement. For example, increasing competence counts for more in the long run than increasing revenues.

2. A second source of Performance Goals are the specific requirements of the sub-unit of the organization. Like the organization itself, every part of it must outperform its counterpart at least among its competitors and comparable organizations generally. So those are added to that part of the organization's P/Gs it now owns.

3. From the explicit or implicit accomplishments designed into every individual role description. Every person who has a role in the organization must minimally outperform his or her counterparts in the competitors' organizations. The organization competes, every component competes, every person competes – to outperform all others. P/Gs are there to make clear the criteria on which all others are to be bested.

4. From your wildest hopes and dreams. What does
it take to outperform all others? Coaches know. And
they establish performance goals to be surpassed,
both individually and collectively, until those levels of
performance become habitual. Then you are prepared.
Until tomorrow, when you raise the bar, because
yesterday's performance will *always* enable another high-
performance organization (or person) to out-perform
you. This is not a resurrection of the once-fashionable
Management by Objectives. Performance goals are not
management, but *performance*, tools.

The **purpose** of performance goals is to develop throughout
the organization the *capacity* to devise viable *plans* for meeting
specific goals. Implicitly, the purpose of P/Gs is to make *necessary*
the *development* of all of the human and other *resources* required
to carry out the plans devised to achieve them. Achieving those
goals is obviously vital to the existence and the future health of
the organization. But even more important over time is developing
the internal capabilities of the organization for devising and
carrying through plans for achieving objectively measurable goals
on a time-line, no matter what gets in the way. Making plans and
then executing them is where an organization's inner strength
comes from.

The ultimate achievement here is the full capability and
readiness to achieve goals, no matter what happens. This process
will never work perfectly. And no one controls the final outcome.
But the ownership of planning and execution throughout the
organization (not just at the top) is the key to real achievement.

Performance Goals are necessary to the present – to spell out
what's required – whether that is productivity, Return on Time,
margins, quality, customer care, or just plain competence. P/Gs
are necessary for preparedness. P/Gs are necessary to remind their
owners of what they might otherwise forget. P/Gs are necessary
for raising the level of performance at every touch point in the
organization, continuously.

P/Gs illuminate the path. What isn't owned won't be done. What isn't necessary and what doesn't have consequences won't be on the front burner. That's what great P/Gs are for.

Performance goals are relatively worthless –

- If they have no "teeth" in them. That is, if a viable plan and its implementation are not **necessary.** That is, if people don't believe there will be serious consequences for failure either to devise a plan or to carry it out, then they are no more than a bureaucratic exercise. A great tool abused.

- If they don't contribute mightily to getting you where you want to go. They may be perfect in some other sense. But the performance of P/Gs can only be measured by the contribution they make to the movement of the organization from what it is to what it is intended to be.

If the organization's role is its ultimate goal, then performance goals are all of the intermediate goals required to get there – daily, weekly, monthly, quarterly, annually. They represent all of the tactical plans throughout the organization for carrying out – measurably – the organization's role(s) and its mission in the world.

Learning Plans

Another tool. Every person in the organization who has a role must have a Learning Plan (an L/P). An L/P is a set of personal P/Gs that address a person's shortfalls – skills, conceptual skills, perceptual inadequacies, attitudes that hinder performance, follow-through orientations, habits, etc. – with respect to that person's Role Description and/or P/Gs. These need to be treated, by the person and his or her leader, merely as problems to be solved. Not as shortfalls of the *person*, but as specific shortfalls in that person's present *performance* or that person's preparedness for future *performance*.

For example, most of the errors that occur in the typical organization are a result either of shortfalls of competence, or of a failure to be totally attentive to what one is doing. People can change themselves to avoid either cause. A learning plan sets forth how, when, and what the measures of changed performance will be.

It may be a shortfall of understanding. Or of the mental or emotional wherewithal to perform at the level required. Or of sheer energy levels, or inhibiting habits. New hires have shortfalls. But so do CEOs and long-timers. A role without a learning plan is not as lofty or as demanding as it must be.

All this raises the question of assessing performance. Who does it? Both the person(s) involved and the leader. What's required in the way of performance is spelled out and agreed to in the R/Ds and P/Gs of the people involved. Since the measures of performance are objectively measurable and on a time-line, any shortfalls are as obvious to the incumbent as they are to his or her leader. All that's needed is some interpretation. They do this together. Who *owns* the problem then? The incumbent of the role who exhibited that shortfall.

N.B. Leaders ("bosses") are not there to pass judgment. They are there to help people continuously improve their performance in their role. So they have to function as coaches, to make self-leaders of their people. They are there, as all leaders are, to set impossible (to those people) goals, and then to help those people capacitate themselves to achieve those goals. The aim is the performance of the organization, not games of dinking around with the problems of the day, or of who's the smartest.

Thus the need for a learning plan, devised and implemented by the incumbent of the role and the P/Gs that accompany it. Don't aggregate the problem. Organizations can't learn. Only people can learn. Any real learning is a change in the person's ability to measurably perform his or her role. "Organizational Learning" is just pop hype.

There is such a thing as learning mode, as we have seen. It is the opposite of the knowing mode, where people compete to see whose opinion (usually derived from past "experience") wins. Both are matters of habit. There are habits of performance. And then there are habits that lead in the direction of shortfalls. A person in the learning mode is a person who is looking diligently and continuously for ways of improving his or her performance in his/her role.

People in the knowing mode assume they already know what they need to know – and their performance deteriorates over time until it becomes inadequate.

So, what the Learning Plan says, implicitly, is "get thee into the learning mode."

Being in the learning mode is always the key driver for raising performance to the next, and then the next, level.

Since the way *you think* is the indispensable tool, you might want to keep in mind that –

- Most people are lazy, quite self-satisfied, and in their comfort zone where their everyday performance is concerned.
- Most people are not going to be diligent about the hard work and effort required to improve their performance at anything except perhaps their hobbies or other leisure time activities.
- If they don't have to change for the better, they won't.
- Improving performance is the only kind of change that matters in the long term.
- What people and organizations don't get better at, they will be bested at.
- Learning is *the producer of growth and hence of real life*, and the more such real life an organization has in it, the more formidable its performance will be.

Measures (or "Metrics")

You're familiar with the old saw, "What gets counted gets done." This is intended to suggest that people and organizations will do what gets counted. Revenues are counted, and thus are deemed very important, even though they may not be achieved. If you go to school or have a job, attendance may be counted, and punishments or rewards are handed out for attendance or the lack thereof. So what gets counted does not necessarily drive *achievement*. It merely makes clear what is considered important by the society or by the teacher or the boss.

We pay attention to what gets measured. But any organization may be measuring the wrong things.

There's also the old saw, "What is counted is not necessarily what counts." So it seems to have been long understood that counting begins with what is easy or conventional to count. But what we count may not be the most important things we need to pay attention to.

Accountants count what is typically counted. But what they count may not account for what most needs counting.

As a good example: We count certain things (like income and expenses) to arrive at a bottom line, which we take to be a good measure of the economic health of an organization. That it may be. But what you are counting here is a byproduct of other things that may be more important if you want to enhance the performance of the organization. The bottom line does not drive performance. It is a thin, historical (rear-view mirror) measure of past performance. What gets ignored is what *drives* the bottom line.

Competence, for example. What accountant measures *that*? Or zeal. It affects the bottom line significantly. Is it measured? Or simply doing what one has signed up to do. Who measures *that*? Which comes first in the typical organization – performance or paycheck? Are you counting what drives *performance* in order to get more of it?

Or are you counting dollars, assuming that by counting dollars we'll get more of them?

Can you get better outcomes merely by measuring outcomes? Or do you need to measure the performance of the organization by measuring the performance (and the readiness or preparedness) of each of its components?

The destiny of the organization is determined at every moment of every day by how competently people perform in their roles. (Assuming, of course, that the right roles have been conceived and the Role Descriptions comprehensively identify those competencies.) Many try to see what is going on through certain financial and other reports prepared *after the fact* by those who are going through the motions, who are engaged in activities, not accomplishments, and often are themselves deeply in the knowing mode.

But it isn't these after-the-fact reports that make a difference in the performance of the organization. It is:

- How masterful people are in their roles (which is measured by where they are on the learning curve of their role descriptions).
- How diligently and creatively they are implementing their plans for achieving the goals set forth in their performance goals.
- How competently and creatively everyone in the organization is dealing with the shortfalls and problems that emerge.
- How much intelligent *zeal* there is behind the pursuit of real accomplishments.
- How adequate the systems are for pushing and pulling real achievement.

These are what drive the bottom line. They are therefore what most needs counting. Measure everywhere the *performance* you need to get you to where you intend to go. If you do, the bottom line will take care of itself. It is the *result*, not the *cause*, of performance.

Decide what's needed, put that into the role descriptions and performance goals, and then measure (objectively) progress and performance. Simple and obvious.

Maybe that's why it is so rarely done to great effect. More to reflect upon:

- Without measurement, there is no accountability.
- Goals that are not achieved by plan will be achieved only by accident.

Problems

It may seem odd to consider "problems" as tools. But they can be.

It may be that you are given the problems you confront in order to learn what *your* shortfalls or inadequacies may be (this is old wisdom). You live in a pop culture where it is most often assumed that problems are "out there," independent of you. That may not be the best perspective to take if you intend to be a leader, if you intend to be instrumental in the pursuit of real achievement. We continue to try to make the world acquiesce to our egocentricities. It can be done. But building a huge dam is not the same kind of accomplishment as making a great organization. The concrete does not need to collaborate with the engineer. Great organizations, by contrast, require widely distributed and decentralized ownership of the performance of each of its many parts.

So a *problem* can best be enlisted to tell us what's wrong with us – not what's wrong with the economy or with the technical details of the product. If you can learn from your problems how you need to change, you will move ahead. If you can't, those problems will become a recurring part of your environment.

The price of not seeing problems as mirrors, as telling us more about ourselves than they do about our environment, is one that we pay over and over again as new problems arise from the old ones. (We see this everywhere. Look at medicine, or at the legal system.)

So the leader sees problems as challenges to his or her growth and development. Great leaders see problems as a tool for making himself or herself a better leader, and thus a tool for enabling the organization to learn what is required to better perform.

- A "problem" can be a turn-off or a turn-on. That's the "mirror" part.
- If it is a turn-off, nothing much ever changes and the same old problems return again and again.
- If it is a turn-on, what we get turned-on to is our own faulty perceptions, ineptness, and incompetencies. Fixing those provides great ROI.
- That's what problems can tell you if you let them. Leaders let them.

- There is no performance of any role that could not
  be improved upon every day forever, if the problems
  encountered are seized upon as tools of changing ...
  of improving ... the performance of every role.

Composing Organizations

How the organization is "composed," how it is invented
and engineered, is another tool for altering, in this case for
optimizing, its performance. This is accomplished by optimizing
the performance of all of its parts as they work in concert with
themselves and with each other.

"Structure" is far too wimpy a word for this purpose. It is
much more like composing a symphony that will be dramatically
unfolded by its virtuoso players than it is like a building or a bridge
or even a spaceship. There is a "score." The score exists in all of
the plans of the role incumbents to achieve their performance goals.
But it is only in concert with all of the players that the overall
effect is achieved. The score helps to keep everyone on the same
page. Competence in role moves in two directions. The first is the
performer's mastery of his or her role. The second is the competent
performer's ability to listen at the same time to all of the other
players, and to contribute as much to those others' performances as
they contribute to their own.

And all of this while the concert is in progress. And what is
the conductor (the leader) doing all of this time? First of all, he or
she is the only virtuoso on stage who is in a position to determine
what the whole thing *should* sound like – the performance of the
whole and how the audience experiences it. And he or she is the
only virtuoso on stage on whom all the others depend to influence
their individual performances for optimizing the performance of the
whole. In other words, he or she leads them from where they are to
where they ought to be.

This is but a metaphor. The more you appreciate its
implications for yourself and your organization, the more value it
has. You have to compose the organization. This means determining
in advance how it is supposed to work (how it gets from here to

there through the masterful performance of people in each of their roles). Note that there are as many symphonies as there are great composers. And there are as many different performances as there are great conductors and great orchestras. How you compose the organization will always be less important than how well it can be made to perform. The design of the organization does not by itself drive performance.

What this means is provocative. It means that a great orchestra can make a poor score sound good. A mediocre orchestra can make a great score sound mediocre or worse. There is always this underlying interdependence.

The best of all possible organization designs will not work with incompetent performers in *any* role. A conventional organization design can be made to perform exceedingly well if there are outstanding performers in every role.

So we're back to the original logic. If you want a high-performance organization, you have to have people in every role who are on the path to becoming the best in the business in their role. If you want top performance out of the virtuosos in every role, you have to design the organization in such a way that it is *possible* for them to perform at an optimum level, and that it is also *necessary* that they do so. You cannot get optimum performance without leveraging both at the same time. *Possible* is, as you know, a function of competence and of "smart" systems – the kind that enable optimum performance on the part of really competent people. And *necessary* is. as you know, a function of habits of high performance coupled with the demands of the role.

In addition: In the same way that the best symphony performances will emerge in response to the best audiences and the best competition, the performance of your organization will always depend upon how good your suppliers are and how good your competitors are. (Good here refers to performance, not likeability – to demanding-ness, not comfort.) So you always have a vested interest in whether they contribute to your laziness and complacency, or whether their own aims keep you continuously challenged (in the right direction, of course).

So you have to fit and compose your organization to the circumstances of the existing marketplaces and other conditions of all of your stakeholders. If the labor market is tight, design to it. Do what you have to do to overcome that constraint in the pursuit of your own aims. Don't just talk about it. If it enhances *their* performance, design around or even *into* your customers and/or suppliers. If market or technological intelligence is critical, design for it.

If you want to be different, design differently. Fashions in organization design come and go. You may be tempted. Don't be. No one has your particular cause, or your players. No one else has *you*. Design to where you want to get to, not to what is fashionable. What is fashionable is conventional. And no conventional design will provide you with a competitive advantage.

- Composers hear the performance internally and then write the score.
- What would the score look like that would get you to the performance required by your organization's role?
- What is your role as leader before, during, and after your organization's moments of truth?

Smart Systems

In an earlier chapter, we explored "dumb systems" as one of the obstacles/barriers to high performance, to real achievement. "Smart systems," the other end of the continuum, are tools for enhancing and elevating the performance of the organization.

It has long been known to field generals that the advantage always falls to the organization having the best information systems and the timeliest information. It isn't that information in and of itself improves performance It does not. It isn't that technology in and of itself improves performance. It does not. There is no substitute for competence.

There is no substitute for great goals, zealously pursued. There is no substitute for an organization that works the way it needs to work in order to outperform all others.

There is no substitute for the right design. There is no substitute for leadership. There is no substitute for systems – technological, cultural, and mandated – that function to make consistently outstanding performance possible, and *necessary*.

Smart systems provide the intelligence infrastructure for what has to be accomplished. Smart people who are masterful in their roles can make good use of smart systems, as we have seen. Inadequate or marginally competent people will only be enslaved by them.

Smart systems make it possible for people who are already masterful (in their roles and in the hand-offs between and among roles) to see relevant facts more quickly, or more meaningfully, than they would otherwise – to see and/or "hear" the slightest discrepancies between what is happening and what needs to be happening. A smart system enables you to look at what is going on from different perspectives, in different combinations, along different trend lines or time frames. A smart system enables you to simulate various scenarios, to assess different outcomes of a different mix of actions. A smart system enhances your grasp of what is going on and what you might do about it by providing you with the intelligence you need – whether or not you knew you needed it.

Data-basing and shuffling information around is a game IT people play. But if the system isn't smart, which most are not, it isn't going to help you very much. What you can't do without conventional "information" systems, you generally can't do with them. Smart systems are designed to underwrite the *role descriptions* and the *performance goals* that constitute the current operating fabric of the organization. They do not provide performers with what's available. They provide the intelligence and the perspectives those people *need* in order to fulfill their roles, and to exceed their performance goals, while providing synergy with other roles, and vice versa.

Smart systems are just now on the horizon. They are not an extension of your average IT. They are a paradigm or two removed. But neither are high-performance organizations merely an extension of mediocre ones. They are a paradigm or two beyond.

You can't devise smart systems apart from having a cause that cannot be achieved without them.

Here are some other considerations:

- *If* you know exactly what you want to accomplish and you have a compelling plan for getting there, the intelligence systems by which you determine where you are and what needs to be done will be apparent.
- If you don't, you'll have to be content with the conventional information technology that you can afford, promising much but delivering little.
- Why? Because mediocre performers are content with mediocre systems. They're used to them.
- And because smart tools cannot be designed by people who are not themselves top performers.
- No tool is better than its user, including the tools used by IT designers to design systems for your use.
- No matter how much you pay or where you get it, you will never be able to import something that can compensate for marginal competence.
- The higher the level of the role, the more valid this is.
- By and large, government regulations are not designed to contribute to enhanced performance. Neither are most information systems.

Consider the average retail clerk, held up and down and all around by various systems. Could the average person potentially do all of these –

1. Know where all of the merchandise is, including colors, sizes, sources, uses, related items, etc., etc.?
2. Know how to order and stock and do all of the paperwork (or electronic entries) required?
3. Know how to display and market the goods, including upselling?
4. Actually be able to deal with customers and to help customers solve their problems?
5. Astonish everyone down line with their performance?

The answer is … absolutely.

So could the average manufacturing or commercial employee. But most systems are designed for people who are no better than marginally competent. And now we're stuck with people who can't or won't perform because the systems they use will not permit them to be anything more than marginally competent. Their jobs require a few minimal *activities*. The *accomplishments* are presumably to be provided by the system – or by the manager.

One more example, of a different kind of system. We pay certain people (salespeople in some businesses) to do their job, and then we reward them with a commission or a bonus for doing what they signed on to do. Similarly, we've come to pay chief executives an astronomical level of compensation, and if they fail or get sticky fingers, pay them more for leaving than for staying.

Those strike me as being *dumb* systems.

Any way of doing things in an organization, if it becomes MO (the way things are done because they're done that way) engenders a *system* by which things are done. The *system* is now in charge. People can't grow in competence and performance if they are working for the system. The system should be working for them.

But this can happen only if it is **necessary** for people to capacitate themselves to be the best in the business in the role they are in.

To sum up:
- The systems that enable every role and connect all of the working parts of your organization can be dumb … or smart.
- The systems that interconnect your organization with its customers, suppliers, and other stakeholders can be dumb … or smart.
- The systems you put in place for measuring, for compensation, for rewards and punishments, can be dumb … or smart.
- A system is smart if it is measurably moving you from where you are to where you want to be. If it isn't, it's a dumb system.

Your call.

POINTS TO PONDER

+ What makes the three parts of the role description different "tools"?

+ In a changing world, role descriptions are forever provisional.

+ The P/Gs throughout the organization should exceed the P/Gs of the organization.

+ Where performance is concerned, you either get better or you get worse. There is no status quo in a high-performance organization.

+ Which of the 4 sources of P/Gs is most important?

+ It is the plans for achieving P/Gs, and how well executed they are that underwrites future performance, not the outcomes.

+ There is no "learning organization" unless everyone has a learning plan with "teeth" in it.

+ If people don't have to get better, most won't.

+ What's important, not what's convenient, has to be measured.

+ A problem is a tool. So is how the organization is designed a tool.

+ A smart system is a valuable tool only if the other tools have been made to do their work.

Chapter 16 More - Power - Tools

They're all "power" tools, of course – when used by a powerful person in just the right situation in the most powerful way. What makes them powerful is the level of mastery with which they are understood and employed. It is not even necessary to be able to talk about them. To make them work for you because you are so good at putting them to good use at just the right time, in the right way – that's the measure of their worth in your thinking and in your *performance* as leader.

The leadership tools that follow by no means exhaust the list of tools you need in your toolbox. One is more important than another *only* because that's what the situation calls for. Some are more universal than others, that is, some may be more pertinent than others to most or all situations.

For example –

Communication

We're revisiting here, but doing so in order to make some different, highly valuable, observations on this most fundamental of all subjects. If you get involved with yourself or others about anything whatsoever, you're awash in the process and the products of communication.

- It's difficult to live with the facts, even though you know what they are. Fact: there is not a world out there which you and I perceive more or less as it is. What we make of that world, and how that world grasps and informs us, always depends on the workings of our own minds, *on how we interpret it.*

- The way you perceive and interpret the world depends upon the meanings you *have* to give to it. What you "see" and how you think about it is both enabled and constrained by what you have to do so with – your own mind.

- What you say or do is interpreted by others, in the same way that what they say or do is interpreted by you. Whatever something means is a product of someone's mind.

- Try as you will, there's no way around all of this.

That's the crux of communication.

But there are lessons here that are not so obvious, lessons of immense practical value.

1. With what we've got to do it with, you and I have to build up a *picture* of the way things are and the way they work. There are no *theories* in the world apart from us. All those are ours, imposed upon the world we see it, and as we understand it.

2. Like all the rest of us, you observe, you take account of what certain others say or do, and you yourself say stuff and do stuff. All this has to be interpreted by you and others. We deal with the meanings of things – which are human inventions. Meanings are all human minds can deal with.

That's a given. What is not given is what it is we need to know in order to avoid predators, to find or avoid a mate, to find food, and when and where it's safe to sleep. These are all metaphors of real practical value to any leader. Competition, alliances, margins, and financial security: everything depends upon how you take the world into account. All the rest of it hinges on that. That's the *thinking* part of it. From that comes who we *are*, and how we do what we do.

3. We believe that communication is mostly about telling ourselves and other people stuff. It's far more about the quality of the intelligence we can provide to ourselves about the world we want to maneuver in.

4. You can't pay attention to the world when you're talking. The opportunity costs are huge and play out way into the future. That's why the most useful form of communication begins with a question.

5. There is no safety in numbers. Large numbers of people have *always* been wrong, in science as well as in popular delusions. That's the lesson of history. Neither the number nor the celebrity of people who believe something has ever obligated the world to conform. "Truth" cannot be trumped by any humans you know. It is what it is. It does not communicate itself to us. Nor can we communicate it. Whatever is meaningful is made so by humans.

6. So you have to pick the people who inform you carefully, beginning with yourself. Communication is indifferent to the outcome. It can as readily sink you as save you.

Remember the bit about a tool not being any better than the person who wields it? Here we have the fundamental example. No communication is any better than the person who engages in it. Just because you believe what people tell you does not make it true. By listening to the wrong people, you may fail at any endeavor you might undertake – from life to leadership. An organization that fails is not one that has "financial problems." It is one that didn't have the right interpretations about *what mattered* in the world in which it operated. It was first about communication.

The financial part is a result of poor or inadequate communication. The organization didn't know what it needed to know in order to survive and thrive. Leaders succeed or fail for the same reason.

The tool here is to be especially skeptical of all *you* know, and to be at least skeptical of what others say – especially if what they say is easy for you to believe.

Here are some thought-prodders about the (communication) infrastructure of all things human:

- The snake in the Garden of Eden was not in the tree. It was in Eve's mind. She was talking to herself.
- This "snake" that misleads us still exists, for all of us.
- To know something requires you to assume you know it because it is true. No assumption gets to be true just because you believe it.
- *Consequences* are the reality of what takes the measure of any belief or assumption.

Truth is a red herring. That's never the real issue. The real issue is where you are taken by what you know. Not whether it is true or not. Every leader is saved by this realization. What are the consequences if you believe what someone says to you? What are the consequences if you interpret what is going on this way or that way? What are the consequences if you listen to yourself?

The tool here is *how not to be* **duped**. Ultimately, you can only be duped by yourself. And you can limit that. In any struggle between doubt and certainty, cast your lot with doubt and then proceed with certainty, rather than the other way around.

Leader's lesson

The only test of how valid your (or others') view of the world may be will come only with the consequences. Tough, but pragmatic. As follows:

- Communication is only academically (and thus trivially) about content. It is mainly about the consequences.
- Your mind is your master tool. It mediates the world for you whether "inputting," "outputting," or just talking to yourself. Get your thinking right and the rest will follow, leaders say.

Questions

Questions are the most powerful tools you could employ. Asking just the right question at just the right time in just the right way of just the right source will serve you better than anything else

270

you can do. A virtuoso question-asker can generate more pertinent intelligence in just a few minutes than a person of little curiosity, with comfortable certainty, can generate in days, weeks, or years. That's why great leaders are great question-askers, a key lesson most people are too lazy and too full of themselves to learn how to do.

Other lessons for leaders?
- Whether valid or not, most people will not divulge their candid perceptions if they imagine revealing those might jeopardize their interests (usually status quo or interpersonal politics).
- A good and potent question always trumps present understanding.
- Given a choice, great leaders will choose a potent question over a comfortable statement of fact, especially when they are talking to themselves.
- Most managers make four statements to every question they ask. Leaders ask four questions to every statement they make.
- Defeat or failure can almost always be traced to a question not asked.
- Being smart in the real world is not measured by how much you know, but the rate at which you can learn by asking the right questions.
- Not being able to figure out what question to ask is like not being able to figure out what key to strike next when playing the piano. Think about it.
- It is not mainly what you don't know that can thwart your endeavors. It is what you know that just ain't so.
- Leader, lead thyself. (By, perhaps, asking some questions?)

Communication *SYSTEMS*

Don't confuse any of that with communication *systems*.

A communication *system* is what connects or networks people. It can simply evolve from frequent use, or it can be engineered. A communication system that connects people who think alike will ensure that they do not change unless they change together. The glue that holds them together is that they want to go on being who they are, and they want the others to go on being who *they* are. They will share fashions of being, doing, saying, knowing, and having – collectively (which is the only safe way). Belonging to any communication *system*, from love affairs to occupations, will influence you in ways that endorse your membership in that system.

Managers converse most easily with other managers, assemblers with other assemblers, secretaries with other secretaries, engineers with other engineers. People can't talk shop, even if it's only television fare, with other people whose worlds do not overlap theirs (whose minds are not similarly furnished).

More to think about:

- Communication always takes the path of least resistance. The more used communication channels are, the more they are likely to be used. Observe your own patterns.
- Politicking thrives as a driver of all communication systems. Gossip always has political undertones.
- Communication is readily used as the primary means of maneuvering and manipulating. Everyone is a victim of whatever is going on in *any* communication *system*. *Meetings*, for example, are quasi-impromptu theater. The only way to know the plot is to participate in developing it. Otherwise, you will be no more than a spectator.

Meetings are also ad hoc communication systems. The reason they are so notoriously inefficient and unproductive is that the participants usually have their own agendas, and none of those is the agenda for the group as a whole.

Meetings over coffee or over a beer work better. That's because there is no official agenda. It's only when the participants are regular members of the same communication system that meetings work as well as they do. If a meeting is not required because people talk to each other productively all the time anyway, meetings might then be modestly productive.

The communication systems that interconnect an organization with its stakeholders (e.g., customers, suppliers, etc.) are fraught with difficulties. The way customer behavior is interpreted, for example, is created more in the internal conversations about that customer than by anything that occurs in communication *with* that customer.. Did you ever notice that the image flight attendants have of passengers never seems to fit *you*?

Or that the image passengers have of flight attendants is a matter of indifference to those folks, who are busy talking to each other in order to maintain their shared stereotypes of the passengers, and the passengers are doing the same with respect to their shared stereotypes of the flight attendants?

Perceptions and beliefs about customers, for example, are not created by what customers do or do not do, but by what we *say* about what they do or do not do. Most basic ideas, attitudes, stereotypes, etc., that people take for granted are actually products of the communication system(s) they belong to. That's why it is so difficult to change people. They're going to be the way they are as a result of the communication systems they participate in. So you have to change or modify those systems.

Consider further:

- A communication system is a system. It can be dumb or smart.
- Smart communication systems are a prerequisite to preparedness and of exceptional performance anywhere in the organization.
- Leaders who can create and engineer smart systems *for themselves* might therefore be competent to design smart communication systems throughout the organization.
- Those who can't create smart communication systems for themselves will bring their faulty communication systems to bear on all the rest of the organization.

So what are the keys to designing smart communication systems?

- Competent people in every role. They will make it happen.

- All any leader has are interpretations (explanations, descriptions, etc.) – whether his own or those of others, or some combination of both.
- Everything has to be interpreted in terms of *something*.
- The tool? Interpret *everything* in terms of your goals.
- Make it possible *and* necessary for everyone around you to do the same. Smart systems are built that way.

Doing More With Less

You've heard much in recent years about getting "lean" – lean manufacturing, lean thinking, you know the drill. If you've done your homework, you also recognize that most of all that un-lean outpouring is merely old wine in new bottles. The idea of doing more with less has been around literally forever. Henry Ford could outdo any of the lean authors. So could the 18th-century industrial innovator Robert Owen. And every medieval craftsman understood lean.

You don't need an elaborate corporate program for pushing and pulling the idea of doing more with less. You have to practice it yourself, and preach it. Get more done with less talk. Accomplish more in less time. Reward people who accomplish what needs accomplishing with the tools and resources at hand (bricoleurs). If you reward people on the basis of how big their empire is, that's what you'll get – more people accomplishing less.

There's a bit of logic here worth thinking about. The more you divide up tasks (once known as division of labor), the more coordination is required. Costs increase exponentially, simply because coordinating things is always more expensive than the cost of doing those things themselves.

Doing more with less is about three things:

1. Continuously elevating and enlarging the competencies of every person in every role in the organization.
2. Making it *necessary* for every person to measurably enhance the performance of everyone above, below, and each side of them.

274

3. Recognizing and rewarding those people who make themselves wholly dispensable by getting their roles performed so well without them they are no longer needed. Give these people tenure and a little time to find some other role they would like to take on. Then you win twice. So do they.

Lean is about eliminating waste. The two greatest sources of waste in the typical organization are those of wasting people, and wasting time by talking too much. Talking about something is not the same thing as doing it. And the cost of talk is typically the most significant hidden cost in any organization.

Yes, you can take out all of the non-value-added activities. But competent people will do this for you because they won't put up with it. Competent people know *you* represent overhead. They know that eliminating overhead is fundamental to doing more with less. Are they willing, through their own efforts, to cover your compensation and perks? If not, you're not the leader they need and want.

Doing more with less starts at the top. If you are in it to amass material goods and the glitziest new things for yourself – from cars to management panaceas – you've set the tone.

To ponder:

• If you don't play it that way, then it likely won't get played that way elsewhere in the organization, from the top down.

• How many people does it take to get your role accomplished? How many hours a week? With how much in the way of resources?

• Think about it. But only to the ends of accomplishing more with less.

Here, some practical tips about doing more with less:

• Want your organization to be more effective? Tell people to stop talking about it and go do what needs to be done.

- Want to save some money? Cut the number and the length of meetings by 50%.
- Observe the increase in productivity and cut them in half again.
- Tell people to engage their minds before engaging in *any* communication. If they haven't got what it takes to get engaged, fix that first.
- The aim of communication needs to be thought of in terms of its consequences. People who don't know what these should be are wasting everyone else's time. Sunk costs.
- Forty to sixty per cent of the operating costs of the average organization are the costs of communication. Begin trimming costs in your own office first?
- The next time someone tells you how much things are going to improve by adding people or a computer program, let him bet his job on it. He's asking the organization to bet on it.

The effectiveness of a telephone conversation is usually inversely related to the time spent on it. E-mail? That's a place where people who can't communicate go into hiding to hassle other people who are also likely to believe that computers improve their mental capabilities.

The more masterful people are at what they do, the less they waste time, effort, materials, or other people's lives.

- Start there.
- And don't waste time looking for substitutes.
- There aren't any that are even 10% as good.

Words

Let's try some more with less here. Just to show ourselves and the rest of the world that we can do it.

Some lessons:

- Words (or any other form of mental representation) are the tools of thought.

- If you think it a bit odd to look at words as tools, try doing anything without them.
- The right word in the wrong place is a waste. The wrong word is always waste.
- People without the right words waste themselves and others. Look no further than your own experience.
- As tools, words are no better than the person who sends them or receives them.
- People who don't have the words to influence others when it would advantage the performance of those others or the organization are a part of the waste.
- People who are not capable of being influenced when that would advantage their performance or the performance of the organization need to be fixed, or replaced.
- Not having the right tools in your toolbox when you need them = wasted opportunity.
- People who speak or listen only in clichés lay to waste everything they encounter. You could be guilty of that. Or those around you could be.

Power

Power is an indispensable tool. If you don't have power over yourself, you can't make much on purpose of the raw material that is you. That's a waste of the raw material. If you don't have power in the eyes of others, they'll conclude they could waste their time and effort in better places. If you don't have the power, ultimately, to make happen what has to happen, it's unlikely to happen.

Power isn't something you came with. It's given to you by others. If you don't use it for the reasons they granted it to you, or if you can't change their thinking about what it's for, it will evaporate. Power is as power does. If you intend to change the order of things, you have to have the power to do so. Those changes will ultimately be determined as for the good, or the bad. That's a value thing. But power is not. It is simply a necessary thing.

As a tool, power can be no better than the person who wields it. So, it's what you accomplish together that counts. A carpenter builds a great or a shoddy house depending on how competent he is at making use of the tools at his disposal. The same with leaders. They can build great or shoddy organizations depending upon how competent they are at making use of the tools in their toolbox. Especially their power, which is always provisional. The power of the tool in the carpenter's hands is a function of how capable he is of wielding it to make something worthwhile.

Power is amoral. Leadership is not.

You have to know when to use it, and how. The best use of power lies in influencing the world (and the people in it) so you don't have to use it. The nail knows the kind of power the carpenter has. So the carpenter never has to talk about it – never has to threaten the nail with it in order to get the nail to do its job.

Here's the bottom line:

- Leaders are frugal. They seek no more power than they need. But they do not attempt great achievements without the power needed to achieve them.
- The path to real achievement can make huge demands on power, especially will-power. And on the kind of power required to seduce others to your cause.
- If you haven't got the power to see it through, get that first.
- How do you measure your power? By how far you and your people will go to transform your mission into reality.

Just a couple of thought-prodders for their power to provoke:

- For most people over history, it has been powerful gods who have been behind both permanence and change in the world.
- Having abandoned that explanation, we now look to our leaders to provide what was once provided by the gods.
- Without the power of that expectation on their part, you can't make it happen.

278

Dissatisfaction

Without dissatisfaction, there is no change. Without dissatisfaction with the present, given some imagined future, there will be no significant change. People don't undertake significant change unless they feel the necessity to do so. And that necessity will come from some level of dissatisfaction with their present state.

When Henry V addressed his troops at Agincourt, he created an imagined end to the day that was far different from what appeared to be certain: annihilation by the overwhelming numbers of French and their weapons. When Columbus addressed the mutineers on the voyage to a new land which no one (including Columbus) was certain could be reached, he played upon the uncertainties of their position. If they journeyed on, they *might* all die for lack of food or water; but if they turned back, it was certain they would all die. When Joshua Lawrence Chamberlain addressed the Union deserters he was to guard, he gave them a reason for fighting on, making their present situation a source of dissatisfaction. It isn't enough to paint a compelling picture of the future.

You have to make people dissatisfied with their present circumstances. As I'm sure you know, most commercial advertising is based on just those premises. Followers want someone who will take away their dissatisfaction with things as they are. Leaders make certain they first have those dissatisfactions.

The leader may even have to create that sense of dissatisfaction. Or it may already exist. Either way, the leader's mission is to take people out of their dissatisfactions with the present state of things to a world that promises to be far more satisfying to them.

Summarizing:

- If you are not driven by your dissatisfaction with the present state of things, There is little hope that you will ever be called to lead anything.

- If your would-be followers are not dissatisfied enough to put up with the ordeal of change and to bring to bear the efforts required for achieving some other conditions of life, you won't have followers.

- The whole process is not a rational one. It is an emotional one. You have to lead with your – and your followers' – feelings.
- There is a leap of faith required. People have to be seriously dissatisfied to make that leap in your direction.

Seductiveness

Attention-grabbing term. All it means is that all leaders are "seductive" – that is, that there is something about who they are that captures the imagination and fires the hearts of those who would be followers. The bigger the leap of faith required, and the more uncertain or difficult the path ahead with the leader seems to be, the more the would-be followers have to be seduced by how that leader *thinks*, who he *is*, and how he *does* what he does, all of which is a measure of his or her seductiveness.

Seduction always involves complicity and/or collaboration. This is the leader's aim: to gain the voluntary commitment of others. When Martin Luther King, Jr. was speaking so eloquently of his "dream," he was aiming to seduce his listeners to a cause he believed to be a just cause. This is what all leaders do.

If you do not have the stomach for or the skills for seducing others to your cause, there will be no cause, there will be no leader, and happenstance will rule.

More on this ever-fascinating tool:

- Leaders are seducers. They have been seduced by their cause. For there to be such a cause for others, they have to be seduced – by it, by you, or both.
- The problem is not that there are seducers. Always have been, always will be. The problem is, whose ideas ought you to be seduced by? The problem is, are the potential leaders who would be good for you the ones who have the most potent skills for seducing you? Or, coming at it the other way around, are those who can readily seduce you good for you?

- A variation on the old saw, "Lead, follow, or get out of the way" – "Seduce and be burdened with followers, be seduced and suffer the consequences, or get out of the way!"

Those are the tools.

Unreasonableness

Being addicted to his or her cause, the leader has no choice but to be unreasonable. People who have never been *had by* a cause will perceive that leader as being unreasonable. They would be using the wrong criteria. To a person who has to achieve his or her aim, whatever has to be done is reasonable, no matter how unreasonable that may appear to aimless people.

All great leaders have been *capable* of great wrath. That may be the tool that gets the key message across – you are either with me or against me. There is no neutral position.

A compelling corollary: If you don't kill complacency, it will kill you and your cause.

 Think about it.

Those who intend to be leaders will be unreasonable about incompetence, about laziness, about indifference, about self-absorption, about dereliction of duty, about carelessness and waste, about negativity, about analysis-paralysis, about stupidity, about lack of attention or zeal, about sycophancy or other forms of kissing-up, about politicking, about the inability to set goals and devise plans for achieving them, about duplicity, etc. Whatever doesn't contribute to the cause works against it. Compelling leaders are so unreasonable about immaturity and about lack of character that they do something unreasonable about it every day.

In other words:
- Real achievement requires unreasonableness.
- If you are not ruthless about what really matters, about what *will* you be ruthless?
- There is no change without unreasonableness (as G. B. Shaw said).

- If you are not as unreasonable as your adversaries, both within and outside your organization, you will be their victim.
- Having the "courage of your convictions" may mean being strategically unreasonable about them.

Reputation

There is who *you* imagine you are. And then there is who people *say* you are. As a tool, the crafting of your reputation can be just as important as your crafting of yourself.

Best example: If you have a reputation for being ruthless with respect to your cause and others' performance in their roles, then it's unlikely you will ever have to *be* ruthless. If there are things you don't like doing, or aren't very good at, then craft your reputation in such a way that *you* don't have to do it because your reputation (which always precedes you in the perceptions of others) has already done it for you.

As Gracian wrote:

> *"You must not only have certain characteristics to be an effective leader. You must be **seen** as having those characteristics."*

Some implications:
- Sharpen that tool diligently and daily.
- What you have to *be* in order to lead others in your cause exists in two places – in your eyes and in the eyes of your followers. It takes both.
- If you had to choose, your reputation will always be the better real-time tool.

Luck

Have we said enough about the role of luck in all human endeavors? If you actually picked your parents, then you probably don't need to think about luck. If you didn't, then you'll know that things turn out the way they do for reasons you cannot control. Whatever you want to call those other uncontrollable forces are what we are calling "luck" – just the throw of the dice.

Those who are not prepared cannot be lucky. They will be deemed unlucky. As Jean Cocteau once put it,

> *"We must believe in luck. For how else can we explain the success of those we don't like?"*

Leaders have long known, for example, that there is as much luck in not getting what you want as there is in getting what you want. So they are very prudent about taking credit – or blame – for outcomes which they cannot control. Stephen Leacock said,

> *"I am a great believer in luck, and the harder I work the more I have of it."*

That's what achievers think of luck. It's all of the hard work you put in to prepare yourself.

More to consider ...

- If you want to be seen as unlucky when things go badly for you, then when things go well you would have to attribute that to getting lucky, wouldn't you?
- If a person who cannot count finds a four-leaf clover, is that person lucky?
- Leaders make themselves an ally of luck.

We've let George Bernard Shaw into our arena before. Let's give him a shot at this one:

> *"People are always blaming their circumstances for what they are. I don't believe in circumstances. The people who get on in this world are the people who get up and look for the circumstances they want, and if they can't find them, make them."*

Leaders may fail. But they fail in an all-out attempt to accomplish something that has them "by the skin and the hair." They never fail by being victims of circumstances. Unacceptable. They succeed because they risk everything to avoid being merely victims. Victims *can't* succeed. That's why they believe their fate turns on luck. For the compelling leader, luck turns on taking their fate into their own hands. They are not caused. They *cause*.

Think, then, on these:

• The prepared mind is prepared for whatever happens.

• Great leaders, as we have seen, take the randomness out of events. The determination with which they pursue their cause deflects randomness.

There are of course many, many other tools. In fact, all of the particulars of your thinking are tools. They will serve you well. Or ill. Who you are is an ever-present tool. So, too, are others' images of you. And how *they* think. What you do not bring into alignment with your cause and the journey to it will bring obstacles to carrying it out. Then you would be dealing with the symptoms of a much deeper problem. If you don't fix that problem (usually consisting of failures of competence and of conscience) you will forever be plagued and harassed by the symptoms.

The ultimate tool, then, may be your capacity for distinguishing symptoms from their source, and your capacity for aligning all of those sources to your cause. For example, if you know how to make an organization that is actually *good* for people, people who want a higher quality of life and know what that requires of them will be attracted to your place. Great coaches don't need to spend nearly as much as poor ones on recruiting.

Great leadership provides its own self-fulfilling prophecy.

POINTS TO PONDER

+ Leaders are the arbiters of the meaning of things in an organization.

+ The "facts" you have to work with are interpretations.

+ The communication that matters most is how you gather and interpret what bears upon your performance and your cause.

+ How would you describe a "smart" communication system?

+ The inescapable measure of communication lies in its consequences.

+ Questions are the best tools you could have in your toolbox.

+ What questions would you ask to make it necessary for your people to communicate primarily (80/20) by questions?

+ Have you ever been exposed to a dumb communication system?

+ *Bricoleurs* are the ultimate "lean."

+ Communication is the best waster of time and money.

+ Which words are tools?

+ Power is amoral.

+ Reputation is a tool.

+ How can "luck" be a tool if who you are is a tool?

PART V

Codes, Values, Beliefs, & Stratagems

Wherever there have been people engaged in some mutual endeavor, there have been codes of conduct. Whenever any person today engages in any human activity, he or she is guided by a code of conduct, of which they may be blissfully unaware. But behavior is guided and channeled. And such codes of conduct, once internalized, serve that purpose.

In addition, the values and beliefs that comprise the core of who people are and how they think and feel also play a usually hidden, always tacit role. The leader who does not know how his or her own beliefs and values color what they see and what they say will be a victim of how others use those to resist and manipulate the leader.

The values and beliefs that are necessary for the pursuit of the leader's cause have to be in place: tacitly. Values and beliefs that are not a part of the people involved do not play a role. What you post on the walls of your place, no matter how elegantly framed, are merely words on the wall. They don't do anything.

Every leader needs to align these. In addition, there are a few core stratagems that need to be a part of how the leader thinks, who the leader is, and thus how the leader leads. That is what's ahead in the next three chapters.

Chapter 17 Codes of Conduct

Everyday behavior – at work or at play – is *all* guided, invented, carried out, and evaluated on the basis of *some* "code of conduct." What this means is that people have at least some vague, usually tacit, sense of *what* they are supposed to do in the situations they encounter. And the habits – which are well-worn codes of conduct – to drive what they take to be the appropriate behavior in those situations.

They have a similar set of assumptions about how others should be conducting themselves in those situations. When people, intentionally or not, venture outside of those understood codes of conduct, they will be misunderstood by others, be ostracized or chastised by others, or they may have a sense of shame or guilt at having breached what would have been appropriate behavior. Or all of these.

There are rules of engagement. Without such rules implicitly observed, human interaction would be chaotic. It wouldn't make any sense. You couldn't make sense of it. Thus such rules of conduct, which constitute a sort of internalized code, are fundamental to making sense of your own and others' behavior.

The important point here is that these implicit codes of conduct will take you *somewhere*. There have always been rather explicit codes of conduct for warriors like the Samurai, for military units, and for any organization that has a cause – like the Mafia or the Catholic Church.

The next most important point is that the codes of conduct most people in the modern world bring with them into your organization are highly unlikely to provide adequate support for what you are committed to accomplish.

Thus – and this is the crunch issue – you may have to formulate a code for the conduct of the people in your organization which *will* underwrite your cause and the journey required to pursue it.

But let's be clear. The codes of conduct that actually guide and inform people's behavior (and hence attitudes) are unrelated to anything you might have printed up and posted in conspicuous places on the walls at your place. The only codes that function are those that have been internalized by people. Only those that have become routine habits for people. The only code that makes a difference is the one that has become a part of who those people *are* – their *character.* You can pretend. But company policy is not at all the same thing as a code of conduct. People might obey rules imposed upon them. But their hearts and minds won't be in it.

It is when people live by a code of conduct that they have one. If they don't have the one they need, you have to inculcate it.

So the challenges to leaders are always these two:

1. How to formulate a code of conduct that, widely internalized, will be what is needed to get you where you want to go.

2. How to get that code of conduct widely and deeply internalized.

Here's How

First, there is no reason why you would want to concern yourself with a code of conduct at your place unless you are committed to achieving extraordinary performance. You can take people as they cross your threshold and devote much of your time to the problems that come from the fact that most people have no aim in life – "Whatever happens, happens." But if you do have that kind of commitment, then you will need to concern yourself with a code of conduct that may be necessary to underwrite the extraordinary performance required.

This is the idea behind the "Code of the Samurai," with which you are probably familiar. Any great achievement that requires the interdependent performances of many people has to be underwritten by a code of conduct. Orpheus – the only chamber orchestrate that has never had a "conductor" – would be an example. Why don't troops under fire break and run? Code of conduct. Why are some people diligent about their commitments? Code of conduct.

A code of conduct that has no consequences for shortfalls is not in fact a code that will make any difference to people. The consequences, whether applied by the person to himself or applied from outside, must be in keeping with the significance (to the mission) of the shortfall.

Second, the code of conduct you want to be internalized throughout your organization has to be evident and exemplified in every encounter people have with the leaders and executives in your organization – beginning with you. You have a operational code of conduct when anyone who visits your place could accurately infer what it consists of from the way every key person comports himself or herself. This is not Monkey see, monkey do. But if the top people can violate a code of conduct at will, then everyone else has an excuse for doing the same.

Third, you have to recruit and select people (or retain them, or not) according to how close their personal code of conduct already is to the one you want everyone to adhere to. Or, that these are people who can readily adopt the code of conduct you see as necessary to your journey to real achievement. This may appear to you altogether obvious. But most organizations hire for experience or for other credentials when it is this right stuff that counts in the crunch.

Fourth, you need to invent and customize the systems by which your organization operates so that they provide just the kinds of pushes and pulls required to get the code of conduct in place and to keep it in place. This includes compensation systems. If you reward A while hoping for B, you probably won't get much B, but you will get a lot of A.

The systems by which you account for things and make persons clearly accountable have to be thoroughly consistent with your code of conduct. If you make it possible – and *necessary* – for people to work diligently at becoming virtuosos in their roles, you have to have systems that provide the right pushes and pulls for that to happen. For example, if it's the only way people can get recognition and reward at your place, they will climb the proverbial corporate ladder to get it, and no real gain in performance will actually occur. It is competence in role that counts, not competence at climbing the corporate ladder.

Fifth, it is a struggle at the outset. And everything has to be exaggerated to be noticed. But once there begins to be a critical mass of people who have internalized the code of conduct needed to support the journey to great achievement, the culture of the organization will kick in and make the code appear to be natural (because it is embedded in the culture) and inescapable, since the culture is a system that envelops everyone.

Worth thinking about –

- The codes for becoming mediocre are ubiquitous, easy to adopt, and have been adopted by most people. That's why, in an open struggle between mediocrity and achievement, mediocrity has the critical mass, and will almost inevitably win.
- If the code required to become the best were that prevalent, people who wanted to be mediocre would be struggling against the current.
- Once the culture of your organization takes over from a critical mass of people, what once appeared to be extraordinary performance will simply be the standard level of performance. Kind of a reverse perversity!

So What Is A Code Of Conduct *About?*

A code of conduct is about the human criteria you believe are critical to getting on and staying on the path to the real achievement you have envisioned. It is what informs and drives the everyday ways of thinking and action in your organization that you believe are necessary to make progress on your mission every day. It is about those personal traits and generic orientations you believe your people would have to internalize in order to achieve any or all of the goals of the organization.

Just a reminder: the actual code of conduct that is behind the everyday thinking and actions of your people is what could reasonably be inferred by observing them. When people in your organization observe you, they infer your code of conduct. Is the one that guides your present thinking and behavior going to get you to where you intend to go? If not, designing and exemplifying the one that will ... is a basic tool for making it happen.

It will become clear to you if we go to example. What follows is a sort of generic list of the kinds of orientations that would be required to move an organization in the direction of real achievement. This list is not intended to be either comprehensive or exclusive. You may think of other criteria that would suit your situation better.

And none of the following criteria is intended to exclude any other possibilities. We'll look first at the themes you may need to drive your story going forward. And then we'll circle back to put some meat on these bare bones.

A generic code might have the following themes. They are not a description of how you are now. They are intended to describe how you and your people need to *be* to get to where you are committed to going.

- We will become virtuoso **communicators**.
- We will be **courageous**.
- We will become an organization of "**bricoleurs**."

- We will become heroic, world-class **inventors** of a better way.
- We will become a **humanizing** organization.
- We will become an organization of **learners**.
- We will become an organization of **leaders**.
- We will become a **community** of **interdependent achievers**.
- We will make **great lives** by doing **great work**.
- We will kill **complacency** and **mediocrity**.
- We will be joined in **common cause**.
- We will become an organization of **dragon-slayers**.
- We will relentlessly equip and prepare ourselves to do our **duty**.

If you achieved all of this – or any similar list – you would clearly have an outstanding organization. Even if you did no more than try to instill this code in every member of your organization, you would stand apart as unique and extremely capable. You wouldn't have to worry about things like customer service. Your customers and clients would be astonished by their treatment every day in every way by the people who had internalized this kind of internal guidance system.

But getting there: that's the rub. It's all in the implementation. So you first have to make certain that you understand every one of these themes deeply, for two reasons: one, so that you exemplify the terms of this code in everything you do and say, and second, so that you can explain what each of these topics means to the person you're talking to, no matter how skeptical or reticent that person might be.

Explaining The Code

Explain first to yourself, until you and the theme are indistinguishable. Then you can explain it to others and answer any questions others may have about it, because you are now the source of it. That's how well you have to understand what you are talking about when you talk about a code of conduct. Challenge yourself with as many of the toughest questions as you can imagine might be asked of you. Nothing less will serve you when you are being grilled about the whys and the hows.

Using the same list as above, here are some ideas that might serve as starters for explaining every major theme (to yourself or others):

• "We will become virtuoso **communicators**."

A. We will say what we mean and mean what we say.

B. This requires becoming virtuoso thinkers about anything we want to talk about, and fully engaging our minds in every encounter.

C. We will become virtuoso question-askers – ever more masterful at acquiring the intelligence we need to fulfill our roles, and at providing the information or intelligence others need to carry out their roles whenever, wherever, or however our performance or that of any of our customers or our suppliers is at stake.

D. We will study and practice and raise our competencies as communicators every successive day.

• "We will be **courageous**."

A. The depth of our commitments to ourselves and our mission will provide all of the courage we need to do the right thing, every time.

B. Attempting the impossible involves risk and failure. We will recognize that what is inexcusable is failing to push the envelope, whatever the tasks – individual or collective.

C. We will recover from our mistakes with speed, without compunction or blame, and move boldly ahead.

- "We will become an organization of **bricoleurs**."
A. As *bricoleurs*, we will accomplish what has to be accomplished with the tools and resources at hand.
B. Our daily purpose will be to outperform ourselves as we outpace all of our competitors, actual or potential.

- "We will become heroic, world-class **inventors**."
A. We will invent a better way of doing everything we do, *before* it becomes necessary to do so.
B. Tomorrow we will re-invent better ways of doing things, better products and services, better systems. We will get better at everything we do.

- "We will become a **humanizing** organization."
A. We will perform our roles in such a way that every person who comes into contact with us during the course of our workday will be the better for it.
B. We will never expect less than the best of ourselves, and we will equip ourselves to be invaluable resources to others along the same path of growth and development.

- "We will become an organization of **learners**."
A. We will look at life as an opportunity for continuous, lifelong learning, because we will understand that growth through learning is the source of life and of the qualities that make life most meaningful and exciting.
B. We will forever be in pursuit of what it takes to be the best in the business, and we will never cease learning how to deliver it.

- "We will become an organization of **leaders**."
A. We will demonstrate this by leading ourselves in extraordinary ways.

B. We will provide invaluable leadership to our customers, our suppliers, our competitors, and all of our other stakeholders.

C. Where our mission is concerned – which is everywhere at all times – we will learn to lead, to follow, or to get out of the way.

• "We will become a human **community** of **interdependent achievers.**"

A. We will do that by putting the needs and interests of the organization first, the needs and interests of our fellow members second, and our own needs and interests last.

B. There is no other way to create a community of interdependent people.

C. If there is a better way of creating the kind of totally effective and engaging organization we all want and need, we will invent it.

D. We will become the model for all those who seek a better way of doing things, and a better way of life while doing it.

• "We will make **great lives** by doing **great work**."

A. There is no other way.

B. We will know that the better we are at what we do, the more engaging it will be and the more gratification there will be in doing it.

C. Creativity is a function of discipline. We will have so much of the latter we can enjoy all we wish of the former.

D. "Work," as one wise man said, "is love made visible." We will show the world how much we care about ourselves and others by the excellence we put into everything we do. We will show others how much we care about ourselves and about them by the rate of growth of our performance.

- "We will kill **complacency** and **mediocrity**."

A. We will actively resist the forces of mediocrity in ourselves.

B. Having succeeded in that most difficult of tasks, we will help others to do the same.

- "We will be joined in **common cause**."

A. We will have a deep sense of interdependence in the mutual pursuit of our common cause – our mission.

B. Those outcomes of all our doing and saying that move us along the path toward our mission we will recognize as contributions.

C. Those outcomes that do not move us along that path we will recognize as dis-contributions. Our common cause will judge each of us on our contributions.

D. There are no observers or critics in an organization that has a great mission. There are no neutral thoughts, actions, or attitudes in an organization committed to real achievement. Everyone is an indispensable player.

- "We will become an organization of **dragon-slayers**."

A. Wherever there is a belief, a myth, a practice, or a habit that impedes us on our path, we will slay it.

B. Every explanation of why something can't be done is a loathsome dragon. There is no "can't." There is only inventing a "how" to accomplish what has to be accomplished.

- "We will continuously equip and prepare ourselves to do our **duty**."

A. Whether to our fellow members, to our customers, or to ourselves, we will never fail to carry through the duty we have signed on to fulfill.

B. We will never fail to *see* what our duty is in any
situation, present or future – nor will we fail *to equip
ourselves* to fulfill that duty, whatever it takes.

If you're thinking these seem to be fairly lofty goals, yes they
are. These days, the common inclination is probably to smirk.
That's because mediocrity loathes every form of excellence that
offends it – or any serious attempt to rise above it. There is more
comfort in being in the middle of the crowd than in the much
smaller company of achievers, but far more life and excitement in
the latter.

Yes, these are lofty words, *ideals*. If a code like this were
the core of your organization's culture and thus of your people's
consciences, you would likely achieve your mission. But if the
ideals of such a code as the one above make *you* uncomfortable,
it may simply mean that you have not personally escaped the
clutches of the most irresistible dragon of all. That would be the
dragon that comes of knowing that if you are not compelled by a
cause, you will be approved of by the majority of people (who are
mediocrities) rather than by the small minority of people who are
achievers. Reaching for something significantly above where most
people are will take you out of your comfort zone. If you can't get
out of it, real achievement may be out of your reach.

Some thought-prodders:

• If you have lofty goals, these can be described,
  understood, and held in mind only with such
  lofty words.
• But nothing much happens if you don't have what
  it takes to make reality out of such ideal blueprints.
• No matter how hard you try, you cannot achieve
  something great out of commonplace thinking.
• The aim of a code of conduct is to give voice to who
  you *intend* to be.
• Without it, you will forever be who you are.

Here's what it might feel like to add one to the mix. For example –

- We will each perform our roles with the **sense of urgency** that says we may not be here tomorrow if we don't.

Indeed, we may not be here tomorrow if we don't undertake our roles with that sense of urgency about them. Those are the words.

What kinds of pushes and pulls would you have to provide as leader in order to make that orientation the order of every day?

There is no common cause without a shared code of conduct. It's what makes a team out of a collection of individuals. It is what's needed to make a coherent organization on its way to real achievement out of a bunch of "employees." You want people who exemplify what it takes to get where you intend to go. That's what a code of conduct can do.

- Everyone is guided by an implicit code of conduct. It will take you where *it* leads, not where self-indulgence would mislead you.
- The one you do not design for your destiny is one that you will merely pick up from someone or something else.
- The code of mediocrity is one of the most powerful forces on earth.
- If you and your people do not consciously and aggressively struggle against it, you will inexorably be drawn into it.
- You can't achieve your own chosen destiny by going where everyone else is going.

That's why the most ideal code of conduct you can devise and implement is not just a good thing to do. It is a necessary thing to do.

POINTS TO PONDER

+ *Any* way of thinking, being, and doing will get you somewhere. The issue is: do you have the one you need?

+ A "code of conduct" is a set of habits that function like rules of engagement.

+ The "code" of mediocrity is obviously the one most people subscribe to.

+ Do you have a code of conduct? Is it getting you where you want to go?

+ A code of conduct lives only as it is invariantly practiced.

+ If people in your organization cannot explain what each point in the code means in practice, then there is no commitment to it.

+ Your destiny and the destiny of your organization are a function of how your actual code of conduct is working.

+ Why does a code of conduct describe the "ideal"?

+ Having a code of conduct for making a high-performance organization is, simply, necessary.

+ In practice, those you do not influence with your code of conduct will influence you with theirs.

Chapter 18
Values & Beliefs – the Tacit Mediators

Every code of conduct implies a set of values and beliefs. And every set of values and beliefs implies a code of conduct. You may like the idea of using either the one or the other. Or both. What's provided in this short chapter is a possible set of values and beliefs that are most needed if you intend to pursue real achievement, like making a high-performance organization.

But first, consider this:

In case you weren't paying attention in Chapter 16, when people speak to you, everything they say is cooked in and filtered through their personal values and beliefs. When *you* listen or observe, every observation and every interpretation you make is constructed out of and woven through with *your* values and beliefs.

Additionally, most of the dragons that affect our lives and everything we do with others abide in the values and beliefs that we can't help having and imputing to the world. Perhaps it is time to explore these matters more explicitly.

What matters? The two most basic for our purposes are these:

One, there are those values and beliefs that abound in the world around us that will function as serious or even defeating impediments to any endeavor we may engage in.

Two, without the *needed* values and beliefs – without that right stuff – no one is going to lead themselves or their organizations to any significant level of real achievement.

This is not a detour. Nor is it an academic or a philosophical digression. It is practical, pragmatic, fundamental. There is a tremendous potential advantage in being able to figure out how this tacit dimension of values and beliefs – that mediates all human perception, thought, and behavior – will be either furthering your cause, or impeding it. Quickies ...

- Leaders have to know what propels their cause or what constrains it – whether in themselves or others.
- Values and beliefs either serve you or impede you. There are no neutral values or beliefs.
- You will win or lose in this tacit dimension. It is to your advantage to understand it deeply.

Values And Beliefs Are ...

Values and beliefs are not something people have. They are what *have us*. Whether on the input side (listening, reading, observing) or the output side (speaking, writing, thinking, or doing), the values and beliefs that have people in their clutches – in their *thrall* – are what mediate everything. We do not deal with the world directly. The world does not affect us directly. All of our "minding" of the world or ourselves is mediated, filtered, spun through our values and beliefs. They are what every thought, every perception, every choice or decision, and every bit of behavior must pass through. *We* are ... what *they* are.

People are not born with any values or beliefs. Our values and beliefs infiltrate the most basic parts of our being from those around us. They are like contagious diseases, spread by those who are had by them to newcomers to the group. Those newcomers are admitted to full-fledged membership in that group (family, culture, tribe, whatever) only if and when they are properly infected and taken over by the values and beliefs that distinguish and characterize that group (religious, occupational, familial, community, whatever). People have to be indoctrinated before they qualify for full membership. High-performance organizations do it that way.

Values and beliefs are both imported and exported. We are infected by other people who are *had by* certain values and beliefs. And, properly indoctrinated, we become carriers who, intentionally or not, try to infect others. We cannot live in *any* human group without exhibiting reasonably acceptable evidence that we are had by the same core values and beliefs as the others in that group.

Some groups are less permissive than others. It's unlikely you will ever be acknowledged as an a *bona fide* software engineer unless you *think* like those other engineers around you do – which is to say, unless you exhibit certain values and beliefs that are reasonably consistent with theirs. There is little possibility of successfully *pretending* to be reasonably consistent with the values and beliefs of the Mafia or a big-rig network on the highways. You are either one of them or you are not.

If you are one of them, you will think and do and say and have as they do. Or you will, simply, not be admitted. If you want to be seen and accepted as an executive, you may have to act like one, dress like one (up *or* down), and talk like one. You must exhibit the values and beliefs of this group, or you may never be quite accepted.

More thought-prodders:

- Whatever the human group, tribe, subculture, etc., if you want to be one of them, you have to exhibit the same values and beliefs as they do.
- The most compelling evidence you can exhibit is that you are an effective carrier – that is, that you have effectively infected others.
- If you are merely pretending, you will be found out. It is only when your values and beliefs are *tacit* – only when they are driving you without your conscious awareness that you can be considered a bone fide member of that group.
- Your values and beliefs mediate the world for you, and mediate you for all the rest of the world.

The Software Of Thought And Behavior

It may seem strange to present such ideas in a book like this. Or to present them in such an unconventional way. But, as we have seen, it is conventional understandings that predict well to your being mediocre. You can't achieve something that is beyond average with an average or conventional way of thinking. Real achievement is not commonplace. And getting there requires thinking about the factors critical to that endeavor in a very unconventional way.

None predict to the outcome more than your values and beliefs and the values and beliefs of those people who have to make it happen. If you aren't had by the right set of values and beliefs for undertaking and carrying through the struggles and difficulties you will encounter on the path to real achievement, you won't get very far.

If you don't in fact know what values and beliefs you are had by, you will likely attribute any impediments on your journey to the wrong source. The right source would be you.

Desire is not an achievement. You will remember where we started: many try, few succeed. If you truly value your aim or your cause, you have to value all of the efforts – mental, physical, and spiritual – required to get there. If you believe in your cause, you have to believe in whatever it takes to get there.

There is no necessary correlation, as we have seen, between what people say and what people do. There *is* a close correlation between what people value and believe and what they accomplish.

Values and beliefs are the software that energizes, guides, channels, filters, and screens all of our attention and all of our actions. What we value and what we believe not only defines who we are, but how things will turn out for us in the end.

Some provocations along those lines –

- If you don't value accomplishment over activity, your life will be more or less a random sequence of activities.
- If you don't get the software right, the hardware isn't going to make much difference one way or the other.

306

- What you don't understand of your own values and beliefs will make you a mere victim of them. The ones you haven't consciously chosen will penetrate you from outside sources.

- What you don't understand of the values and beliefs of others – whether enemies, competitors, friends, or partners – will leave you naked and vulnerable on the playing field.

- Values and beliefs are not what make the world go 'round. They *are* the world around which everything else revolves.

The Right Stuff

The right values and beliefs are "the right stuff."

If *you* don't have the right stuff, then you are not going to accomplish anything extraordinary, either individually or as a leader of others. And if those key others are not right-minded, right-hearted, and right-spirited (if they don't have the right stuff), then your mission will likely fail. You can always hope, of course, that you get lucky, or that your competitors are less well equipped and prepared than you are. In that case, you may have some ordinary success. But it will not be *your* accomplishment. Being the least-worst is not much of an accomplishment.

The right values and beliefs are critical because values and beliefs do not take us where *we* want to go. They take us in the direction *they* go. Their direction and their ends are inherent in them. They are blind to everything but their own ends. Get them right, and they will carry you along to where you want to go. Get them wrong, and they will carry you along to wherever *they* just happen to be headed.

The Field Of Play

We thrive, or we fail, not because of our values and beliefs. But as a consequence of how those values *play us out* in all the rest of the world – the real world. Think of the world as a game in which we are players. In this game, the outcomes are beyond any person's control. We adapt, or we cease to be players. It is this world in which we have to accomplish. We either make things happen for our own purposes in this world, or we will simply be a byproduct of it. It is in the real world that leaders succeed, or fail.

We got Machiavelli wrong because we looked at what we interpreted, what we thought he meant, through the lenses of our modern view of the world. What he advised his prince was to perform superbly those values and beliefs that would perpetuate the state, and to eliminate within himself those that would put the security of the state in jeopardy.

That's it. Seems like good advice even today. The Roman Empire had a good long run. But it was eclipsed by a world outside of it that had passed it by. The values and beliefs that had made it great in times past led to its fall. In the more recent years before the so-called consumer revolution in our own country, there was an acquiescence to shoddy products and services that made it possible for many large organizations to grow and flourish for reasons other than quality, customer service, and the like.

We still don't get it. Organizations fail today because they cannot rid themselves of the values and beliefs that made them successful but which no longer have that relevance on the changed playing field. What was good for General Motors may have been what was good for the country at some point in history, as that much-repeated quotation had it. But not today. When people had to be grateful for whatever they could get, good intentions may have sufficed. But these days you would be prudent to have product liability insurance, and to value a good lawyer over good intentions. Traditional values and beliefs have increasingly been replaced by fashionable ones.

So here are some thoughts to ponder –
• It isn't values and beliefs as such that make the difference.
• It is how they play us out in the complex, dynamic world of sometimes conflicting values that makes the difference.

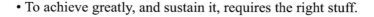

• To achieve greatly, and sustain it, requires the right stuff.

The Contrary Values And Beliefs You Are Up Against

Here's what you are up against. And thus what you have to change if you need certain values and beliefs working for you rather than against you.

1. In general, work is not very highly valued these days. But the values that are not put into one's work cannot appear in the products or the services you provide. What people don't value about the work they do devalues the products of their work.

2. Training people to say "Have a nice day" is not the same thing as equipping them to produce a nice day for customers and others. Saying, "Have a miserable day," isn't going to make it happen, unless it has already been made so, as for example by the perfunctory treatment you get from most flight attendants, retail clerks, and those who anonymously aim their road rage at you.

3. An old Hungarian proverb has it that people should be rewarded for how well they do what they do, not for their position in an organization. We value our celebrities more than our plumbers. When everyone becomes a talk-show host (or devotee), who will fix the plumbing?

4. We are greatly concerned with our rights and our entitlements. But our duties and responsibilities are rarely mentioned.

5. We espouse certain values, but live by very different values. People will be as hypocritical with customers and fellow-workers as they are in their private lives.

6. Great performance is wholly incompatible with easy hypocrisy. The logic is inescapable.

7. The level of character you and your people do not *routinely* exhibit (basic values are consistent because they are habits) can be no part of the assessment that customers, suppliers, or investors make of you.

8. You cannot perform at a level of character you do not have.

9. People who can't give to the organization more than they expect from it are deadbeats, and need to be dealt with accordingly.

10. What you don't value won't value you.

What They Might Have To Be

Well, you get the point. What follows is an example of the kinds of values and beliefs that can underwrite real achievement. They work only if they are a part of who you and your people are. These are unlikely to be your present everyday, always practiced values and beliefs. They are the kinds of values and beliefs to aspire to if you intend to pursue great achievement.

Here is a possible list of values and beliefs that can make a difference (because they have made a difference):

Some Guiding Values and Beliefs

We believe that good work, superbly done, is the richest source of human dignity and quality of life.

• *Can you imagine ... what the performance of an organization would be like if most of the people in it were actually driven by that belief?*

We believe that the world passes by those who do not change with it.

• *Isn't it the case that people who stop learning, and thus changing, actually lose ground simply because the world is changing around them? Can you imagine ... that world trying to keep pace with people who are learning every day?*

We believe we should never belittle ourselves by setting mediocre goals.

• *Aren't mediocre goals the way mediocre people achieved their mediocrity in the first place? Think small – be small?*

We believe in being forever dissatisfied with our performance.

• *Isn't it always the case that people who are satisfied with their performance go stale? Can you imagine ... a whole organization of strivers?*

We believe that, to fulfill our moral obligation to ourselves and to others, DUTY must come first.

• *Obligation? Duty? Can you imagine...a whole organization of people who put their duty to others and to the organization* first? *Their customers would be astonished, wouldn't they?*

We believe that people should be the masters of their own destiny.

• *Can you imagine ... a person who says to the world, "Make of me what you will"? Can such a person actually be empowered?*

We believe that the future belongs to those who ask the right questions.

• *What is the right question* here? *Or can a person escape the problem by pretending to have no future in mind and play the role of victim?*

We believe that trust and respect must be mutually *earned*.

• *Can trust and respect simply be traded? Or does it seem to you things work better if you and the other person actually have to* earn *the trust you then deservedly offer or receive?*

We believe that the primary measure of our success lies in the quality of life we provide to each of our stakeholders, internally and externally.

• If your customers are not better people as a result of their interactions with you, are you?

Well, it must be obvious how powerful it can be to have the right values and beliefs as widely and deeply distributed, and internalized – made into habits – as possible. The above may not be just the right ones for you. But if you depend upon the hodge-podge collection of values and beliefs that people bring to your place from their friends and the media, you will be struggling, for the rest of your life, with the problems these can create. It may be to your advantage (even to try) to get people on the same page with respect to the beliefs and values needed to pursue your cause.

Leadership Lessons: Some Reminders

Before launching into the next chapter on the "core stratagems," it might be useful to briefly reprise some of the basics explored thus far.

- The way your mind works determines who you *are*. Who you are determines what you *do* and *how* you do it. Fix the source, not the symptom.
- People who haven't assumed responsibility for their own destiny will have difficulty understanding people (like you) who have. The solution: hold them responsible for their own destiny.
- You don't control all of the outcomes. No one can. What you can control is everyone's preparedness for achieving your goals, come what may.
- Instrument yourself and the people of your organization in such a way that you don't merely have a cause, but so that cause has *you*. Let the cause be the immediate and the ultimate boss.

- There are only two basic reasons why people do what they do. One is that they *can* (competence and wherewithal). The other is that it is *necessary* (conscience, cultural systems, or even to avoid unwanted consequences).
- If you want to know what people *mean* by what they say, look at what they do.
- The meaning of communication is exclusively in the consequences.
- The only measure of performance is performance.
- The primary necessity for better performance lies in the level of dissatisfaction with previous performance. People have a comfort zone only with your permission.
- People's habits (including your own) will take you where *they* go, not where *you* intend to go.
- A person's experience (or credentials) is not the same thing as that person's performance in the role they have for making your great achievement a reality.
- Most of what you have to learn about extraordinary achievement you have to learn by doing it.
- You must unrelentingly value the future you envision over the realities of the present, which you understand full well, and value. That future has to be as real to you today as is the present.

So, when you're ready, let's move on.

Points to Ponder

+ How *do* values and beliefs affect performance on the job?

+ Values and beliefs are either enablers or constraints on your path.

+ What makes most values and beliefs "tacit"?

+ How would you explain to someone else what it is that values and beliefs "mediate"?

+ We don't "have" values and beliefs. They "have" us.

+ If you don't get this—the "software"—right, the "hardware" (the people doing the work of the organization) won't make much difference.

+ The values and beliefs you don't choose will choose you.

+ Organizations either have "the right stuff" (which is...?) or they don't.

+ The values and beliefs that enabled you to be successful in the past may not enable you to be successful in the future.

+ The best values and beliefs are usually the most fashionable ones.

+ It's easy to recognize "deadbeats" in any organization.

+ How would you change or improve upon the values and beliefs in this chapter?

+ You must value the future you envision more than the realities of the present.

Chapter 19 — The Core Stratagems

In this chapter, we will confront head-on the core stratagems for the pursuit of real achievement. They have been implicit in much of what we have encountered in the preceding pages. But it is time to call them forth and deal with them directly, now that you have a way of understanding them as they have to be understood.

The *Strategic Distribution* Of The *Ownership* Of Problems

The first of these core stratagems is all about the *strategic distribution* of the *ownership* of problems. That's a lot of words packed together. A brief overview and then we will unpack them.

Most broadly, what this means is that the actual organization is not what's on the organization chart. The actual organization is structured around *who* owns *what* problems, and the processes that connect them. More informally, what this means is that what makes the organization work is determined by what person or group owns what problems, because this is what determines the flow of information to those nodes, and where decisions and initiatives originate that affect what others do.

In the past, we strove to locate this ownership in the offices of the managers of the organization. This was the "Who reports to whom?" kind of organization structure. But it never worked perfectly because there was always someone fouling up the works by taking ownership of a problem and dealing with it more or less unilaterally. The idea was that because they were at the head of the pyramid structure of the conventional organization, managers were the "brains." It was up to them to do the thinking, make the decisions, and see to it that others did what they were told to do.

The point is that the underlying organization structure will always depend upon who owns what problem. And the power of this logic predicts that if you get this right, you will have the blueprint for a high-performance organization.

Let us then unpack our terms in reverse order. (It will simply work better for you that way.)

1. How **problems** get dealt with depends upon who owns them. A problem that no one owns is a problem that is unseen. To see a problem and talk about it is what makes any problem real. How it is seen and made real in talk about it depends solely on who sees it, or who brings it into existence by how they talk about it. How it is dealt with depends entirely on who deals with it. We've considered all this before. What we want to bring to the fore here is that people's attention is always focused on *their* problems (as they understand them). And what moves people to action is the significance (to them) of where they are vs. where they are trying to get to by dealing with the problem. Problem: If an entrepreneur is the only person in her enterprise, she is the problem-seer, the problem-definer, and the problem-solver. What she does at work depends upon the problems she owns. Others may see different problems, and define them and go about solving them differently. Unless she persists in owning them, which is more often than not the case.

2. To **own** a problem simply means to have the responsibility for it – in many ways: for anticipating it, for seeing it, for defining it, for doing something about it, and for being accountable for the consequences of all of these, especially for what is done, or not done, about it. What deserves your careful consideration here is that

people treat the problems they own very differently from the problems others own. You do.

Some people gladly own problems they ought not to own. You have undoubtedly done this more than once in your lifetime. There are many people who would be okay with having someone else own *all* of their problems – certainly all of their problems they prefer not to deal with.

In any system that involves people dealing with each other to some end, here's the crux: If the person who ought to own the problem is not the one who owns it, the system becomes dysfunctional. Here's an example which you may not be familiar with: If a parent "owns" the problem of the child's learning to walk and interferes, this typically delays that ability on the part of the child for two or more months.

Another universal example: In a schoolroom, if the teacher owns the problem of the students' learning, and the students do not own the problems of their own learning, very little learning beyond rote recall takes place. The system is dysfunctional because the problem is owned by someone other than the person who should own it.

In the same way, if the boss owns the problem of the subordinate's performance, so that the subordinate doesn't or can't own that problem, the system is dysfunctional. All kinds of problems will arise that are attributed to causes other than the key cause. If the problem of the performance of the company is owned solely by the chief executive, the whole organization is dysfunctional. That's a problem that ought to be owned by everyone in the organization – like the problem of quality. If the system is dysfunctional, it cannot be fixed by fixing the people in it, or by applying a recipe on top of it. It can only be fixed by fixing the system, and that means making sure that the person or persons who ought to own the problem do in fact own it. As soon as your spouse's happiness becomes your problem, the system is dysfunctional. In the same way, if you own the problem of the employees' satisfaction, you will find that there is no way for you to succeed and you will forever be engaged in dealing with problems that are unrelated to your cause.

"Ownership" means that the person who ought to own the problem owns it.

Here are two generic caveats:

- One, if a person who works at your place does not own the problem of his or her personal destiny, that person will never be able to understand why you would choose a cause or a destiny for your organization. Or why that should be of any concern to that person.

- Very important to remember: You should never require a person to own (to be accountable for) anything that is not reasonably within that person's control. Preparedness and competence are. Outcomes aren't.

People who have no obligation for the health and welfare of the larger system to which they belong will be a dead-level drag on the spirit and the economy of that system, including your own organization.

The paradox here is that:

- It is only by owning the problems of their own personal destinies that people can come to a realization of their inescapable *interdependence* with others in any larger endeavor.

- People who do not own the problem of their own performance and their destinies in life cannot see that they have to put into the larger whole what they want to get out of it.

You have to fix that disability first.

3. The **strategic distribution** of the ownership of problems simply refers to the need to get the ownership of every problem rightly situated. To repeat, if *you* own the problem of the performance of the people in your organization, you will struggle and struggle with a problem you cannot solve. That's because, ultimately, they

are the only ones who can solve the problem of their own performance, and therefore they should own that problem.

There's always a logic involved. If a person or a department owns the problem of quality, then none of the rest of the people have any need to own that problem. If customer service is owned by a small group of people, then the other people in the organization don't have to own that problem. If conformity to government regulations is a problem that is owned by a person or a department, then no one else has to own that problem in their workplace. If recruiting is a problem owned by the HR department, others don't have to get involved. The problem of recruiting people ought to be owned by everyone in the organization. The logic is this: *who* ought to own *what* problems in order for the performance of the whole to be raised ... daily?

If you let it be assumed that people get paid at your place for performing *their* petty problems and concerns at work, that's what will happen. People get paid (if "Mother" has it to pay) for performing their *roles*. If they don't own their performance in their roles, someone else (you?) will have to.

How much of your performance in your role gets siphoned off in this direction? All because the ownership of problems has not been strategically distributed. Because the people who ought to own the problem can't (competence) or won't (their feelings of the moment) means that others get drawn into owning problems they shouldn't own.

Rise to the challenge of the strategic distribution of the ownership of problems within your organization and your organization can then rise more fully to the challenges it faces in the larger world.

- The leader cannot get the level of competence and performance needed by decree or exhortation.
- What should he (or she) do with this problem?

319

Some thought-prodders:

- The problems that people don't own will serve them as an excuse in advance for any shortfalls in their performance, as they see it.
- The problems that people don't *own* will be problems they will feel no responsibility for.
- If you believe that you exhibit your superiority by being the go-to problem-solver for your people, then you will be an unseen and therefore insoluble cause of those problems.
- And ... thus you will function as the chief inhibitor of the growth of your people's competencies and consciences.
- Your first duty? To not be a part of the problem, so that you might be a part of the solution.
- Your second? Selecting and casting people so that they own the problems of their own performance and the performance of the part of the organization for which they are accountable, so that you can concentrate on the performance of the whole.
- The more sense people have of owning the vital problems of the organization, those that they encounter, the more tied they will be to the life and the destiny of the organization.

Making Possible What's Necessary ... And Making Necessary What's Possible

That is not intended to be a cute play on words. It is intended to engage you in trying to figure out what all that means. In what way do those words constitute a core stratagem?

The first part of it – **making possible what's necessary** – means that one's goals and purposes require certain preconditions, like stamina or commitment or competence. What you are not equipped to do you will not do because you cannot. So this refers to equipping oneself (or others) with whatever is required to carry through those goals and purposes.

People have to own the problem of capacitating themselves to carry out the accomplishments called for in their roles. But some impediments to their performance may have to be removed by you. If the organization is not structured (remember problem ownership?) so that they can effectively perform their roles, you may be the one who has to fix that problem because they can't. If they do not have the resources they need, or the information infrastructure required, you may have to enable them by providing those. This is part of what is meant by making the necessary accomplishments possible.

You may have the wrong people. You may not have exactly the right roles for your "story" to unfold as intended. You may not have the right business strategy. You may not have the kinds of "smart" systems that would enable performance even if you have all the rest of it right. These are all enablers. If they're not right, it isn't going to happen. You make it possible by getting all of the preconditions right, so that your people have no excuse for not owning the problem of their own performance in their roles.

The other half of it is **making necessary what's possible**. You don't know what's possible. No one does. What is commonplace today was at one time considered impossible. Heavier than air vehicles really can fly. The Pony Express, which never really made money, was the fastest way of getting information around in its day. The internal combustion engine was not possible – until someone figured out how to make one. History is replete with examples of how what was considered impossible came to be a part of our everyday lives.

When someone says, "That's not possible," they mean that they themselves, constrained as they are by their own thinking, beliefs, and attitudes, can't figure out how to do it. Nay-saying is not a *test* of what's possible. Only doing it is.

The art of all great leaders has been their uncanny creativity in making **necessary** what no one has yet seen or experienced, what's believed to be "impossible" – that is, the art of making **necessary** whatever might *be possible*.

The lesson is this:
- What "can't" be done reflects no more than a failure of imagination.
- It is the leader's task to make it **possible** for people to first imagine that something could be accomplished, and then to make it **necessary** for them to accomplish that.
- Making necessary what's possible is the process of making reality out of imagination. That's what Columbus did. That's what Gandhi did. That's what the world's first heart transplant surgeon did. That's what leaders do. What leaders have always done.
- That's what you could do. If you can figure out how to make necessary what you want to achieve.
- Doing it, accomplishing it, is what makes it possible. Reality always trumps prophecy.
- Declaring something to be "impossible" is prophecy based on no more than one's own disbelief in oneself.

Accomplishments, Not Activities

Because it is also true of the larger culture, the cultures of most organizations permit, channel, even encourage people to think and do in terms of **activities**. "I have to study" is an activity that students use to identify their burdens in life. "I have to go shopping" is the second most time-consuming activity in America. "I have to go to work" is an activity. And what we do, most of the day at work, consists of *activities*. The typical job description is more often than not a list of *activities*.

When the time for evaluation comes, and the cowardly manager meets the aggressive employee in the arena, the argument is, frequently, "But I'm doing my job, aren't I?!" Since that consists mainly of some activities, what recourse does the cowardly manager have?

What you want and need are **accomplishments**. But those are rarely in the job description. They are left implicit, mainly in the daydreams of the manager. As we have seen, a job description is a good example of doing **A** while hoping for **B**. We list the activities but hope for the accomplishments.

Real meaning in life lies mainly in the pursuit of a worthy goal or a purpose, not in the mindless repetition of activities. People can get *engaged* in activities. But if they are not means to much larger ends, sheer activities suck the life out of people.

There is a real "catch" in this whole endeavor we are exploring in this book. It is this: If you don't understand how to accomplish your goals, you won't. But it is only when you do accomplish your goals that you will fully understand how. Nice paradox. But that's the way it is.

To get right into the differences between "activities" and "accomplishments," let's go to some specifics:

- For people who have no particular aim in life, an *activity* will seem to them like an *accomplishment*.
- In organizations, an accomplishment is a measurable contribution to the aims or the cause of the organization.
- Making it necessary for people to distinguish between activities and accomplishments is an ongoing task of leadership.
- People must make themselves capable of accomplishing what is required of them in their role.
- An accomplishment that is not understood at the outset, or which cannot be objectively measured, creates problems.
- The more closely related an accomplishment is to the goals of the organization, the more meaningful it is to the person.
- The accomplishment is *accomplishment-mindedness*. If people are not accomplishment-minded, they will not be accomplishers.
- What you want to achieve is that ordinary people will thrive on doing common things uncommonly well.
- Sheer activity requires just as much effort with a fraction of the return on accomplishments.

Relationship

This core stratagem operates so unnoticeably it is often given no thought at all. It is simple but powerful.

Here it is in its briefest form –

- If two or more people intend to collaborate to some mutual end (collaborate, negotiate, make love, whatever), their *relationship* determines what can be done, and how.

- Just as it is your relationship with your customers that determines what's possible, or how much collaboration can be expected, it is your relationship with your people that determines what you can do with them, and how you have to do it.

- What can and can't be done is a function of the relationship.

Choice

To provide good and effective leadership, you must perceive and treat every person's circumstances and problems as a matter of choice. *Their* choice. This has to begin with you. You have to be the exemplar of seeing yourself as the owner of all of your circumstances.

You have to assume that people are the way they are *by choice*. A person is always the result of a whole series of choices (or failures to choose) over a long period of time. Choices in the past bear upon outcomes far into the future.

And we know that outcomes are always uncertain and uncontrollable. But people do have a choice about having a purpose in life or not. And people do own the problem of how well their ongoing choices contribute to their purpose in life.

Indeed everything is going to turn out the way it turns out. But equipping oneself and preparing oneself to pursue worthy and chosen ends are conditions over which every person has control. That is what you (or I, or they) *choose*. We choose to be prepared and equipped to accomplish something on purpose. Or we choose *not* to be equipped and prepared.

CHAPTER 19 • THE CORE STRATAGEMS

A person who doesn't "get" that is not going to be very useful to you in furthering the choices you make about what kind of organization to have in order to pursue a cause that is yours by choice.

- The alternative to choosing your own or your organization's destiny is being a *victim* of whatever forces happen to push you this way or pull you that way.
- What isn't accomplished by choice you cannot take credit for.
- The choices you do not make determine the destiny you or your organization cannot have.
- People cannot choose who they are at the moment. But they always choose the competencies that enable them to *perform* to their advantage in a given situation. Preparedness.

Get Everyone In The Learning Mode

It seems likely that for every ten dollars spent on change in the past 20 years or so, we've realized a return of fifty cents or less. We're looking back on billions spent in the name of change.

There is only one form of *sustainable* change. And that's when people change – in relevant and significant ways – their ways of thinking, of being, and of doing. And that kind of change occurs only when people learn something that makes it necessary for them to remodel how they think, to alter who they are, or to re-tool their ways of doing things.

Real learning is the source of real change. And real learning is possible only for those people who are in the learning mode. People don't get more competent day after day because they are told to do so. People don't equip and prepare themselves for outstanding performance because they are told to do so. Or even if they agree that they should. People don't get smarter and more capable if they are fed larger amounts of information or even of larger amounts of "knowledge." They have to have goals that they have to achieve.

If they have to change in order to carry out those goals, they will do so. That's why everyone in the organization needs to have a learning plan, as we have seen. This is a plan for systematically eliminating shortfalls in their ability to accomplish what's given in their role, and with respect to the performance goals they have signed onto.

Couple that learning plan with objectively measured performance and an inescapable necessity for performing, and you will have an organization that will outperform all others.

- The premise here is simple. Performance in any role whatsoever can be improved upon every day...forever.
- Learning opens minds. Knowing closes them down.
- Learning requires a question. You have to think about that. Knowing leads to making statements. You don't have to think about that.
- If you want people to think about what they're doing, they have to be in the learning mode.

There are two ways to grow an organization: outside-in and inside-out. Outside-in simply means that the organization grows to meet the demands of its customers or clients. Inside-out means that people grow in their competencies and capabilities, and this opens up more of the world to the organization.

Which way would you choose? To be victim or cause?

When people are in the learning mode, their insatiable curiosity about their work – and about everything that affects their performance one way or the other – is a powerful source of real and lasting change.

It is performance that needs changing. And the people who can best figure out how to change performance for the better are the ones who are demonstrating that they *own* their performance in their role – today, tomorrow, and beyond.

Some ponderables:

- Most resistance to change is at the top of the organization.
- That's because the more elevated one's position, the more in the knowing mode that person is likely to be.

- People at the top may want change. But they themselves often do not want to – or *can't* – change.
- Unfettered learning coupled with competence is a far better source of the right change than is managerial decree.
- The lesson for leaders: Demonstrate what being in the learning mode looks and feels like. Then expect no less from others.
- People are going to take you where they're going unless you lead them elsewhere.. Make their competence and their growth necessary. Then they'll take you where it would otherwise be impossible to go.

Bring Life Back Into Work

- If you apply the leadership lessons provided in this book, you **will** bring life back into work.
- If you cannot select – or develop – people who have the level of competence in their roles that enable them to give their hearts and minds to their work, you cannot have an organization that performs greatly.
- To the extent your people cannot give life to their work, your organization's performance will be life-less.

Real life and real growth are two aspects of the same thing. The life you or your people cannot have at your place is a life you cannot have. Learning is the source of real growth, which is growth in competence. And real growth is the source of life. To talk about bringing life to work accomplishes nothing. But you can do so by making necessary the kind of learning that enhances needed competence and thus performance. Learning produces growth. And growth = life.

Some thought-prodders:

- The more of a purpose in life one has, the more life one has.

- The sense of being fully alive you have in the present comes from the future cause you are serving.
- Every person is the steward of his or her own future. And every person is responsible for the future of the organization in which they are interdependent with others.
- Whether for an infant or a CEO, a real, delicious sense of life comes not from where you are but from what you are committed to achieving.
- And life comes from growing the capabilities required to get there.
- The leader is thus a life-maker. How the leader thinks determines who she *is*.

And who she is determines what she does, and how she does it.

When the leader learns how to use the powerful tools required to make a high-performance organization, that leader will also become a life-maker for those who are her followers.

POINTS TO PONDER

+ The strategic distribution of the ownership of problems. Why "strategic"? Why, and how, "ownership"?

+ How problems get dealt with depends upon who owns them.

+ The "right" problems should be owned by the "right" person(s), meaning ... ?

+ The actual organization would be a picture of who owns what problems.

+ If you were going to conduct a seminar on "Making Possible What's Necessary, and Making Necessary What's Possible," how would you begin?

+ Reality always trumps any prophecy about what's possible.

+ Most people never learned how to distinguish accomplishments from activities.

+ There are some things – like making a high-performance organization – that can be understood only by doing it.

+ Relationships determine what can be expressed, with what consequences.

+ Leaders must take this stance: who people are and how they perform is a result of choices they have made. Why?

+ Becoming more competent requires being in the "learning mode."

+ About LIFE: Learning = Growth, and Growth = Life. The good leader is thus a life-maker.

+ Why are these the "core" stratagems?

PART VI

Envoi

So, these are the kinds of provisions you need to undertake your leadership journey. The rest is up to you.

It's good to know as much as you can at the outset of your journey. But, as ancient wisdom has it, when it comes to matters like leadership, what you have to learn ... you have to learn by doing.

You have to practice thinking like a leader – thinking the way a leader thinks. You have to practice being who you have to be, who you envision being, who awaits you at each stop on your road to a high performance organization. You have to practice seeing and saying – living in and through – the world you are trying to get to. Your progress will always come in small advances. It's all about who you are, and thus about how you think and do in this world in order to lead yourself and others toward the world you envision.

The way there, all that has preceded in these pages, could hardly be summarized. Nothing of all that you have to do can be reduced to a scheme, a formula, or a set of secrets or rules. You're the person who has to author the story of your leadership. You do this – always remember – with what you have to do it with.

The purpose of this book is to provision you with much of what you need to do it with. But what's here, explicitly and implicitly, will of itself do nothing for you. You have to do what has to be done. How it all turns out will be a measure of you, not of all the rich and powerful ideas got from the world's wisdom and from years and years of hands-on experience and reflection. If all the preceding enables you in some small way to achieve great success on your journey, then our journey together to this point has been mutually rewarding.

This book does not end with the next chapter. It ends with what you do with all of this. It is for the purpose of tidying up and providing you with a thinking pad for launching your journey.

There is always time to have some fun with what we think we know, just in case there are better ways of thinking about it. Let these next two pages provoke one or more of those.

Chapter 20

A Short Course on Real Achievement

In all the world, there is no human experience that can compare to the exercise of the deeply-rooted competencies required for the pursuit of a great and worthy cause.

Something to think about.

Few people have had such an experience. That's because few people have been a part of pursuing, alone or with others, a great and worthy cause. This is in spite of the fact that it is the most humanizing experience that any person can have.

If you have a vision, and if you have the kind of tenaciousness that can develop within you the kinds of competencies required for seeing that vision through to reality, you are called to leadership. As a leader, you are in a position to provide that unique human experience – the pursuit of a great and worthy cause – for yourself and for all of those who contribute to the pursuit of a great and worthy achievement.

This is your privilege, because of your position. This is your moral obligation, because of your position.

As you think, so will you be. As you are, so will you do. To fulfill any task in this world, think your way through to accomplishing it. You have to be the person who makes it necessary. You have to *be* what needs to be done.

You can do what needs to be done only if you are fully competent to do so.

If you are "had by" the cause of making a great and high-performance organization, you need to make a part of who you are the competencies required of you in order to carry out that task. That's what you have in your hands.

You will need to provide the leadership required to make it possible, and necessary, for your people to develop the deep competencies required for seeing it through. The more competent people are in their role, the more pleasure they have in their work, and thus the higher the quality of their lives. It's win-win. In fact, the more competent people are at what they do, the more they can play at what they do. Useful creativity is a function of extreme competence.

If you succeed, be humble. Others conspired with you to make it happen. You were blessed.

If you do not succeed, go back and fix the only things over which you have control: how you think, who you are, and how you do what you do. Make all of the tools required an integral part of who you are.

This guidebook can provide you with much of what you need for the thinking part of it. How you make that a part of who you are, and how you use it to color what you do and how you do it, will be a product of putting it into practice. It will be your utter determination that puts it all together, fitting you to the tools you need, and fitting the tools you need to you. Sometimes the right tools make even that passionate determination possible.

Envoi is the greeting I give you as we part ways here. Let us part with a shared vision, that of the real journey, which now lies ahead of you.

Acknowledgements

My thanks to those dozens and dozens of chief executives and top managers who have challenged my ideas over the years, and as a result made them work better in their many and various organizations. There have been so many, and they have been so different, that it would be misleading to put them all on the same page. What we have learned from our partnerships has been its own reward.

My thanks, also, to the many thinkers and practitioners who, over the past eight millennia, have provided a rich legacy for our own present day thinking about this infinitely challenging subject.

And to my friends and colleagues who have read and critiqued one or more of this book's several incarnations, and have gently nudged me until I just had to do it in a way the might vindicate their belief in what I had to say.

They will know who they are. In any event, this is what they all made possible.

About the Author

Lee Thayer is best known for his acerbic wit, his engaging style, his sense of humor, and for the depth and breadth of his intellectual resources. Accompany those traits with his accomplishments and the work he does in this complex world of ours, and you begin to get an idea of Thayer's vision for the "thinking, being, and doing" of leadership.

Thayer's goal is to visualize the ideal, and then to figure out how to get there by starting with the actualities of the present circumstances.

Dr. Lee Thayer,
author of *How Executives Fail:
25 Surefire Recipes for
Sabotaging Your Career*
(2007)

Like some of the rest of us, he wants to leave this world a better place. And he's doing it – organization by organization. Many say that in his craft he has no peer. His approach is as unique (often counter-intuitive) as it is powerful. It is a life-changing experience for those who are fortunate enough to work with him.

Thayer's work begins with an invitation from an exceptional and exceptionally committed CEO – to partner with that CEO for the purpose of transforming his or her organization to an outstanding level of performance, while learning the kind of leadership required to deserve a great organization. (A high-performance organization is one that does everything it does better than anyone else – and improves upon that every day – giving that organization a *sustainable* competitive advantage.)

Thayer gets into "the trenches" with those who are going to make it happen, to help them every step of the way. As he says,

> *"It isn't what you know that creates excellence. Ninety-five percent of it is in the implementation. For that, you need a guide and a mentor – someone who's been there in all kinds of conditions."*

Dr. Thayer's career as a pioneer and influential innovator in the design and development of high-performance organizations – and in the kind of leadership required of the top executive to achieve that – has spanned more than four decades. It has often been observed that he has rattled more CEOs' cages than anyone else.

Having come from a high-level executive position in industry himself, coupled with his experience as a jazz performer and arranger and his university degrees in the humanities, engineering, and psychology, Dr. Thayer has developed a revolutionary and practical framework for understanding *what it takes* to lead the way to creating great organizations, in the '*how*' as much as the '*why*'. He and his CEO partners often have to **invent** the pushes and pulls required to achieve the kind of excellence that others can't figure out how to copy.

Early on in his career, he served as consultant to several of the Fortune 500 and other notable companies, such as IBM, AT&T, Westinghouse, Boeing, Curtiss-Wright, Pratt-Whitney, McDonnell Douglas, Phillips, Shell, General Motors, Sealtest Foods, and Hallmark. He has consulted with the U.S. Air Force, the Postal Service, numerous banks and other institutions, universities around the globe, and West Point.

He was the consultant behind the now well-known success story at Johnsonville Foods – which Tom Peters referred to as "the most remarkable example of organizational transformation" he had ever seen.

He has taken his extraordinary problem-solving skills to the Scandinavian countries (esp. Finland and Norway), to Australia, to the UK and most European countries, and to Canada, Mexico, and China. Today, he limits his work to small to medium-sized organizations where, as he says, the impact is more immediate and measurable.

His other "career," as a distinguished university professor in major universities both here and abroad (e.g., the Harvard Graduate School of Business, The University of Amsterdam, Queensland University of Technology in Australia, Universidad Complutense in Mexico, etc.) was an ongoing research project he "put up with" for thirty-five years, before "retiring" in 1991 to devote full time to his passion which, as he has described it in interviews, is

"... to help committed CEOs and other top executives transform themselves into leaders and their organizations into healthier, more vigorous, and more adaptive high-performance organizations."

Doing so, many have observed, has brought life back into those organizations, and has lifted the quality of life of its employees, both at work and at home.

Dr. Thayer has been invited to work in most of the major leadership development programs in the U.S. and abroad, to share the wisdom he has gained during his many years of working and coaching "in the trenches" with his carefully-selected CEOs to make outstanding performance a way of life. Thayer has conducted hundreds of seminars and has spoken before thousands of top executives. He has served as the manager of dozens of organizations and projects, including work for the National Science Foundation, the U.S. Office of Education, and NASA.

He has been recognized as a Ford Foundation Fellow, as a Danforth Teacher, and as a Fulbright Scholar.

Truly a Renaissance man himself, Dr. Thayer is one of the most sought after seminar speakers and consultants in America.

Index

Consequences 66, 68
Conventional thinking/wisdom 2,
  36-39, 130–132
Core stratagems 315–330
  accomplishments, not activities
    322–323
  bringing life back into work
    327–328
  choice 324–325
  get everyone in the learning mode
    325–327
  making necessary what's possible
    321–322
  making possible what's necessary
    320–321
  relationship 324
  strategic distribution of the
    ownership of problems
    315–320
Crawford & Matthews 252
Culture of Narcissism, The 176

D

De Pree, Max i, 211
Dilbert 189
Dissatisfaction 24, 42–43, 279–280
  energizes leaders 141
  essential to change 279
Dorner, Dietrich 199
Dragons
  as mental obstacles 113–122
Dumb systems 159–168
  communication essential to all
    systems 165–166
  identifying 166–167
  predictability vs. adaptation
    163–165
  vs. smart systems 161–163
Duty 100

E

Einstein, Albert 61, 64
Empowerment
  as a buzzword 147–148

as becoming competent 148
  measuring 152–153
Excuse Factory, The 173
Explaining things 71-73

F

Fashion
  in management ideas 102
Faust 175
Followership 211
Ford, Henry 61
Four covenants, the 210-212

G

Gates, Bill 208
Geneen, Harold 188
General Swartzkopf 206
Genghis Khan 203
God's instruction 191
Goethe 85
Gracian 282

H

Habits 22–24
  as drivers of mediocrity 135–138
Henry V 279
High-performance 1
  competence 10
  organization as being
    good for people 10–11
Hope is not a method 37
*How Executives Fail: 25 Surefire
  Recipes for Sabotaging Your
  Career* 30, 199, 337, 340

I

Indispensable tools, two 229
Interdependence 25–26
Iverson, Ken 219

J

Joan of Arc 208
Jobs, Steve 115

Success
  formula 3
Sun Tzu 35, 107, 193

T

"Talk does not cook rice" 55
Tecumseh 203
Telling the story 219
Thinking
  about bosses vs. leaders 126–128
  about management vs. leadership
    124–126
  about what you "deserve" 33–36
  about who you are 36–39
  conventional thinking =
    conventional results 36
  stretching exercises 1–17
  tools 14
Thompson, D'Arcy 75
Thoreau 57
Time 107
Tipping Point, The 76
Tools for making it happen
  229–250
  "composing" the organization
    260–262
  accountability 236–238
  adapting to inescapable logic 240
  capacitation 238–239
  casting people in the right roles
    241–242
  communication systems 271–274
  dissatisfaction 279–280
  doing more with less 274–277
  how you think (indispensable)
    229
  learning plans 254–256
  luck 282–284
  making performance possible
    and necessary 233–234
  measures or metrics 256–258
  performance goals 251–254

  power 277–278
  preparedness/readiness 234–235
  problems as tools 259–260
  questions 270–271
  reputation 282
  role description 243–249
  seduction 280–281
  smart systems 262–265
  unreasonableness 281–282
  who you are (indispensable) 229
  words 276–277
TQM 3

U

Under-empowerment 147–158
Unreasonableness 281-282

V

Values and beliefs 303–314
  as "the right stuff" 307
  as software of thought and
    behavior 306–307
  contrary ones you're up against
    309–310
  examples that support great
    achievement 310–312
Victimization
  as a way of life 171–173

W

Walton, Sam 115
Welch, Jack 206, 219
Wooden, John 59
Woods, Tiger 89

Y

Yoda 4

Also by Lee Thayer:

How Executives Fail:
25 Surefire Recipes for
Sabotaging Your Career
(WME Books, 2007)

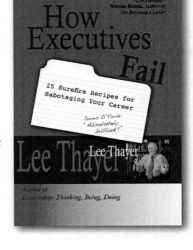

Early praise for *How Executives Fail* –

Warren Bennis: *"The best 'insurance' book
on leadership I've read. It's terrific!"*

Ralph Stayer: *"Thayer's seminal thinking
on leadership is the foundation for all that
I have done at Johnsonville Sausage."*

James O'Toole: *"... original, funny, and
useful little gem of a book."*

Michael Norris: *"There is no set of ideas on leadership more
profound ... than Lee Thayer's latest illumination of what really
counts for leaders who want to make a dent in the Universe."*

Pat Murray: *"Thayer teases us solidly onto the path of superior
and sustainable performance by revealing how most executives
fail. What a coup!"*

Order Lee Thayer's books
direct from the publisher:
www.WMEBooks.com
Or call toll-free: 1-877-947-BOOK (2665)

Many have observed that "rattling the cages" of executives
and CEOs is what Dr. Thayer ***does best***.

If you'd like to listen in or "rattle back," visit his new blog,
The Leader's Journey with Lee Thayer:

http://leethayer.typepad.com